FAITH, HOPE, LOVE

WHAT REALLY MATTERS

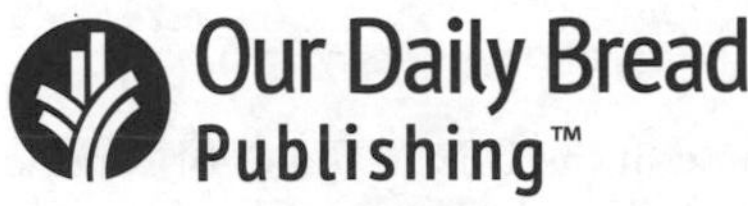

What Really Matters: Faith, Hope, Love

Interior design by Sherri L. Hoffman

ISBN: 978-1-62707-946-4

Printed in the United States of America
20 21 22 23 24 25 26 27 / 8 7 6 5 4 3

Introduction

What really matters in life?

That question could be answered in hundreds of ways.

Some seek fame, thinking that if everyone knows his or her name, life will take on new importance.

Others hold a political agenda tightly and seem ready to sacrifice everything for their way to become the norm.

Advertising encourages us to pursue a perfectly manicured lawn, the newest electronic devices, or just the right car, while the news shows us those searching for enough food to eat and a safe place to live.

What would you say really matters in your life? Are you striving for something that you feel will promise true happiness?

Although many things are important to us, Paul in 1 Corinthians 13 hinted that some things are more important than others. He explained to his readers that certain gifts from God eventually would no longer be needed. To contrast the temporary nature of those gifts, he mentioned three things that we will have with us always—even into the future kingdom of God.

What we will enjoy into eternity are faith, hope, and love. Our faith, by the power of the Holy Spirit, will never diminish. Our hope for the future glories the Father has in store for us will continue. And, of course, Jesus, who is love personified, will always be with us. God's love, which is unfathomable and unending, will shine on us forever.

In this collection of *Our Daily Bread* articles, we have focused on those three eternal traits of the redeemed. If they will serve us well as we enjoy the glories of heaven, they will definitely serve us well as we tread the pathways of earth.

Our faith is the anchor of our existence, for it tethers us to our wonderful Savior, Jesus Christ.

Our hope is the encouraging draw that moves us forward, for we know who gives us the strength to press through each day with confidence in Him.

And love is the basis of it all. It controls how we interact with others, how we treat those less fortunate, and how we stay in fellowship with our heavenly Father.

All three—faith, hope, and love—need to be hallmarks of our life, characteristics that control what is important to us—not just in the future but in our everyday lives.

Faith, hope, and love. That's what really matters in life.

DAVE BRANON, GENERAL EDITOR
AND *OUR DAILY BREAD* WRITER

Faith, Hope, Love

Faith, Love, and Hope

READ 1 THESSALONIANS 1:1–3

We always thank God for all of you and continually mention you in our prayers. —1 THESSALONIANS 1:2

For ten years, my Aunt Kathy cared for her father (my grandfather) in her home. She cooked and cleaned for him when he was independent, and then took on the role of nurse when his health declined.

Her service is one modern example of the words of Paul, who wrote to the Thessalonians that he thanked God for "your work produced by faith, your labor prompted by love, and your endurance inspired by hope in our Lord Jesus Christ" (1 Thessalonians 1:3).

My aunt served in faith and love. Her daily, consistent care was the result of her belief that God called her to this important work. Her labor was borne out of love for God and her father.

She also endured in hope. My grandfather was a very kind man, but it was difficult to watch him decline. She gave up time with family and friends, and she limited her travels to care for him. She was able to endure because of the hope that God would strengthen her each day, along with the hope of heaven that awaited my grandfather.

Whether it is caring for a relative, helping a neighbor, or volunteering your time, be encouraged as you do the work God has called you to do. Your labor can be a powerful testimony of faith, hope, and love.

LISA SAMRA

The glory of life is to love, not to be loved; to give, not to get; to serve, not to be served.

Faith

Will You Be Around?

READ JAMES 4:13–17

Do not boast about tomorrow, for you do not know what a day may bring. —PROVERBS 27:1

When the medical examination of a seventy-eight-year-old man was over, his doctor recommended that he come back in six months for another checkup. At this suggestion the patient shook his head and said, "Doctor, I don't think I'll be around then."

"Nonsense!" replied the physician with a hearty, reassuring smile. "You'll be around for years yet."

The older man gave his doc an odd look, then nervously cleared his throat. "I mean," he explained, "I'll be in Florida in six months. I go there every January."

Although this little anecdote may bring a smile, I'm more interested in the question it raises and the lesson it suggests. Is there any assurance that you will be around tomorrow, next month, next year? While it is right to make plans for the future, we must always do so with a consciousness of life's uncertainty. Life, James reminds us is "a mist that . . . vanishes" (4:14). That's why we depend on "the Lord's will" (v. 15).

Look ahead six months. Will you be around? Let this question prompt you to live so faithfully that whether "here" or "there" it'll make no difference!

RICHARD DEHAAN

Defer not till tomorrow to be wise;
tomorrow's sun for you may never rise.

Hope Is Our Strategy

READ MICAH 7:1–7

But as for me, I watch in hope for the L*ORD*, *I wait for God my Savior; my God will hear me.* —MICAH 7:7

My favorite football team has lost eight consecutive games as I write this. With each loss, it's harder to hope this season can be redeemed for them. The coach has made changes each week, but they haven't resulted in wins. Talking with my coworkers, I've joked that merely wanting a different outcome can't guarantee it. "Hope is not a strategy," I've quipped.

That's true in football. But in our spiritual lives, it's just the opposite. Not only is cultivating hope in God a strategy but clinging to Him in faith and trust is also the only strategy. This world often disappoints us, but hope can anchor us in God's truth and power during turbulent times.

Micah understood this reality. He was heartbroken by how Israel had turned away from God. "What misery is mine! . . . The faithful have been swept from the land; not one upright person remains" (7:1–2). But then he refocused on his true hope: "But as for me, I watch in hope for the LORD, I wait for God my Savior; my God will hear me" (v. 7).

What does it take to maintain hope in harsh times? Micah shows us: Watching. Waiting. Praying. Remembering. God hears our cries even when our circumstances are overwhelming. In these moments, clinging to and acting in response to our hope in God is our strategy, the only strategy that will help us weather life's storms.

ADAM HOLZ

What does it take to maintain hope in harsh times?
Watching. Waiting. Praying. Remembering.

Hope

This Could Be the Year

READ 1 THESSALONIANS 4:13–18

We who are still alive and are left will . . . meet the Lord in the air. And so we will be with the Lord forever. —1 THESSALONIANS 4:17

My dad was a pastor, and on the first Sunday of each new year he preached about the return of Christ, often quoting from 1 Thessalonians 4. His point was always the same: "This could be the year Jesus will return. Are you ready to meet Him?" I'll never forget hearing that sermon at age six, thinking, *If that's true, I'm not sure I will be among those He's coming for*. I felt certain my parents would be going to heaven, and I wanted to go too. So when my dad came home after church, I asked how I could be sure. He opened the Bible, read some verses to me, and talked to me about my need for a Savior. It didn't take much to convince me of my sins. That day, my dad led me to Christ. I will be forever grateful to him for planting these truths in my heart.

In an increasingly chaotic world, what a hopeful thought that this could be the year Jesus returns! More comforting still is the anticipation that all who trust Him for salvation will be gathered together—relieved from this world's suffering, sorrow, and fear. Best of all, we'll be with the Lord forever!

JOE STOWELL

Perhaps today! —Dr. M. R. DeHaan

Chipmunk Chatter

READ ISAIAH 41:10–13

Do not fear; I will help you. ISAIAH 41:13

I had laid out some landscape netting in my yard, upon which I was going to spread decorative stones. As I was preparing to finish the job, I noticed a chipmunk tangled up in the netting.

I put my gloves on and gingerly began clipping away at the netting. The little guy was not happy with me. He kicked his hind feet and tried to bite me. I calmly told him, "I'm not going to hurt you, buddy. Just relax." But he didn't understand, so in fear he resisted. I finally snipped the last restricting loop and sent him scampering home.

Sometimes humans feel entangled and react in fear of the Lord. Through the centuries, He has offered rescue and hope to people—yet we resist Him, not understanding the help He provides. In Isaiah 41, the prophet quotes the Lord as saying, "For I, the LORD your God, will hold your right hand, saying to you, 'Fear not; I will help you' " (v. 13 NKJV).

As you think about your situation, how do you see God's role? Are you afraid to turn things over to Him—for fear that He might harm you? He is good and He is near, wanting to free you from life's entanglements and give you hope. You can trust Him with your life.

DAVE BRANON

Faith is the best antidote for fear.

Love

Love Revealed

READ 1 JOHN 4:9–16

This is how God showed his love among us: He sent his one and only Son into the world that we might live through him. —1 JOHN 4:9

When a series of pink "I love you" signs mysteriously appeared in the town of Welland, Ontario, local reporter Maryanne Firth decided to investigate. Her sleuthing turned up nothing. Weeks later, new signs appeared featuring the name of a local park along with a date and time.

Accompanied by a crowd of curious townspeople, Firth went to the park at the appointed time. There she met a man wearing a suit, and he had cleverly concealed his face. Imagine her surprise when he handed her a bouquet and proposed marriage! The mystery man was Ryan St. Denis—her boyfriend. She happily accepted.

St. Denis's expression of love toward his fiancée may seem a bit over-the-top, but God's expression of love for us is nothing short of extravagant! "This is how God showed his love among us: He sent his one and only Son into the world that we might live through him" (1 John 4:9).

Jesus is not merely a token of love, like a rose passed from one person to another. He is the divine human who willingly gave up His life so that anyone who believes in Him for salvation can have an everlasting covenant relationship with God. Nothing can separate a Christian "from the love of God that is in Christ Jesus our Lord" (Romans 8:39).

JENNIFER BENSON SCHULDT

We know how much God loves us because
He sent His Son to save us.

Are You Connected?

READ JOHN 4:1–14

He said to me: "It is done. I am the Alpha and the Omega, the Beginning and the End. To the thirsty I will give water without cost from the spring of the water of life." —REVELATION 21:6

For thirty-five years a hospital in the American Midwest relied on a firefighting sprinkler system for the safety of its patients. But then officials discovered that it had never been attached to the city's water main. The pipe that led from the building extended four feet underground—and stopped!

The medical staff and the patients had felt complete confidence in the system. They thought that if a blaze broke out, they could depend on a nearby hose to extinguish it. But theirs was a false security. Although the costly equipment with its polished valves and well-placed outlets was adequate for the building, it lacked the most important thing—WATER!

This illustrates the condition of many people regarding salvation. They have never been united to Jesus Christ—the source of Living Water! Although they are morally upright, deeply religious, or members of a church, they are lacking "the righteousness that comes from God on the basis of faith" (Philippians 3:9). This puts well-meaning people in eternal peril.

Have you accepted Christ as your Lord and Savior? Only the righteousness of God received by faith will give you the assurance of salvation. Be certain that you are united to Him. He alone can forgive your sins and supply you with "the water of life"!

Paul Van Gorder

Faith in Christ is the connecting link between man's sin and Divine forgiveness.

JANUARY
8

Hope

Hope's Sure Foundation

READ HEBREWS 11:1–6

My God will meet all your needs according to the riches of his glory in Christ Jesus. —PHILIPPIANS 4:19

Lessons on faith can come from unexpected places—like the one I learned from my 110-pound, black Labrador retriever named Bear. Bear's large metal water bowl was located in a corner of the kitchen. Whenever it was empty, he wouldn't bark or paw at it. Instead, he would lie down quietly beside it and wait. Sometimes he would have to wait several minutes, but Bear had learned to trust that I would eventually walk into the room, see him there, and provide what he needed. His simple faith in me reminded me of my need to place more trust in God.

The Bible tells us that "faith is confidence in what we hope for and assurance about what we do not see" (Hebrews 11:1). The foundation of this confidence and assurance is God himself, who "rewards those who earnestly seek him" (v. 6). God is faithful to keep His promises to all who believe and come to Him through Jesus.

Sometimes having faith in "what we do not see" isn't easy. But we can rest in God's goodness and His loving character, trusting that His wisdom is perfect in all things—even when we have to wait. He is always faithful to do what He says: to save our eternal souls and meet our deepest needs, now and forever.

JAMES BANKS

Don't worry about tomorrow—God is already there.

Too Much Love?

READ EPHESIANS 5:22–33

In this same way, husbands ought to love their wives as their own bodies. He who loves his wife loves himself. —EPHESIANS 5:28

The apostle Paul suggested that the husband has the primary responsibility for fostering love in a marriage. He must show his wife that he deserves her trust and devotion. No one wants to submit to a tyrant or be controlled by a dictator, and Ephesians 5 doesn't ask a woman to do that. In these verses, the husband is told three times that his major task is to express Christlike love to his wife. Only as a husband patterns his actions after Christ's love for the church can he expect his wife to respect him, as verse 33 explains.

A young man once went to talk to well-known Bible teacher Harry Ironside (1876–1951). "I love my wife too much!" he said to Ironside. "In fact, I've put her on such a high plane, I fear it's sinful." "Do you think you love your wife more than Christ loved the church?" inquired Ironside. The husband didn't dare say he did. "Well, that's the limit to which we may go," Ironside explained, "for we read, 'Husbands, love your wives, even as Christ also loved the church, and gave himself for it' (Ephesians 5:25 KJV). Every tender act of love expressed toward your life partner is proper and spiritual!"

The word *love* in Ephesians 5:28 doesn't refer merely to romantic affection but also to the highest relationship possible. It involves commitment, sacrifice, and even a willingness to die for the one loved. We can never show too much of this kind of love.

HENRY BOSCH

A successful marriage requires falling in love many times—but always with the same person.

Faith

Guidance in the Fog

READ PSALM 119:105–112

Your word is a lamp for my feet, a light on my path. —PSALM 119:105

Some fishermen in the Gulf of Mexico had taken a small boat to their favorite spot about five miles from land. They enjoyed themselves and had no difficulty until late afternoon when a dense fog suddenly moved in. By the time they realized what was happening and got the motor running to head back, they were completely engulfed in the "soup" and could see only a few yards ahead. With hearts pounding, they tried to figure out the way to shore.

Then one of them remembered that he had a small compass. Even though its tiny pointer defied their sense of direction, they agreed to trust it. The men later admitted that periodically they would shout above the noise of the motor, "I don't think the compass is working. I'm sure we're headed the wrong way." But they allowed its needle to be their guide. After a very long time, they finally saw the dry images of land emerging. With uncanny precision they had been guided out of the fog to within a few yards of the dock from which they started.

That's the kind of confidence we can have in the Word of God. Like that compass, it shows us the way. It may not enable us to see as much as we would like to, but it will always enable us to see as much as we need.

MART DEHAAN

The Bible is like a compass—it always points the believer in the right direction.

Another Day

READ MARK 16:1–7

"Don't be alarmed," he said. "You are looking for Jesus the Nazarene, who was crucified. He has risen! He is not here. See the place where they laid him." —MARK 16:6

For many people, their last glimpse of Christ was of a dying form on a cross. This is embodied in the story of Scottish philosopher Thomas Carlyle as he stood one day before a cross in France. Upon that cross was a representation of the forlorn Jesus. As Carlyle looked at it, he was heard to say, "Poor fellow, Your day is past!"

No, Mr. Carlyle, when the Savior died on Calvary, His day was not past. He rose from the grave, and right now He is in heaven, exalted at the right hand of God the Father. We would never minimize the sacrificial death and vicarious atonement of our Lord, but this is not the whole basis of salvation. Writing of the gospel, Paul emphasized the fact that Christ not only died for our sins and was buried but that He also "was raised on the third day according to the Scriptures" (1 Corinthians 15:4).

The empty tomb points to the glorious truth that after Jesus died He had another day.

But there is more! We have the sure hope that we someday will be ushered into His presence. Because our Savior was victorious over the grave and became "the firstfruits of those who have fallen asleep" (v. 20), we don't need to fear the day when we will die. Our confidence is in our living Lord, who assures us that for us there is another day—one that is eternal!

PAUL VAN GORDER

Christ's empty tomb is the shining gateway to heaven!

JANUARY
12

Love

A Powerful Prayer

READ LUKE 6:27–33

Bless those who curse you, pray for those who mistreat you. —LUKE 6:28

Pastor Kefa Sempangi preached a sermon in his church in a country with a ruthless dictator. Outside the church stood five of that dictator's secret police, submachine guns at the ready. In the church were widows whose husbands had been brutally slain by the police. After Kefa finished his sermon, the gunmen followed him to his office. "We have come to kill you," said the leader. "Do you have anything to say?" The pastor's knees shook and his voice cracked as he said, "I wish to pray for you, that God will not judge you for what you are about to do."

The leader interrupted, "What's wrong with those people—why do they look so happy? Even the widows seem to have peace." The pastor explained that the life Jesus gives cannot be taken away, even by death. The men listened, their facial muscles relaxing. The leader said he had never felt love, and he asked the pastor to pray for him. The police then turned and left. Several months later, the leader came to know Christ.

Prayer for persecutors does not always bring freedom nor end mistreatment. Stephen died with words of forgiveness on his lips (Acts 7:60). But his prayer affected Saul, who later became the apostle Paul.

We may never face such extreme circumstances. Yet we will face family members who are spiteful or fellow workers who don't like our faith. Their words may cut deep. Ask God to show His love through you. That's an extremely powerful prayer.

DENNIS DEHAAN

Where prayer focuses, God's power falls.

When Dreams Don't Come True

READ JEREMIAH 29:1–14

"For I know the plans I have for you," declares the LORD, *"plans to prosper you and not to harm you, plans to give you hope and a future."* —JEREMIAH 29:11

Shattered dreams.

It happens all the time. A man dies unexpectedly just before retirement, leaving his wife to face conditions far different from those of which she had dreamed. A young man is an outstanding baseball pitcher in college. He is drafted by a major league team and anticipates making it to the big leagues. But his hopes are dashed when he realizes he can't get batters out at the next level.

Shattered dreams. These words aptly describe what happened to a large group of Jewish people in 597 BC. They were uprooted from their land and transported to Babylon as exiles. It appeared that all their hopes were gone. But before long, some false prophets told them that God would intervene and bring about their return very quickly if they would resist their captors. The people started dreaming again. Their hopes were high!

Then along came Jeremiah, who shattered their dreams by telling them the prophets had been lying to them. He explained that the Lord planned on keeping them in Babylon for seventy years. Jeremiah said that eventually they would discover that God's plan was for their good.

It's good to dream big dreams. But if they don't come true, let's turn our eyes to God in humble trust. His plans are always best!

HERB VANDER LUGT

No one is hopeless whose hope is in God.

Faith

Locked Out!

READ MATTHEW 25:1–13

He replied, "Truly I tell you. I don't know you." —MATTHEW 25:12

It's a strange feeling to be locked out of your own house. One evening, it happened to me.

My family had just left for the evening, and I had gone outside to close the garage. When I went back to the house, I discovered that the door had blown shut, and it was locked. Since I had no key, I inspected all the windows, hoping to find some other way to get in, but everything was tightly secured. Because I had no way to communicate with Marge, I had no choice but to remain out in the chilly air until my family returned.

As I sat there for several hours, I thought about how hopeless and dreadful it will be for all who are "locked out" of the heavenly home for eternity! Having waited too long to receive Christ, they will suddenly face the terrifying reality that the door of salvation is closed to them forever!

In Matthew 25, Jesus told the parable of the ten virgins. Five of them had prepared for the appearance of the bridegroom, and when he came, they "went in with him to the wedding" (v. 10). Later, however, when the five foolish virgins tried to gain entrance, the door was shut! In response to their pleas, "Lord, Lord, open the door for us," they heard him answer, "I don't know you" (vv. 11–12).

The way of salvation is still open. Won't you accept the blessings of redemption through faith in the Savior. Don't risk being "locked out"!

RICHARD DEHAAN

It is never too early to decide for Christ, but the time will come when it will be too late!

A Second Chance

READ LAMENTATIONS 3:22–33

Because of the LORD's great love we are not consumed, for his compassions never fail. —LAMENTATIONS 3:22

On January 15, 2009, 155 people on US Airways Flight 1549 thought they were going to die. During takeoff from New York City, their plane struck a flock of geese, disabling both engines. In a powerless glide, the captain maneuvered over the densely populated area, then announced: "Brace for impact." Less than ninety seconds later, the crippled plane made a water landing in the frigid Hudson River, where boats and ferries quickly arrived to rescue the passengers and crew, all of whom survived. People called it the "Miracle on the Hudson" and praised the pilot and crew. One grateful passenger said simply, "We have a second chance in life."

In times of crisis, we grasp the importance of every hour. During our ordinary routine, however, we often forget that each day is a second chance. "Because of the LORD's great love we are not consumed, for his compassions never fail. They are new every morning; great is your faithfulness. I say to myself, 'The LORD is my portion, therefore I will wait for him' " (Lamentations 3:22–24).

We can choose to live with thankfulness for God's mercy and grace, with confidence in His faithful care, and with hope because He is with us forever. Today, God offers us a second chance in life. Let's make the most of it!

DAVID MCCASLAND

Our God is a God of second chances.

The Love of Rules

READ ROMANS 13:1–10

Love does no harm to a neighbor. Therefore love is the fulfillment of the law. —ROMANS 13:10

When I taught writing, I explained that it's generally better to use short words or phrases first in a series, as in "arts and letters" and "life, liberty, and the pursuit of happiness." Early in my career, I explained to authors that it just sounds better this way, but then I discovered a "rule" about this. And I learned that authors are more likely to accept editorial changes when I can point them to a rule than when I just say, "Trust me."

This is typical of human nature. We have a love/hate relationship with rules. We don't like rules, but we're unsure how to determine right from wrong without them.

God had a relationship with Adam and Eve that was based on loving trust. The only rule necessary was one that protected them from knowledge that would end in death. But when disobedience broke the trusting relationship, God added more rules to protect the wayward couple and their offspring.

In Christ, God proclaimed once more that the good life He wants for us is not about rules but a relationship. As Paul wrote, all the commandments can be summarized in one word: love. Because we are "in Christ," we can enjoy peace with God and others—not because there's a rule, but because there is love.

JULIE ACKERMAN LINK

The greatest force on earth is not the compulsion of law but the compassion of love.

Small Faith in a Big God

READ MATTHEW 17:14–21

He replied, "Because you have so little faith. Truly I tell you, if you have faith as small as a mustard seed, you can say to this mountain, 'Move from here to there,' and it will move. Nothing will be impossible for you." —MATTHEW 17:20

Faith—we all wish we had more of it, especially when facing mountainous problems.

Most of us are well practiced in faith. We sit down in chairs without checking them out; we use microwave ovens without analyzing how they work; we put keys in doors and expect them to open. We don't go around moaning, "If only I had more faith in chairs, in microwaves, in keys." We depend on these objects because we see them as reliable—not because we've worked up great feelings of confidence.

Jesus didn't say to His disciples, "Have more faith in God." He simply said, "Have faith in God" (Mark 11:22). Bible teacher Stuart Briscoe writes, "Faith is only as valid as its object. You could have tremendous faith in very thin ice and drown . . . . You could have very little faith in very thick ice and be perfectly secure."

When facing trials, many of us want mountain-size faith. But Jesus taught that faith the size of a mustard seed is sufficient—if planted in the soil of God's greatness.

What is your mountain today? Plant your mustard seed of faith in God, turn your mountain over to Him—and you can rest in His faithfulness.

JOANIE YODER

Have faith in God—not faith in faith.

Locked into Love

READ ROMANS 8:31–39

Praise the LORD. Give thanks to the LORD, for he is good; his love endures forever. —PSALM 106:1

Several years ago, the city of Paris removed forty-five tons of padlocks from the railings of the Pont des Arts pedestrian bridge. As a romantic gesture, couples would etch their initials onto a lock, attach it to the railing, click it shut, and throw the key into the River Seine.

After this ritual was repeated thousands of times, the bridge could no longer bear the weight of so much "love." Eventually the city, fearing for the integrity of the bridge, removed the "love locks."

The locks were meant to symbolize everlasting love, but human love does not always last. The closest of friends may offend each other and never resolve their differences. Family members may argue and refuse to forgive. A husband and wife may drift so far apart that they can't remember why they once decided to marry. Human love can be fickle.

But there is one constant and enduring love—the love of God. "Give thanks to the LORD, for he is good; his love endures forever," proclaims Psalm 106:1. The promises of the unfailing and everlasting nature of God's love are found throughout Scripture. And the greatest proof of this love is the death of His Son so those who put their faith in Him can live eternally. Nothing will ever separate us from His love (Romans 8:38–39).

Fellow believers, we are locked into God's love forever.

CINDY HESS KASPER

Christ's death and resurrection are the measure of God's love for me.

When Life Falls Apart

READ ROMANS 8:18–25

The creation itself will be liberated from its bondage to decay and brought into the freedom and glory of the children of God. —ROMANS 8:21

Life is full of frustrations. The car breaks down. The house always seems to need another fix-up job. We get sick or injured. And a look in the mirror reminds us we're not getting any younger.

Even in this age of high technology and medical advances, we have to admit that things fall apart. No matter how many inventions and new products we come up with to make life easier, things will continue, as they always have, to deteriorate. And we will continue to face the inevitable process of decline, which Paul described as the "bondage of decay" (Romans 8:21). We simply cannot avoid "our present sufferings," which are a part of living in this fallen world (v. 18).

Yet there is hope. We as Christians can look forward eagerly to "our adoption to sonship, the redemption of our bodies" (v. 23). Paul called that grand expectation "the glory that will be revealed in us" (v. 18).

So, the next time another one of your modern conveniences lets you down, making you aware that life isn't getting any easier, shift your attention away from this deteriorating world. If you are trusting in Christ, remind yourself that God will someday make us and our world eternally perfect. Then all our frustrations will end.

DAVE BRANON

Heaven's delights will far outweigh earth's difficulties.

Faith

Hold On

READ PHILIPPIANS 3:12–4:1

I have fought the good fight, I have finished the race, I have kept the faith. —2 TIMOTHY 4:7

Tianmen Mountain in Zhangjiajie, China, is considered one of the most beautiful mountains in the world. To view its towering cliffs in all their glorious splendor, you must take the Tianmen Shan cable car, which covers a distance of 7,455 meters (4.5 miles). It's amazing how this cable car can travel such long distances and scale such steep mountains without any motor on the car itself. Yet it moves safely up these spectacular heights by keeping a strong grip on a cable that is moved by a powerful motor.

In our journey of faith, how can we finish the race well and "press on toward the goal to win the prize for which God has called [us] heavenward in Christ Jesus"? (Philippians 3:14). Like the cable car, we keep a strong grip on Christ, which is what Paul meant when he said, "stand firm in the Lord" (4:1). We have no resources of our own (See John 15:5). We depend fully on Christ to keep us moving forward. He will take us through the greatest challenges and lead us safely home.

Toward the end of his earthly life, the apostle Paul declared, "I have fought the good fight, I have finished the race, I have kept the faith" (2 Timothy 4:7). We can too. We must simply keep a strong grip on Christ.

Albert Lee

Keeping the faith means trusting God
to faithfully keep you.

Max and the Orphaned Calf

READ 1 THESSALONIANS 2:1–7

We were like young children among you. Just as a nursing mother cares for her children, so we cared for you. —1 THESSALONIANS 2:7–8

My friend Max runs a small farm as a hobby. Recently when he checked on the cows he is raising, he was surprised to see a newborn calf! When he bought the cows, he had no idea one was pregnant. Sadly, the mother cow had complications and died shortly after her calf was born. Immediately, Max purchased some powdered milk so he could feed the calf from a bottle. "The calf thinks I'm its mother!" Max told me.

The tender story of Max's new role with the calf reminded me of how Paul likened himself to a caring mother in dealing with the believers at Thessalonica: "We were gentle among you," he said, "just as a nursing mother cherishes her own children" (1 Thessalonians 2:7 NKJV).

Paul adopted a nurturing attitude when teaching people. He knew believers needed the "milk of the word" for spiritual growth (1 Peter 2:2 NKJV). But he also gave special attention to the concerns of those he cared for. "We dealt with each of you as a father deals with his own children," Paul said, "encouraging, comforting and urging you to live lives worthy of God" (1 Thessalonians 2:11–12).

As we serve each other, may we serve with the tender loving care of our Savior, encouraging each other in our spiritual journey (Hebrews 10:24).

DENNIS FISHER

God pours His love into our hearts
to flow out to others' lives.

Love

Letting God Choose

READ GENESIS 13:9–13

So Lot chose for himself the whole plain of the Jordan and set out toward the east. The two men parted company. —GENESIS 13:11

We may have secret longings too deep to utter to others—perhaps a desire for marriage, or a work or ministry we'd like to perform, or a special place to serve. We can take those longings to God: "Lord, You must choose for me. I will not choose for myself."

Genesis 13:10–11 tells us that Lot made his own choice about a desire he had. He "looked around and saw that the whole plain of Jordan toward Zoar was well watered, like the garden of the LORD. . . . So Lot chose for himself the whole plain of Jordan."

The plain of Jordan, with its rich soil and copious water supply, looked best to Lot. But the land was polluted with wickedness (v. 13). Pastor Ray Stedman wrote that "Lot, presuming to run his own life, 'chose for himself,' and, deceived by what he saw, stumbled blindly into heartache and judgment. Abram, on the other hand, was content to let God choose for him. . . . Abram saw it in its true light." Lot chose for himself and lost everything—his family, his fortune, his favor with man.

It is always the best course for us to let God choose and to follow His direction, knowing as we do that all our heavenly Father's choices are prompted by infinite wisdom and love.

DAVID ROPER

Contentment comes when we want God's will more than our own way.

Concrete Love

READ 1 CORINTHIANS 13

If I give all I possess to the poor and give over my body to hardship that I may boast, but do not have love, I gain nothing. —1 CORINTHIANS 13:3

The story is told of a child psychologist who spent many hours constructing a new driveway at his home. Just after he smoothed the surface of the freshly poured concrete, his small children chased a ball across the driveway, leaving deep footprints. The man yelled after them with a torrent of angry words. His shocked wife said, "You're a psychologist who's supposed to love children." The fuming man shouted, "I love children in the abstract, not in the concrete!"

I chuckled at the alleged incident and groaned at the play on words, but the story rang true for me. While I agree in principle with the concept of self-giving love, I find myself failing to express it to the people I live and work with each day.

First Corinthians 13 describes Christian love in terms of its tangible expression: "Love is patient, love is kind. It does not envy, it does not boast, it is not proud. It does not dishonor others, it is not self-seeking, it is not easily angered, it keeps no record of wrongs" (vv. 4–5).

As a theory, love isn't worth much; as a practice, it is the world's greatest treasure. When footprints are in the driveway, people discover whether our love exists in the abstract or in the concrete.

DAVID MCCASLAND

Love is an active verb.

Faith

Unlikely Heroes

READ JUDGES 2:7–19

Then the LORD raised up judges, who saved them out of the hands of these raiders. —JUDGES 2:16

The book of Judges is an account of God's people descending into spiritual indifference and rebellion. After the death of Joshua, the leader of the Hebrews, the next generation "forsook the LORD, the God of their ancestors, . . . They followed and worshiped various gods of the peoples around them" (Judges 2:12).

This dismal record of wavering allegiance hardly seems the place to find spiritual heroes, yet four people from the book of Judges—Gideon, Barak, Samson, and Jephthah (chapters 4–16)—are named in the New Testament book of Hebrews (11:32). Along with Noah, Abraham, Moses, and other notables, they are commended for their faith.

The book of Judges, however, presents these men as flawed people who responded to God's call during a time of spiritual darkness in their culture. The Bible honors them for their faith, not for their perfection. They were recipients of God's grace as surely as we are.

In every generation, God raises up people who are true to Him and to His Word. The measure of their lives and of ours is not the absence of failure but the presence of God's gracious forgiveness and the faith to obey His call. Even today, God's champions are unlikely heroes. Could you be one of them?

DAVID MCCASLAND

Faith in Christ can make extraordinary heroes out of ordinary people.

Confident Hope

READ PHILIPPIANS 1:19–26

For to me, to live is Christ and to die is gain. —PHILIPPIANS 1:21

Dr. Bill Wallace was serving as a missionary surgeon in Wuzhou, China, in the 1940s when Japan attacked China. Wallace, who was in charge of Stout Memorial Hospital at the time, ordered the hospital to load his equipment on barges and continue to function as a hospital while floating up and down rivers to avoid infantry attacks.

During dangerous times, Philippians 1:21—one of Wallace's favorite verses—reminded him that if he lived, he had work to do for the Savior; but if he died, he had the promise of eternity with Christ. The verse took on special meaning when he died as a martyr while falsely imprisoned in 1951.

The apostle Paul's writing reflects that kind of deep devotion—the kind we can aspire to as followers of Jesus; enabling us to face trials and even danger for His sake. It is devotion enabled by the Holy Spirit and the prayers of those closest to us (v. 19). It's also a promise. Even when we surrender ourselves to continued service under difficult circumstances, it is with this reminder: when our life and work end here, we still have the joy of eternity with Jesus ahead of us.

In our hardest moments, with hearts committed to walking with Christ now, and with our eyes firmly fixed on the promise of eternity with Him, may our days and our acts bless others with the love of God.

RANDY KILGORE

Sacrifices offered to God are opportunities to showcase His love.

Love

An Atheist's Witness

READ 1 JOHN 3:11–18

Jesus replied: "Love the Lord your God with all your heart and with all your soul and with all your mind." —MATTHEW 22:37

Aware that love of God and neighbor is a central teaching of Scripture, I did my doctoral dissertation on "The Concept of Love in the Psychology of Sigmund Freud." I learned that this influential thinker, who had no faith in God, nevertheless stressed the supreme importance of love.

Freud wrote, for example, that the best way to "escape from the cares of life" and "forget real misery" is to follow the path "that expects all satisfaction to come from loving and being loved." In this point, Freud was in agreement with the Bible, which focuses on love.

Scripture teaches that "God is love" (1 John 4:8). It also teaches the importance of "faith expressing itself through love" (Galatians 5:6). So the great problem we all face is how to rid ourselves of sinful self-love while sincerely loving God and our neighbor (Matthew 32:37–39; 1 John 3:14). The gospel—with its message of the life-transforming love of Christ—provides the only answer to that problem. Paul declared in Romans 5:5, "God's love has been poured out into our hearts through the Holy Spirit."

Have you experienced the infilling of God's love? Only when you trust Jesus as Savior will the Holy Spirit of love begin to flow in and through you.

VERNON GROUNDS

God pours His love into our hearts
to flow out to others.

Faith Women

READ MARK 15:39–47

Some women were watching from a distance. Among them were Mary Magdalene, Mary the mother of James the younger and of Joseph, and Salome. In Galilee these women had followed him and cared for his needs. —MARK 15:40–41

The Bible tells of a number of women who faithfully served Jesus during his ministry. Here's a list of just a few outstanding women and the specific qualities for which they are remembered:

A Canaanite woman had great faith. *Matthew 15:28*
Anna spoke of Jesus to many in Jerusalem. *Luke 2:38*
A forgiven woman anointed Jesus's feet. *Luke 7:46, 47*
Martha and Mary served and worshiped. *John 12:2, 3*

Many more names could be added to this roll call of godly women whose lives counted for Christ.

In Mark 15 we read of Salome, Mary Magdalene, and Mary the mother of James, who were loyal to Jesus even when He was hanging on the cross. It was said of them that they "followed him and cared for his needs" (v. 41). Their devotion was not diminished by the shameful treatment He received nor were they dissuaded by the jeering mob. Then, early in the morning of the first day of the week they came to the tomb to anoint His body. What a joy it was for them to find an empty tomb and to hear the triumphant words, "He is risen!"

Thank God for consecrated women in every age! Truly they are entitled to a prominent place on the honor roll of faith.

PAUL VAN GORDER

Woman—last at the cross and first at the grave.

JANUARY
28

Hope

Not What It Seems

READ 2 KINGS 6:8–17

Don't be afraid . . . . Those who are with us are more than those who are with [the enemy]. —2 KINGS 6:16

Don is a border collie that lives on a farm in South Lanarkshire, Scotland. One morning, he and his owner, Tom, set out to check on some animals. They rode together in a small farm utility truck. When they arrived, Tom left the vehicle but forgot to put the brake on. With Don in the driver's seat, the vehicle rolled down a hill and across two lanes of traffic before it stopped safely. To watching motorists, it appeared that the dog was out for a morning drive. Indeed, things are not always as they seem.

In a story from 2 Kings 6, it seemed as if Elisha and his servant were about to be captured and carried off to the King of Aram. The king's forces had surrounded the city where Elisha and his servant were staying. The servant believed they were doomed, but Elisha said, "Don't be afraid . . . . Those who are with us are more than those who are with [the enemy]" (v. 16). When Elisha prayed, the servant was able to see the multitudes of supernatural forces that were in place to protect them.

Situations that seem hopeless are not always the way we perceive them to be. When we feel overwhelmed and outnumbered, we can remember that God is by our side. He can "command his angels . . . to guard [us] in all [our] ways" (Psalm 91:11).

JENNIFER BENSON SCHULDT

Things are always better than they seem to be when we remember that God is by our side.

“I Don’t Even Like Her”

READ JOHN 13:31–35

A new command I give you: Love one another. As I have loved you, so you must love one another. —JOHN 13:34

When Missy started her new job in the factory, she was determined to let her light shine for the Lord. But as soon as she met Louise, her work partner, she knew it wasn’t going to be easy. Brassy, defensive, and crude, Louise ridiculed everything Missy did. When Missy tried to befriend her and tell her about Jesus, she was rejected. Louise said, “I tried that. It didn’t work.”

Missy asked God for help. She opened her Bible to John 13:34, “A new command I give to you: Love one another. As I have loved you, so you must love one another.” So Missy kept trying to show love. But all she met was hardness.

After a particularly rough day at work, Missy opened her Bible and cried out to God. Again, her eyes fell on John 13:34. “But I don’t even like her!” Missy complained.

One day Louise sat beside Missy at break and said, “You’re the only person who cares.” Then she poured out a story of heartache and trouble. Missy put her arms around her, and they became friends. Louise attended church with Missy and, after a struggle, opened her heart to Jesus.

This true story has a happy ending, but not all do. Even so, as faithful followers of Jesus, we are to let His light shine brightly through our love.

David Egner

The people we like the least may need our love the most.

Hope

What's in a Name?

READ MATTHEW 1:8–25

She will give birth to a son, and you are to give him the name Jesus, because he will save his people from their sins. —MATTHEW 1:21

"Gip" Hardin, a Methodist preacher, named his son after the famous preacher John Wesley, reflecting Gip's hopes and aspirations for his baby boy. John Wesley Hardin, however, tragically chose a different path than his ministry-minded namesake. Claiming to have killed forty-two men, Hardin became one of the most notorious gunfighters and outlaws of the American West of the late 1800s.

In the Bible, as in many cultures today, names hold special significance. Announcing the birth of God's Son, an angel instructed Joseph to name Mary's child "Jesus, because he will save his people from their sins" (Matthew 1:21). The meaning of Jesus's name—"Jehovah saves"—confirmed His mission to save from sin.

Jesus thoroughly lived up to His name. Through His death and resurrection, He accomplished His mission of rescue. John affirmed the life-giving power of Jesus's name, saying, "But these are written that you may believe that Jesus is the Messiah, the Son of God, and that by believing you may have life in his name" (John 20:31). The book of Acts explains, "Salvation is found in no one else, . . . by which we must be saved" (4:12).

All who call on Jesus's matchless name in faith can experience for themselves the forgiveness and hope He provides. Have you trusted Him by calling on His name?

BILL CROWDER

Jesus's name is also His mission—to seek and to save that which was lost.

Of Spiders and God's Presence

READ EPHESIANS 3:14–19

I pray that out of his glorious riches he may strengthen you with power through his Spirit in your inner being. —EPHESIANS 3:16

Spiders. I don't know any kid who likes them. At least not in their rooms . . . at bedtime. As she was getting ready for bed one night, my daughter spied one dangerously close to her bed. "Daaaad!!!!! Spiiiderrr!!!!!" she hollered. Despite my determination, I couldn't find the eight-legged interloper. "He's not going to hurt you," I reassured her. She wasn't convinced. It wasn't until I told her I'd stay next to her top bunk and stand guard that she agreed to get in bed.

As my daughter settled in, I held her hand. I told her, "I love you so much. I'm right here. But you know what? God loves you even more than Daddy and Mommy do. And He's very close. You can always pray to Him when you're scared." That seemed to comfort her, and peaceful sleep came quickly.

Scripture repeatedly reassures us God is always near (Psalm 145:18; Romans 8:38–39; James 4:7–8), but sometimes we struggle to believe it. Perhaps that's why Paul prayed for the believers in Ephesus to have strength and power to grasp that truth (Ephesians 3:16). He knew that when we're frightened, we can lose track of God's proximity. But just as I lovingly held my daughter as she went to sleep that night, so our loving heavenly Father is always as close to us as a prayer.

Adam Holz

God is always near in spite of our fears.

FEBRUARY
1

Love

Love Letter

READ PSALM 119:97–104

Oh, how I love your law! I meditate on it all day long. —PSALM 119:97

Each morning when I reach my office, I have one simple habit; I check all my emails. Most of the time, I'll work through them in a perfunctory fashion. There are some emails, however, that I'm eager to open. You guessed it—those from loved ones.

Someone has said that the Bible is God's love letter to us. But perhaps on some days, like me, you just don't feel like opening it; and your heart doesn't resonate with the words of the psalmist: "Oh, how I love your law!" (Psalm 119:97). The Scriptures are God's "commands" (v. 98), "statutes" (v. 99), "precepts" (v. 100), and "word" (v. 101).

A question by Thomas Manton (1620–1677), once a lecturer at Westminster Abbey in London, still holds relevance for us today. He asked: "Who is the author of Scripture? God. What is the end of Scripture? God. Why was the Scripture written, but that we might everlastingly enjoy the blessed God?"

It is said of some people that the more you know them the less you admire them, but the reverse is true of God. Familiarity with the Word of God, or rather the God of the Word, breeds affection, and affection seeks yet greater familiarity.

As you open your Bible, remember that God—the One who loves you the most—has a message for you.

Poh Fang Chia

Knowing the Bible helps us know the God of the Bible.

Start Fresh

READ PSALM 86:5–15

[The LORD's] compassions never fail. They are new every morning; great is your faithfulness. —LAMENTATIONS 3:22–23

When I was growing up, one of my favorite books was *Anne of Green Gables* by Lucy Maud Montgomery. In one amusing passage, young Anne, by mistake, adds a skin medication instead of vanilla to the cake she is making. Afterward, she exclaims hopefully to her stern-faced guardian, Marilla, "Isn't it nice to think that tomorrow is a new day with no mistakes in it yet?"

I like that thought: tomorrow is a new day—a new day when we can start afresh. We all make mistakes. But when it comes to sin, God's forgiveness is what enables us to start each morning with a clean slate. When we repent, He chooses to remember our sins no more (Jeremiah 31:34; Hebrews 8:12).

Some of us have made wrong choices in our lives, but our past words and deeds need not define our future in God's eyes. There is always a fresh start. When we ask God for forgiveness, we take a first step toward restoring our relationship with Him and with others. "If we confess our sins, he is faithful and just and will forgive us our sins and purify us from all unrighteousness" (1 John 1:9).

God's compassion and faithfulness are new every morning (Lamentations 3:23). We can start fresh each day.

CINDY HESS KASPER

Each new day gives us new reasons to praise the Lord.

Faith

Faith Mixed with Doubt

READ PSALM 42

Why, my soul, are you downcast? Why so disturbed within me? Put your hope in God, for I will yet praise him, my Savior and my God. —PSALM 42:11

When my close friend Sharon was killed in a car accident, my heart broke. I'm ashamed to admit it, but when life's circumstances hurt that much, my faith is often mixed with doubt. When Sharon died, I cried out to God:

Lord, I sure don't understand you. Why did you allow this death? His answer: "Have you not heard? The everlasting God . . . neither faints nor is weary. His understanding is unsearchable" (Isaiah 40:28 NKJV). "'My thoughts are not your thoughts, nor are your ways My ways,' says the LORD" (55:8 NKJV).

Lord, you are beyond my understanding. But I still wonder: Have you turned your back on the world? His answer: "God is seated on his holy throne" (Psalm 47:8) and "rules forever by his power" (66:7).

Lord, you created this world, but do you care about the pain? Have you forgotten to be good? His answer: I am "good, and ready to forgive, and abundant in mercy to all those who call upon [Me]" (86:5 NKJV).

Yes, Lord, you have been good to me in countless ways, including listening to my doubts and questions about you.

The answers God gives us in His Word may not take away our sadness, but there is comfort in the reality that He is wise, sovereign, and good. Even in the pain, we can praise Him.

ANNE CETAS

Every loss leaves an empty space that only God's presence can fill.

Stop to Help

READ LUKE 10:30–37

"'Love the Lord your God with all your heart and with all your soul and with all your strength and with all your mind'; and, 'Love your neighbor as yourself.'" —LUKE 10:27

Dr. Scott Kurtzman, chief of surgery at Waterbury Hospital in Connecticut, was on his way to deliver a lecture when he witnessed a horrible crash involving twenty vehicles. The doctor shifted into trauma mode, worked his way through the mess of metal, and called out, "Who needs help?" After ninety minutes of assisting and after the victims were taken to area hospitals, Dr. Kurtzman commented, "A person with my skills simply can't drive by someone who is injured. I refuse to live my life that way."

Jesus told a parable about a man who stopped to help another (Luke 10:30–37). A Jewish man had been ambushed, stripped, robbed, and left for dead. A Jewish priest and a temple assistant passed by, saw the man, and crossed over to the other side. Then a despised Samaritan came by, saw the man, and was filled with compassion. His compassion was translated into action: He soothed and bandaged the man's wounds, took him to an inn, cared for him while he could, paid for all his medical expenses, and then promised the innkeeper he would return to pay any additional expenses.

There are people around us who are suffering. Moved with compassion for their pain, let's be those who stop to help.

MARVIN WILLIAMS

Compassion is always active.

FEBRUARY
5

Hope

Selfless Love

READ PHILIPPIANS 2:20–30

[Epaphroditus] almost died for the work of Christ. He risked his life to make up for the help you yourselves could not give me. —PHILIPPIANS 2:30

While serving in Iraq, a nineteen-year-old soldier saw a grenade being thrown from a rooftop. Manning the machine gun in the turret of his Humvee, he tried to deflect the explosive—but it fell inside his vehicle. He had time to jump to safety. Instead, he threw his body over the grenade in a stunningly selfless act that saved the lives of four fellow soldiers.

This almost unexplainable act of self-sacrifice may help us understand why the Bible tells us that there is a kind of love that is more honorable than having great knowledge or faith (1 Corinthians 13:1–3).

This kind of love can be hard to find—leading the apostle Paul to lament that more people care for themselves than for the interests of Christ (Philippians 2:20–21). That's why he was so grateful for Epaphroditus, a coworker who "almost died for the work of Christ. He risked his life" in order to serve others (v. 30).

If we think we could never put our own life on the line for others, Epaphroditus shows us the first step with his selfless example. Such love is neither normal nor common, but it doesn't come from us anyway. It comes from the Spirit of God, who can give us the desire and ability to feel for others some of the inexpressible affection God has for us.

MART DEHAAN

You can measure your love for God by showing your love for others.

Quiet Conversations

READ PSALM 116:5–9

Praise the LORD, my soul, and forget not all his benefits. —PSALM 103:2

Do you ever talk to yourself? Sometimes when I'm working on a project—usually under the hood of a car—I find it helpful to think aloud, working through my options on the best way to make the repair. If someone catches me in my "conversation," it can be a little embarrassing—even though talking to ourselves is something most of us do every day.

The psalmists often talked to themselves in the Psalms. The author of Psalm 116 is no exception. In verse 7 he writes, "Return to your rest, my soul, for the LORD has been good to you." Reminding himself of God's kindness and faithfulness in the past is a practical comfort and help to him in the present. We see "conversations" like this frequently in the Psalms. In Psalm 103:1 David tells himself, "Praise the LORD, my soul; all my inmost being, praise his holy name." And in Psalm 62:5 he affirms, "Yes, my soul, find rest in God; my hope comes from him."

It's good to remind ourselves of God's faithfulness and the hope we have in Him. We can follow the example of the psalmist and spend some time naming the many ways God has been good to us. As we do, we'll be encouraged. The same God who has been faithful in the past will continue His love for us in the future.

JAMES BANKS

Reminding ourselves about God's goodness can keep us filled with His peace.

Faith

Strangers and Foreigners

READ HEBREWS 11:8–16

For he was looking forward to the city with foundations, whose architect and builder is God. —HEBREWS 11:10

I parked my bicycle, fingering my map of the British community of Cambridge for reassurance. Directions not being my strength, I knew I could easily get lost in this maze of roads bursting with historic buildings.

Life should have felt idyllic, for I had just married my Englishman and moved to the United Kingdom. But I felt adrift. When I kept my mouth closed, I blended in. But when I spoke, I immediately felt branded as an American tourist. I didn't yet know what my role was, and I quickly realized that blending two stubborn people into one shared life was harder than I had anticipated.

I related to the Old Testament traveler Abraham, who left all that he knew as he obeyed the Lord's call to live as a foreigner and stranger in a new land (Genesis 12:1). He pressed through the cultural challenges while keeping faith in God, and 2,000 years later the writer to the Hebrews named him a hero (11:9). Like the other men and women listed in this chapter, Abraham lived by faith, longing for things promised, hoping and waiting for his heavenly home.

Perhaps you've always lived in the same town. But remember this: As Christ-followers we're all foreigners and strangers on this earth. By faith we press forward, knowing that God will lead and guide us, and by faith we believe He will never leave nor abandon us. By faith we long for home.

Amy Boucher Pye

God calls us to live by faith, believing that He will fulfill His promises.

It's All about the Love

READ 1 JOHN 4:7–19

We know and rely on the love God has for us. God is love. Whoever lives in love lives in God, and God in them. —1 JOHN 4:16

I saw a sign in front of a church that seems to be a great motto for relationships: "Receive love. Give love. Repeat."

The greatest love that we receive is the love of God. He loved us so much that He gave His Son Jesus, who came to earth, died for us, and rose again to redeem us (1 John 4:9). We receive His love when we receive Jesus as our Savior and Lord. "To all who did receive him, to those who believed in his name, he gave the right to become children of God" (John 1:12).

After we've experienced God's love, we then can learn to give love. "Let us love one another, for love comes from God" (1 John 4:7).

God's love enables us to love our brothers and sisters in Christ. We teach, encourage, and rebuke. We weep and rejoice. The love we give is tender and tough and supportive. We are taught by Jesus even to love our enemies: "Love your enemies, and pray for those who persecute you" (Matthew 5:44). Giving love to others can be challenging in some situations, but it's possible because of the love God has first given to us.

A good plan for our lives today: Receive love. Give love. Repeat.

ANNE CETAS

Receive love. Give love. Repeat.

FEBRUARY
9

Hope

Even Her?

READ JOSHUA 2:1–14

Was not even Rahab the prostitute considered righteous? —JAMES 2:25

Imagine looking through your family tree and finding this description of your ancestor: "A prostitute, she harbored enemies of the government in her house. When she was confronted by the authorities, she lied about it."

What would you do about her? Hide her story from anyone inquiring about your family? Or spotlight and praise her in the legends of your family's story?

Meet Rahab. If what we read about her in Joshua 2 were all we knew, we might lump her in with all of the other renegades and bad examples in the Bible. But her story doesn't stop there. Matthew 1:5–6 reveals that she was King David's great-great grandmother—and that she was in the lineage of our Savior, Jesus. There's more. Hebrews 11:31 names Rahab as a woman of faith who was saved from the fall of Jericho (see Joshua 6:17). And in James 2:25, her works of rescue were given as evidence of her righteous faith.

God's love is amazing that way. He can take people with a bad reputation, transform their lives, and turn them into examples of His love and forgiveness. If you think you're too bad to be forgiven or if you know someone else who feels that way, read about Rahab and rejoice. If God can turn her into a beacon of righteousness, there's hope for all of us.

DAVE BRANON

Whether our sins are great or small,
Jesus is able to forgive them all.

Our Source of Help

READ PSALM 121

My help comes from the LORD, the Maker of heaven and earth. —PSALM 121:2

Twenty-year-old Lygon Stevens, an experienced mountaineer, had reached the summits of Mount Denali, Mount Rainier, four Andean peaks in Ecuador, and thirty-nine of Colorado's highest mountains. "I climb because I love the mountains," she said, "and I meet God there." But one January day, Lygon died in an avalanche while climbing Little Bear Peak in southern Colorado with her brother Nicklis, who survived.

When her parents discovered her journals, they were deeply moved by the intimacy of her walk with Christ. "Always a shining light for Him," her mother said, "Lygon experienced a depth and honesty in her relationship with the Lord, which even seasoned veterans of faith long to have."

In Lygon's final journal entry, written from her tent three days before the avalanche, she said: "God is good, and He has a plan for our lives that is greater and more blessed than the lives we pick out for ourselves, and I am so thankful about that. Thank you, Lord, for bringing me this far and to this place. I leave the rest—my future—in those same hands and say thank you."

Lygon echoed these words from the psalmist: "My help comes from the LORD, the Maker of heaven and earth" (Psalm 121:2).

DAVID MCCASLAND

We can trust our all-knowing God for the unknown future.

FEBRUARY
11

Love

Lavish Expressions of Love

READ 2 CORINTHIANS 9:6–15

You will be enriched in every way so that you can be generous on every occasion. —2 CORINTHIANS 9:11

On our wedding anniversary, my husband, Alan, gives me a large bouquet of fresh flowers. When he lost his job during a corporate restructure, I didn't expect this extravagant display of devotion to continue. But on our nineteenth anniversary, the color-splashed blossoms greeted me from their spot on our dining room table. Because he valued continuing this annual tradition, Alan saved some money each month to ensure he'd have enough for this personal show of affection.

My husband's careful planning exhibited exuberant generosity, reminiscent of Paul's encouragement when he addressed the Corinthians. The apostle complimented the church for their intentional and enthusiastic offerings (2 Corinthians 9:2, 5), reminding them that God delights in generous and cheerful givers (vv. 6–7). After all, no one gives more than our loving Provider, who's always ready to supply all we need (vv. 8–10).

We can be generous in all kinds of giving, caring for one another because the Lord meets all of our material, emotional, and spiritual needs (v. 11). As we give, we can express our gratitude for all God has given us. We can even motivate others to praise the Lord (vv. 12–13).

Openhanded giving, a lavish expression of love and gratitude, can demonstrate our confidence in God's provision for all His people.

XOCHITL DIXON

Generous giving displays courageous confidence in God's loving and faithful provision.

Hope for Skeptics

READ ISAIAH 55:6–13

*So is my word that goes out from my mouth:
It will not return to me empty.* —ISAIAH 55:11

As a workplace chaplain, I'm privileged to be able to talk with many different people. Some are skeptics of the Christian faith. I've discovered three major hurdles that keep them from trusting in Christ for salvation.

The first barrier, surprisingly, isn't an unwillingness to believe that God exists; instead, some doubt that they're important enough for God's attention. Second, some believe they are unworthy of His forgiveness. People are often their own harshest judges. The third hurdle? They wonder why God is not communicating with them if He is out there.

Let's work backward through the hurdles to see what God's Word says. First, God doesn't play head games. He promises that if we read His Word, He will make sure it accomplishes His purpose (Isaiah 55:11). In other words, if we read it we will discover that God is communicating with us. This is precisely why the Bible speaks so often of His grace and mercy toward all (v. 7). His willingness to forgive us is clear. Once we learn that we can hear from God in the Bible and once we see the emphasis on His mercy, it becomes easier to believe we have His attention when we cry out to Him.

God's story is amazing. It can give hope for all of us.

Randy Kilgore

Honest skepticism can be the first step to a strong faith.

Faith

Firsthand Faith

READ JUDGES 2:6–12

After that whole generation had been gathered to their ancestors, another generation grew up who knew neither the LORD nor what he had done for Israel. —JUDGES 2:10

When I was growing up in Singapore, some of my school friends were kicked out of their homes by their non-Christian parents for daring to believe in Jesus Christ. They suffered for their beliefs, but they emerged with stronger convictions. By contrast, I was born and raised in a Christian family. Although I didn't suffer persecution, I too had to make faith my own.

The Israelites who first entered the Promised Land with Joshua saw the mighty acts of God and believed (Judges 2:7). But sadly, the very next generation "knew neither the LORD nor what he had done for Israel" (v. 10). So it was not long before they turned aside to worship other gods (v. 12). They didn't make their parents' faith their own.

No generation can live off the faith of the previous generation. Every generation needs a firsthand faith. When faced with trouble of any kind, faith that is not personalized is likely to drift and falter.

Those who are second, third, or even fourth generation Christians have a wonderful legacy, to be sure. However, there's no secondhand faith! Find out what God says in His Word and personalize it so that yours is a fresh, firsthand faith (Joshua 1:8).

C. P. HIA

If your faith is not personalized, it's not faith.

Loving God

READ 1 JOHN 4:7–21

Dear friends, since God so loved us, we also ought to love one another. —1 JOHN 4:11

Early in our marriage, I thought I knew the ultimate shortcut to my wife's heart. I arrived home one night with a bouquet of a dozen red roses behind my back. When I presented the flowers to Martie, she thanked me graciously, sniffed the flowers, and then took them into the kitchen. Not quite the response I had expected.

It was an introductory lesson in the reality that flowers are not my wife's primary language of love. While she appreciated the gesture, she was mentally calculating the cost of an expensive bouquet of flowers—a budget breaker for a young couple in seminary! And as I've discovered through the years, she is far more interested in my time and attention. When I devote myself to her in an uninterrupted and attentive way, that's when she really feels loved.

Did you ever wonder how God wants us to show that we love Him? We get a clue when we read this note from John: "He who loves God must love his brother also" (1 John 4:21 NKJV). It's that simple. One of the primary ways we show our love for God is by loving our brothers and sisters in Christ. When we genuinely love each other, it brings pleasure to our heavenly Father.

So watch for opportunities to tell Jesus you love Him. He's infinitely worth whatever it costs.

JOE STOWELL

To show your love for God,
share your love with others.

Faith

Happiness and Faith

READ ROMANS 8:29–39

May the God of hope fill you with all joy and peace as you trust in him, so that you may overflow with hope by the power of the Holy Spirit. —ROMANS 15:13

The chorus of the old hymn "At the Cross" concludes with these cheerful words: "And now I am happy all the day!" I don't know about you, but I can't honestly say that just because I know Jesus as my Savior I'm happy all day. I'm a rather optimistic person, but some circumstances don't warm my heart and make me smile.

Troubles may make us wonder: Wasn't our faith supposed to make us happy all the time? Shouldn't Jesus have sheltered us from harm and danger?

Some people teach these things, but the Bible doesn't. God's Word makes it clear that we will have trouble. In Romans 8, for example, the apostle Paul talked frankly about tough times we could face (vv. 35–39). The fact is, Jesus doesn't protect us from all trouble, but His love and His companionship guide us as we go through it.

A more realistic attitude than being "happy all the day" is one stated by a Christian who said, "Now that I'm saved, I'm happier when I am down than I was when I was happy before I was saved."

With Jesus Christ, we can have real joy and make it through even the bad times.

DAVE BRANON

Happiness depends on happenings,
but joy depends on Jesus.

Standing on the Edge

READ JOSHUA 3:9–17

When the people broke camp to cross the Jordan, the priests carrying the ark of the covenant went ahead of them. —JOSHUA 3:14

My little girl stood apprehensively at the pool's edge. As a non-swimmer, she was just learning to become comfortable in the water. Her instructor waited in the pool with outstretched arms. As my daughter hesitated, I saw the questions in her eyes: Will you catch me? What will happen if my head goes under? She had to learn that she could trust her instructors to keep her safe.

The Israelites may have had similar fears. Perhaps they wondered what would happen when they crossed the Jordan River. Could they trust God to make dry ground appear in the flooded riverbed? Was God guiding their new leader, Joshua, as He had led Moses? Would God help His people defeat the threatening Canaanites who lived just across the river?

To find the answers to these questions, the Israelites had to engage in a test of faith—they had to act. "So when the people broke camp to cross the Jordan, the priests carrying the ark of the covenant went ahead of them" (Joshua 3:14). Exercising their faith allowed them to see that God was with them. He was still directing Joshua, and He would help them settle in Canaan (vv. 7, 10, 17).

When we face tests of faith, we can move forward based on God's character and His unfailing promises. By relying on Him, we allow Him to help us move from where we are to where He wants us to be.

JENNIFER BENSON SCHULDT

Fear fades when we trust our Father.

FEBRUARY
17

Love

Bees and Snakes

READ MATTHEW 7:7–11

"If you, then, though you are evil, know how to give good gifts to your children, how much more will your Father in heaven give good gifts to those who ask him!" —MATTHEW 7:11

Some problems have Daddy's name written all over them. For instance, my kids recently discovered bees had moved into a crack in our concrete front porch. So, armed with bug spray, I went out to do battle.

I got stung. Five times.

I don't like being stung by insects. But better me than my kids or wife. Taking care of my family's well-being is at the top of my job description, after all. My children recognized a need, and they asked me to address it. They trusted me to protect them from something they feared.

In Matthew 7, Jesus teaches that we should take our needs to God (v. 7), trusting Him with our requests. To illustrate, Jesus gives a case study in character: "Which of you, if your son asks for bread, will give him a stone? Or if he asks for a fish, will give him a snake?" (vv. 9–10). For loving parents, the answer is obvious. But Jesus answers anyway, challenging us not to lose faith in our Father's generous goodness: "If you, then, though you are evil, know how to give good gifts to your children, how much more will your Father in heaven give good gifts to those who ask him!" (v. 11).

I can't imagine loving my kids more. But Jesus assures us that even the best earthly father's love is eclipsed by God's love for us.

ADAM HOLZ

We can rely on our Father for everything we need.

Valid Entry

READ JOHN 14:1–10

Jesus answered, "I am the way and the truth and the life. No one comes to the Father except through me." —JOHN 14:6

On a teaching trip outside the US, my wife and I were denied entry into our country of destination because of visa problems. Although we were under the assumption our visas had been correctly issued by the country we planned to visit, they were deemed invalid. Despite the efforts of several government officials, nothing could be done. We weren't allowed in. We were placed on the next flight back to the States. No amount of intervention could change the fact that we did not have the proper validation for entrance.

That experience with my visa was inconvenient, but it can't begin to compare with the ultimate entry rejection. I'm speaking of those who will stand before God without valid entry into heaven. What if they were to present the record of their religious efforts and good deeds? That would not be enough. What if they were to call character references? That wouldn't work. Only one thing can give anyone entry into heaven. Jesus said, "I am the way and the truth and the life. No one comes to the Father except through me" (John 14:6).

Christ alone, through His death and resurrection, paid the price for our sins. And only He can give us valid entry into the presence of the Father. Have you put your faith in Jesus? Make sure you have a valid entry into heaven.

BILL CROWDER

Only through Christ can we enter the Father's presence.

Hope

Start with Me

READ 1 CORINTHIANS 13:4–13

Not looking to your own interests but each of you to the interests of the others. —PHILIPPIANS 2:4

I call them Mell Notes—little comments my daughter Melissa made in her Bible to help her apply specific passages to her life.

In Matthew 7, for instance, she had drawn a box around verses 1 and 2 that talk about not judging others because, when you do, "with the measure you use, it will be measured to you." Next to it she wrote this Mell Note: "Look at what you are doing before you look at others."

Melissa was an "others-oriented" teen. She lived the words of Philippians 2:4. Her classmate Matt, who knew her from church nursery through her final days in the eleventh grade when she died in a car accident, wrote of Melissa in a memory book: "I don't think I ever saw you without a smile or something that brightened up people's days." Her friend Tara wrote this: "Thanks for being my friend, even when no one else was as nice and cheerful as you."

In a day in which harsh judgment of others seems to be the rule, it's good to remember that love starts with us. The words of Paul come to mind: "Now these three remain: faith, hope and love. But the greatest of these is love" (1 Corinthians 13:13).

What a difference we'll make when we look at others and say, "Love starts with me." That's a perfect reflection of God's love for us.

DAVE BRANON

Embracing God's love for us is the key to loving others.

Before the Beginning

READ MATTHEW 3:13–17

"Father, I want those you have given me to be with me where I am, and to see my glory, the glory you have given me because you loved me before the creation of the world." —JOHN 17:24

"But if God has no beginning and no end, and has always existed, what was He doing before He created us? How did He spend His time?" Some precocious Sunday school student always asks this question when we talk about God's eternal nature. I used to respond that this was a bit of a mystery. But recently I learned that the Bible gives us an answer to this question.

When Jesus prays to His Father in John 17, He says "Father, . . . you loved me before the creation of the world" (v. 24). This is God as revealed to us by Jesus: Before the world was ever created, God was a trinity (Father, Son, and Holy Spirit)—all loving each other and being loved. When Jesus was baptized, God sent His Spirit in the form of a dove and said, "This is my Son, whom I love" (Matthew 3:17). The most foundational aspect of God's identity is this outgoing, life-giving love.

What an encouraging truth this is about our God! The mutual, outgoing love expressed by each member of the Trinity—Father, Son, and Holy Spirit—is key to understanding the nature of God. What was God doing before the beginning of time? What He always does: He was loving because He *is* love (1 John 4:8).

AMY PETERSON

We are created in the image of a God who is loving and relational.

Love

Praising God's Goodness

READ PSALM 136:1–15

Give thanks to the L*ORD*, *for he is good. His love endures forever.* —PSALM 136:1

Someone in our Bible study group suggested, "Let's write our own psalms!" Initially, some protested that they didn't have the flair for writing, but after some encouragement everyone wrote a moving poetic song narrating how God had been working in their lives. Out of trials, protection, provision, and even pain and tears came enduring messages that gave our psalms fascinating themes. Like Psalm 136, each psalm revealed the truth that God's love endures forever.

We all have a story to tell about God's love. For some, our experiences may be dramatic or intense—like the writer of Psalm 136 who recounted how God delivered His people from captivity and conquered His enemies (vv. 10–15). Others may simply describe God's marvelous creation: "who by his understanding made the heavens . . . spread out the earth upon the waters . . . made the great lights— . . . the sun to govern the day . . . the moon and stars to govern the night" (vv. 5–9).

Remembering who God is and what He has done brings out praise and thanksgiving that glorifies Him. We can then "[speak] to one another with psalms, hymns, and songs from the Spirit" (Ephesians 5:19) about the goodness of the Lord, whose love endures forever!

Turn your experience of God's love into a praise song of your own! Enjoy an overflow of His never-ending goodness.

LAWRENCE DARMANI

For all eternity, God's love endures forever.

Eyewitness

READ 1 JOHN 1:1–7

Through [Jesus] all things were made, without him nothing was made that has been made. —JOHN 1:3

"You don't want to interview me for your television program," the man told me. "You need someone who is young and photogenic, and I'm neither." I replied that we indeed did want him because he had known C. S. Lewis, the noted author and the subject of the documentary we were producing. "Sir," I said, "when it comes to telling the story of a person's life, there is no substitute for an eyewitness."

Christians often refer to talking to others about faith in Christ as "witnessing" or "giving our testimony." It's an accurate concept taken directly from the Bible. John, a companion and disciple of Jesus, wrote, "We have seen, and bear witness, and declare to you that eternal life which was with the Father and was manifested to us—that which we have seen and heard we declare to you" (1 John 1:2–3 NKJV).

If you know Jesus as your Savior and have experienced His love, grace, and forgiveness, you can tell someone else about Him. Youth, beauty, and theological training are not required. Reality and enthusiasm are more valuable than a training course in how to share your faith.

When it comes to telling someone the wonderful story of how Jesus Christ can transform a person's life, there is no substitute for a firsthand witness like you.

DAVID MCCASLAND

Jesus doesn't need lawyers, He needs witnesses.

Hope

Joy in Hard Places

READ HABAKKUK 3:16–19

Yet I will rejoice in the Lord, *I will be joyful in God my Savior.* —HABAKKUK 3:18

For the times when she couldn't take a phone call, my friend left a recording that invited the caller to leave a message. The recording cheerfully concluded, "Make it a great day!" As I reflected on her words, I realized that it's not within our power to make every day "great"—some circumstances truly are devastating. But a closer look might reveal something redeeming and beautiful in my day, whether things are going well or poorly.

Habakkuk wasn't experiencing easy circumstances. As a prophet, he had been shown by God that in coming days none of the crops or livestock—on which God's people depended—would be fruitful (3:17). It would take more than mere optimism to endure the coming hardships. As a people group, Israel would be in extreme poverty. Habakkuk experienced heart-pounding, lip-quivering, leg-trembling fear (v. 16).

Yet despite that, Habakkuk said he would "rejoice in the Lord" and "be joyful" (v. 18). He proclaimed His hope in the God who provides the strength to walk in difficult places (v. 19).

Sometimes we go through seasons of deep pain and hardship. But no matter what our struggle, we can, like Habakkuk, rejoice in our relationship with a loving God. Even when it feels as if we have nothing else, He will never fail or abandon us (Hebrews 13:5). He, the One who "provide[s] for those who grieve," is our ultimate reason for joy (Isaiah 61:3).

Kirsten Holmberg

God's love holds us through our pain and carries us into peace and joy.

Belonging

READ ISAIAH 44:1–5

The Lord who made you and helps you says: "Do not be afraid . . . my chosen one." —ISAIAH 44:2 NLT

I had been out late the night before, just as I was every Saturday night. Just twenty years old, I was running from God as fast as I could. But suddenly, strangely, I felt compelled to attend the church my dad pastored. I put on my faded jeans, well-worn T-shirt, and unlaced high-tops—and drove across town.

I don't recall the sermon Dad preached that day, but I can't forget how delighted he was to see me. With his arm over my shoulder, he introduced me to everyone he saw. "This is my son!" he proudly declared. His joy became a picture of God's love that has stuck with me all these decades.

The imagery of God as loving Father occurs throughout the Bible. In Isaiah 44, the prophet interrupts a series of warnings to proclaim God's message of family love. "Dear Israel, my chosen one," he said. "I will pour out my Spirit on your descendants, and my blessing on your children" (vv. 2–3 NLT). Isaiah noted how the response of those descendants would demonstrate family pride. "Some will proudly claim, 'I belong to the Lord,' " he wrote. "Some will write the Lord's name on their hands" (v. 5 NLT).

Wayward Israel belonged to God, just as I belonged to my father. Nothing I could do would ever make him lose his love for me. He gave me a glimpse of our heavenly Father's love for us.

Tim Gustafson

God's love for us offers us the sense of belonging and identity we all crave.

Faith

Walk of Faith

READ 2 CORINTHIANS 5:1–11

For we live by faith, not by sight.
—2 CORINTHIANS 5:7

Constructed to give people the illusion of walking on air, "Walk of Faith" is a platform of laminated glass at the top of a 385-foot tower in Blackpool, England. An Associated Press photo showed a woman at the edge of the invisible walkway, fists clenched against her face, trying to summon the courage to take a step. She had been told the platform was safe, but she was still afraid.

Sometimes we feel that way about our circumstances. Perhaps a serious health problem has caused us to question the power and the presence of God.

It's encouraging to note that Paul's familiar words "We live by faith, not by sight" (2 Corinthians 5:7) occur in his discussion about being "away from the body and at home with the Lord" (v. 8). He used a powerful metaphor, calling our body an earthly house that's being destroyed, yet he said we have a heavenly building made by God. He spoke of groaning in our earthly frailty and longing for our heavenly home. He concluded that no matter what circumstances we face, we should make it our goal to please the Lord (v. 9).

Our walk of faith can be challenging and sometimes scary. But because God is powerful and present, we can step out in confidence today.

DAVID MCCASLAND

It is better to walk with God by faith
than to go alone by sight.

Loved to Love

READ DEUTERONOMY 10:12–22

And you are to love those who are foreigners, for you yourselves were foreigners in Egypt. —DEUTERONOMY 10:19

The life of pastor Dietrich Bonhoeffer was at risk every day he remained in Hitler's Germany, but he stayed anyway. I imagine he shared the apostle Paul's view that being in heaven was his heart's desire, but staying where he was needed was God's present purpose (Philippians 1:21). So stay he did!

As a pastor he offered clandestine worship services and resisted the evil regime under Hitler.

Despite the daily danger, Bonhoeffer penned *Life Together*—a book on hospitality as ministry. He put this principle to the test when he lived and worked in a monastic community and when he was imprisoned. Every meal, every task, and every conversation, Bonhoeffer taught, was an opportunity to show Christ to others, even under great stress or strain.

We read in Deuteronomy that as God ministered to the Israelites who were leaving Egypt, He instructed them to imitate Him by loving and hosting strangers and widows (10:18–19; Exodus 22:21–22). Likewise, we are loved by God and empowered by His Spirit to serve others each day through kind words and actions.

Who on our daily journey seems lonely or lost? We can trust the Lord to enable us to offer them hope and compassion as we live and labor together for Him.

RANDY KILGORE

The more we understand God's love for us,
the more love we'll show to others.

Love

Learning to Love

READ 1 CORINTHIANS 13

Follow the way of love and eagerly desire gifts of the Spirit, especially prophecy. —1 CORINTHIANS 14:1

Love does more than make "the world go 'round," as an old song says. It also makes us immensely vulnerable. We may say to ourselves: "Why love when others do not show appreciation?" or "Why love and open myself up to hurt?" But the apostle Paul gives a clear and simple reason to pursue love: "These three remain: faith, hope and love. But the greatest of these is love. Follow the way of love" (1 Corinthians 13:13–14:1).

"Love is an activity, the essential activity of God himself," writes Bible commentator C. K. Barrett, "and when men love either Him or their fellow-men, they are doing (however imperfectly) what God does." And God is pleased when we act like Him.

To begin following the way of love, think about how you might live out the characteristics listed in 1 Corinthians 13:4–7. For example, how can I show my child the same patience God shows me? How can I show kindness and respect for my parents? What does it mean to look out for the interests of others when I am at work?

As we "follow the way of love," we'll find ourselves often turning to God, the source of love, and to Jesus, the greatest example of love. Only then will we gain a deeper knowledge of what true love is and find the strength to love others as God loves us.

Poh Fang Chia

Love comes from God. Everyone who loves has been born of God and knows God. —1 John 4:7

Love Your Neighbor

READ ROMANS 13:8–11

For the entire law is fulfilled in keeping this one command: "Love your neighbor as yourself." —GALATIANS 5:14

An anthropologist was winding up several months of research in a small village, the story is told. While waiting for a ride to the airport for his return flight home, he decided to pass the time by making up a game for some children. His idea was to create a race for a basket of fruit and candy that he placed near a tree. But when he gave the signal to run, no one made a dash for the finish line. Instead the children joined hands and ran together to the tree.

When asked why they chose to run as a group rather than each racing for the prize, a little girl spoke up and said: "How could one of us be happy when all of the others are sad?" Because these children cared about each other, they wanted all to share the basket of fruit and candy.

After years of studying the law of Moses, the apostle Paul found that all of God's laws could be summed up in one: "Love your neighbor as yourself" (Galatians 5:14; see also Romans 13:9). In Christ, Paul saw not only the reason to encourage, comfort, and care for one another but also the spiritual enablement to do it.

Because He cares for us, we care for each other.

MART DEHAAN

We show our love for God when we love one another.

Hope

Everyone Has a Purpose

READ 2 SAMUEL 9

Jonathan son of Saul had a son who was lame in both feet. He was five years old when the news about Saul and Jonathan came from Jezreel. His nurse picked him up and fled, but as she hurried to leave, he fell and became disabled. His name was Mephibosheth. —2 SAMUEL 4:4

It's sometimes difficult to reconcile the condition of severely disabled persons with the wise designs of a loving heavenly Father. This includes loved ones who lie helpless as the result of a crippling accident or disease. It all seems so unfair. Scripture indicates, though, that God has a purpose for everyone even though we cannot understand all of His ways.

Nancy Wagner, who cared for a disabled sister for more than eight years, commented, "I asked God to help me to love everything I had to do, and truly He has done just that. Even though it has been so trying physically, the joy has never left me. But why has my sister had to suffer so, scarcely ever free from some type of infection or another, helpless, can't walk, seldom responds, fed by tubes? I don't understand why except for this: I'm the one receiving the blessing. I have learned to love beyond description, and to grow in patience, in tolerance, and in total dependence upon God."

Jonathan's son Mephibosheth was disabled. His name probably wouldn't have been recorded in Scripture if King David had not shown him kindness for the sake of Jonathan. Mephibosheth's difficulty became David's opportunity to show compassion to someone from house of Saul.

God has a purpose for everyone, and it may involve suffering so that others can learn faith, hope, and love.

DENNIS DEHAAN

There is no tragedy on earth that cannot further the purposes of heaven.

Hope

From Wailing to Worship

READ PSALM 30

You turned my wailing into dancing; you . . . clothed me with joy. —PSALM 30:11

Kim began battling breast cancer in 2013. Four days after her treatment ended, doctors diagnosed her with a progressive lung disease and gave her three to five years to live. She grieved, sobbing prayers as she processed her emotions before God for the first year. By the time I met Kim in 2015, she had surrendered her situation to Him and radiated contagious joy and peace. Though some days are still hard, God continues to transform her heart-wrenching suffering into a beautiful testimony of hope-filled praise as she encourages others.

Even when we're in dire circumstances, God can turn our wailing into dancing. Though His healing won't always look or feel as we had hoped or expected it to, we can be confident in God's ways (Psalm 30:1–3). No matter how tear-stained our path may be, we have countless reasons to praise Him (v. 4). We can rejoice in God as He secures our confident faith (vv. 5–7). We can cry out for His mercy (vv. 8–10)—celebrating the hope He's brought to many weeping worshipers. Only God can transform wails of despair into vibrant joy that doesn't depend on circumstances (vv. 11–12).

As our merciful God comforts us in our sorrow, He envelops us in peace and empowers us to extend compassion toward others and ourselves. Our loving and faithful Lord can and does turn our wailing into worship that can lead to heart-deep trust, praise, and maybe even joyful dancing.

Xochitl Dixon

Worship is a heart overflowing with praise to God.

Faith

Quiet Witness

READ 1 PETER 2:11–21

Be careful to live properly among your unbelieving neighbors. —1 PETER 2:12 NLT

Amy lives in a closed country where it's forbidden to preach the gospel. She's a trained nurse who works in a big hospital, caring for newborn babies. She's such a committed professional that her work stands out, and many women are curious about her. They are moved to ask her questions in private. It's then that Amy shares about her Savior openly.

Because of her good work, some coworkers were envious. So they accused her of stealing some medicine. Her superiors didn't believe them, and authorities eventually found the culprit. This episode led some of her fellow nurses to ask about her faith. Her example reminds me of what Peter says: "Dear friends . . . . Be careful to live properly among your unbelieving neighbors. Then even if they accuse you of doing wrong, they will see your honorable behavior, and they will give honor to God" (1 Peter 2:11–12 NLT).

Our everyday lives at home, in our work environment, or at school make an impact on others when we let God work in us. We're surrounded by people who are watching the way we speak and behave. Let's depend on God and have Him rule our actions and thoughts. Then we'll influence those who don't believe, and this may lead some of them to turn in faith to Jesus.

KEILA OCHOA

Our lives speak louder than our words.

A Good Neighbor Policy

READ LEVITICUS 19:13–18

"Do not seek revenge or bear a grudge against anyone among your people, but love your neighbor as yourself. I am the Lord." —LEVITICUS 19:18

One morning my wife and I awoke to find a note from our neighbors on our front door. It read in part, "We've gone away until tomorrow night. Please look after Cleo [the family dog] for us. If she howls and wants to go inside, a spare key is hanging on a nail by the garage door. Thanks." I was glad to read that note because it meant that a strong bridge of trust had been built between us in the two years since they had moved in.

In our Scripture reading, the Israelites were instructed not to rob their neighbors (Leviticus 19:13), to judge righteously (v. 15), not to do anything that would threaten the life of their neighbors (v. 16), and to love and forgive them (v. 18). In this way they would give witness to the nations that Jehovah was the true God and that those who worshiped Him were loving, honest, and just in their personal relationships and in their business dealings.

What was true for Israel is also true for Christians. We too should love our neighbors, and that includes more than just the people who live next door. Jesus defined our neighbor as anyone in need (Luke 10:29–37).

So let's look for ways to develop genuine friendships by lending a hand in time of need. It might mean an emergency run to the hospital or giving a neighbor a half-gallon of milk when we're running low ourselves.

A good neighbor policy may even help bring someone to Christ.

David Egner

One proof of your love for God is
your love for your neighbor.

Home

READ JOHN 14:1–6

In My Father's house are many dwelling places; if it were not so, I would have told you; for I go to prepare a place for you. —JOHN 14:2 NASB

Recently a friend who sold homes for a living died of cancer. As my wife and I reminisced about Patsy, Sue recalled that many years ago Patsy had led a man to faith in Jesus, and he became a good friend of ours. How encouraging to recall that Patsy not only helped families find homes to live in here in our community, but she also helped others make sure they had an eternal home.

As Jesus prepared to go to the cross for us, He showed a keen interest in our eternal accommodations. He told His disciples, "I go to prepare a place for you" and reminded them that there would be plenty of room in His Father's house for all who trusted Him (John 14:2 NASB).

We love to have a nice home in this life—a special place for our family to eat, sleep, and enjoy each other's company. But think of how amazing it will be when we step into the next life and discover that God has taken care of our eternal accommodations. Praise God for giving us life "to the full" (John 10:10), including His presence with us now and our presence with Him later in the place He is preparing for us (14:3).

Thinking of what God has in store for those who trust Jesus can challenge us to do as Patsy did and introduce others to Jesus.

DAVE BRANON

Our search for home ends when we find faith in Jesus.

Hope

MARCH
5

Standing with Courage

READ DEUTERONOMY 31:1–8

Be strong and courageous. . . . Do not be afraid or terrified. —DEUTERONOMY 31:6, 8

While most German church leaders gave in to Hitler, theologian and pastor Martin Niemöller was among the brave souls who resisted Nazi evil. I read a story describing how in the 1970s a group of older Germans stood outside a large hotel while what appeared to be a younger man bustled about with the group's luggage. Someone asked who the group was. "German pastors," came the answer. "And the younger man?" "That's Martin Niemöller—he's eighty. But he has stayed young because he is unafraid."

Niemöller wasn't able to resist fear because he possessed some superhuman antifear gene, but because of God's grace. In fact, he had once held anti-Semitic views. But he had repented, and God restored him and helped him speak and live out the truth.

Moses encouraged the Israelites to resist fear and follow God. When they became fearful after learning Moses would soon be taken from them, he told them: "Be strong and courageous. Do not be afraid or terrified . . . for the LORD your God goes with you" (Deuteronomy 31:6). There was no reason to tremble before an uncertain future; God was with them.

Whatever darkness looms for you, whatever terrors bombard you—God is with you. By God's mercy, may you face your fears with the knowledge that God "will never leave you nor forsake you" (v. 6).

WINN COLLIER

Living unafraid doesn't mean that we don't feel fear but that we don't obey it.

Love

Fear, Love, and Honesty

READ DEUTERONOMY 6:1–9

"You shall not steal. . . You shall not give false testimony against your neighbor." —DEUTERONOMY 5:19–20

Addielou is a crossroads too small for the map. But it has a Baptist church, a feed store, and lots of honesty. Boyd Harmening runs his business on the latter. He opens his Addielou Feed and Farm Supply Store around 7 a.m. and locks up about noon to work his cattle farm. But he leaves the warehouse door open so farmers can pick up feed. All he asks is that they record what they take and sign the clipboard that hangs on the door. They can pay later—and they do.

Most businesses could not operate that way. But in Addielou, honesty works. Why? In part because there is a strong trust between Boyd and his neighbors. But I believe there's a deeper reason—their love for God includes a healthy fear of Him. People who deeply revere and love God learn to trust each other and won't try to cheat each other.

Moses linked fearing and loving God to the Ten Commandments (Deuteronomy 6:1–5), two of which forbid stealing and lying (5:19–20). These two laws form the basis for trust in human relationships. Of course, it would be naive to trust everybody. But if we show ourselves to be trustworthy and honest, people will see that fearing and loving God can make for a more secure world. And we all want that.

DENNIS DEHAAN

Honesty means never having
to look over your shoulder.

Long-Awaited Reunion

READ 1 THESSALONIANS 4:13–18

We who are still alive and are left will be caught up together with them in the clouds to meet the Lord in the air. —1 THESSALONIANS 4:17

As a boy, I had a collie named Prince Boy, a great dog that I really loved. One day, he disappeared. I didn't know if he had been stolen or if he simply ran away—but I was devastated. I searched everywhere. In fact, one of my earliest childhood memories is of climbing a tall tree from which I could scan our neighborhood in hopes of spotting him. I desperately wanted my beloved dog back. For weeks, I was always watching and hoping to see Prince Boy again. But we were never reunited.

There's a much greater sense of loss when we think we'll never again see a loved one who dies. But for those who know and love the Lord, death's parting is only temporary. One day we will be reunited forever!

Paul assured the Thessalonians, "The dead in Christ will rise first. After that, we who are still alive and are left will be caught up together with them in the clouds to meet the Lord in the air. And so we will be with the Lord forever" (1 Thessalonians 4:16–17). The words that provide comfort to the grieving heart are *together* and *we*. These words of reunion indicate that followers of Christ don't ever have to experience permanent separation. For us, death is not a goodbye; it's a "see you later."

BILL CROWDER

God's people never say goodbye for the last time.

Faith

What's Next?

READ ACTS 21:40; 22:1–10

"Now get up and go into the city, and you will be told what you must do." —ACTS 9:6

Having just trusted the Lord Jesus as Savior, an enthusiastic young boy blurted out, "Now what do I do? What's next?" He had the right idea! Although nothing further had to be done to receive salvation, a full life of service and growth still lay ahead.

My favorite Scripture text is Ephesians 2:8–9, "For it is by grace you have been saved, through faith—and this is not from yourselves, it is the gift of God—not by works, so that no one can boast." The Bible makes it crystal clear that we are saved by grace through faith. Human works have nothing to do with redemption. In fact, the best we might offer would never be good enough to meet the Lord's holy, righteous standards. We experience the forgiveness of sin, find peace with God, gain an entrance to heaven, and become possessors of everlasting life by trusting the Lord Jesus Christ and Him alone. It is impossible for anyone to earn these favors!

After conversion, however, we should respond by saying, "Now what do I do? What's next?" There's a very important verse following Ephesians 2:8–9. Verse 10 reads, "For we are God's handiwork, created in Christ Jesus to do good works, which God prepared in advance for us to do."

First there's faith, then comes the "good works." That's what's next!

RICHARD DEHAAN

While we cannot work for salvation,
salvation will cause us to work.

No Wonder!

READ SONG OF SONGS 1:1–4

We love Him because He first loved us. —1 JOHN 4:19 NKJV

"He's perfect for you," my friend told me. She was talking about a guy she had just met. She described his kind eyes, his kind smile, and his kind heart. When I met him I had to agree. Today he's my husband, and no wonder I love him!

In the Song of Songs the bride describes her lover. His love is better than wine and more fragrant than ointments. His name is sweeter than anything in this world. So she concludes that it's no wonder he is loved.

But there is Someone far greater than any earthly loved one, Someone whose love is also better than wine. His love satisfies our every need. His "fragrance" is better than any perfume because when He gave himself for us; His sacrifice became a sweet-smelling aroma to God (Ephesians 5:2). Finally, His name is above every name (Philippians 2:9). No wonder we love Him!

It is a privilege to love Jesus. It is the best experience in life! Do we take the time to tell Him so? Do we express with words the beauty of our Savior? If we show His beauty with our lives, others will say, "No wonder you love Him!"

KEILA OCHOA

God's Word tells us of His love; our
words tell Him of our love.

MARCH
10

Hope

Habits of a Healthy Mind

READ PSALM 37:1–8

Trust in the L*ORD, and do good.* —PSALM 37:3

There is much said today about improving our health by developing habits of optimism, whether facing a difficult medical diagnosis or a pile of dirty laundry. Barbara Fredrickson, PhD, a psychology professor at the University of North Carolina, says we should try activities that build joy, gratitude, love, and other positive feelings. We know, however, that more is required than a general wish for good feelings. We need a strong conviction that there is a source of joy, peace, and love upon which we can depend.

Psalm 37:1–8 gives positive actions we can take as an antidote to pessimism and discouragement. Consider these mood boosters: Trust in the Lord, do good, dwell in the land, feed on His faithfulness (v. 3); delight in the Lord (v. 4); commit your way to the Lord, trust in Him (v. 5); rest in the Lord, wait patiently for Him, do not fret (v. 7); cease from anger, forsake wrath (v. 8).

Because they are connected to the phrase "in the Lord," those directives are more than wishful thinking or unrealistic suggestions. It's because of Jesus, and in His strength, that they become possible.

Our one true source for optimism is the redemption that is in Jesus. He is our reason for hope!

DAVID MCCASLAND

When there's bad news, our hope
is the good news of Jesus.

Serve Heartily

READ PROVERBS 24:30–34

Whoever digs a pit may fall into it; whoever breaks through a wall may be bitten by a snake. —ECCLESIASTES 10:8

Some of mankind's greatest contributions have come from people who decided that no sacrifice was too large and no effort too great to accomplish what they set out to do. Edward Gibbon spent twenty-six years writing *The History of the Decline and Fall of the Roman Empire*. Noah Webster worked diligently for thirty-six years to bring into print the first edition of his dictionary. It is said that the Roman orator Cicero practiced before friends every day for thirty years in order to perfect his public speaking. What stamina! What persistence!

Their diligence can be a model for us as followers of Jesus, for the task we have is so important. As we sense the service God has for us to do, how can we help but serve with enthusiasm and vigor? As we recognize the goals God has for us, how can we let anything else get in the way of accomplishing what God wants us to do? When we serve in the church—whether as a deacon, a teacher, or a part of the praise team, we need to give it our best effort for God's glory.

Paul gave us a clear definition of our duty when he said, "Whatever you do, work at it with all your heart, as working for the Lord" (Colossians 3:23). Our service for Christ, when it is marked by persistent, prayerful, and energetic effort is a sacrifice of service to the One who did so much for us.

PAUL VAN GORDER

We should stop at nothing in our service,
for no Christians has nothing to do.

Love

The Gallery of God

READ PSALM 100

For the LORD *is good and his love endures forever; his faithfulness continues through all generations.* —PSALM 100:5

Psalm 100 is like a work of art that helps us celebrate our unseen God. While the focus of our worship is beyond view, His people make Him known.

Imagine the artist with brush and palette working the colorful words of this psalm onto a canvas. What emerges before our eyes is a world—"all the earth"—shouting for joy to the Lord (v. 1). Joy. Because it is the delight of our God to redeem us from death. "For the joy that was set before Him," Jesus "endured the cross" (Hebrews 12:2 NKJV).

As our eyes move across the canvas, we see an all-world choir of countless members singing "with gladness" and "joyful songs" (Psalm 100:2). Our heavenly Father's heart is pleased when His people worship Him for who He is and what He has done.

Then we see images of ourselves, fashioned from dust in the hands of our Creator and led like sheep into green pasture (v. 3). We, His people, stand in the presence of a loving Shepherd.

Finally, we see God's great and glorious dwelling place—and the gates through which His rescued people enter His unseen presence, while giving Him thanks and praise (v. 4).

What a picture, inspired by our God! Our good, loving, and faithful God. No wonder it will take forever to enjoy His greatness!

DAVE BRANON

Nothing is more awesome than to know God.

Jesus and the Golden Rule

READ MATTHEW 7:7–12

"Therefore, whatever you want men to do to you, do also to them, for this is the Law and the Prophets." —MATTHEW 7:12 NKJV

The concept of The Golden Rule—treat others as you would like to be treated—appears in many religions. So, what makes Jesus's version of the saying so exceptional?

Its uniqueness lies in a single word, "therefore," which signals the generosity of our heavenly Father. Here is what Jesus said: "If you then, being evil, know how to give good gifts to your children, how much more will your Father who is in heaven give good things to those who ask Him! Therefore, whatever you want men to do to you, do also to them" (Matthew 7:11–12, NKJV).

All of us fall short of what we know to be true: We do not love others the way God loves us. Jesus lived out that admirable ethic with perfect love by living and dying for all our sins.

We have a loving, giving Father who set aside His own self-interest to reveal the full measure of His love through His Son Jesus. God's generosity is the dynamic by which we treat others as we would like to be treated. We love and give to others because He first loved us (1 John 4:19).

Our heavenly Father asks us to live up to His commands, but He also gives us His power and love to carry it out. We need only to ask Him for it.

DAVID ROPER

We have committed The Golden Rule to memory; now let us commit it to life. —Edwin Markham

Hope

Hope for the Blues

READ PSALM 62

Pour out your hearts to him, for God is our refuge. —PSALM 62:8

You've felt it yourself, or at least listened to other people talk about it—the blues, times of dark discouragement. Lynette Hoy, in an article for christianwomentoday.com, tells of several steps we can take during those dark times to turn toward Jesus, the Light of the World:

Light up your heart through prayer. Pour out your heart to God when you're feeling overwhelmed (Psalm 62:8). Take your anxieties to Him in prayer (Philippians 4:6–7). And if you journal or write down your prayers, you can look back later to see how the Lord has answered you.

Light up your mind with truth. Read the Word of God every day, at least for a few minutes. Let His truth challenge, permeate, and transform your incorrect thinking that life is hopeless (Psalm 46:1; Romans 12:2).

Light up your life by doing God's will. His will for you is to worship and serve Him. Stay involved in your church where you can worship and fellowship with others and serve Him (Hebrews 10:25). This will help you grow in your trust of God.

When we feel darkness begin to close in on us, we need to turn to Jesus, the Light. He will be a refuge (Psalm 62:7–8) and will give us the strength to keep going.

ANNE CETAS

You won't stumble in the dark if you walk in the light of God's Word.

A Faithful Helper

READ JEREMIAH 20:7–13

But the Lord is with me like a mighty warrior; so my persecutors will stumble and not prevail. They will fail and be thoroughly disgraced; their dishonor will never be forgotten. —JEREMIAH 20:11

As a young boy, my father had to deliver slop to hungry pigs on the farm where he grew up. He hated this job because the hogs would knock him over when he entered their pen. This task might have been impossible except for a faithful helper who accompanied my dad—a German shepherd named Sugarbear. She would maneuver herself between my father and the pigs and hold them back until my dad finished his chore.

The prophet Jeremiah had a difficult job as well. He was called by God to proclaim the Lord's messages to the Israelites. This required him to endure physical abuse, verbal attacks, imprisonment, and isolation. Although Jeremiah struggled with deep discouragement, he had a Helper through all of his trouble. God promised him, "I am with you and will rescue you" (Jeremiah 1:19).

God did not desert Jeremiah, and He will not desert us. We have His continual aid through the power of the Spirit, who lives inside every believer (John 14:16–17). Our great Helper, He gives us hope (Romans 15:13), steers us toward spiritual truth (John 16:13), and pours out God's love in our hearts (Romans 5:5). We can trust that God faithfully helps us as we endure hardship. We can say with Jeremiah, "The Lord is with me like a mighty warrior" (Jeremiah 20:11).

JENNIFER BENSON SCHULDT

Our greatest hope here below is help from God above.

Love

Lost but Found

READ LUKE 15:1–9

"Rejoice with me; I have found my lost sheep." —LUKE 15:6

When we discovered that my mother-in-law had gone missing while shopping with a relative, my wife and I were frantic. Mom suffered from memory loss and confusion, and there was no telling what she might do. Would she wander the area or hop onto any bus thinking it would take her home? Worst-case scenarios spun through our minds as we began to search for her, crying out to God, "Please find her."

Hours later, my mother-in-law was spotted stumbling along a road, miles away. How God blessed us in being able to find her! Several months later, He blessed her: at eighty years of age, my mother-in-law turned to Jesus Christ for salvation.

Jesus, comparing humans to lost sheep, gives us this illustration: "Suppose [a shepherd] has a hundred sheep and loses one of them. Doesn't he leave the ninety-nine in the open country and go after the lost sheep until he finds it? And when he finds it, . . . he calls his friends and neighbors together and says, 'Rejoice with me; I have found my lost sheep' " (Luke 15:4–6).

Shepherds counted their sheep to make sure every one of them was accounted for. In the same way, Jesus, who likens himself to that shepherd, values each of us, young and old. When we're wandering in life, searching, wondering about our purpose, it's never too late to turn to Christ. God wants us to experience His love and blessings.

LESLIE KOH

Amazing grace! . . . I once was lost, but
now am found. —John Newton

The Christian Hope

READ JOB 19:13–27

And after my skin has been destroyed, yet in my flesh I will see God. I myself will see him with my own eyes—I, and not another. How my heart yearns within me! —JOB 19:26–27

I received a letter from a disabled man who told me that he had a sense of victory because of his faith. He had survived a long, delicate cranial operation, but he suffered some brain damage, partial blindness, a high degree of deafness, and mild paralysis. In addition, he spent several months on dialysis after both kidneys failed. He went through an unsuccessful transplant operation and endured another period on dialysis before receiving a replacement kidney.

He admitted that he felt pretty low at times, but he didn't stay down. This man fully believed that God has a loving purpose in everything He allows, and he said he was looking forward to the glorified body awaiting him. He closed his letter by saying, "I can live with my problems, because I know all of these things are preparing me for heaven."

In Job 19, we read not only of Job's bitter lament but also of his expression of hope. Despite losing his wealth, his sons and daughters, and his health, he found consolation! Deep within, he believed that on the other side of death he would see God as His Friend and Savior. With that hope he could triumph over everything—and so can we!

HERB VANDER LUGT

No one is hopeless whose hope is in God.

Love

Giving the Gift of Prayer

READ ROMANS 8:28–34

You help us by your prayers. —2 CORINTHIANS 1:11

"I didn't realize what a gift prayer was until my brother was sick and you all prayed for him. I cannot tell you what a comfort your prayers were!"

Laura had tears in her eyes as she thanked me for the prayers of the people in our church for her brother, who was facing a cancer diagnosis. She continued, "Your prayers have strengthened him in this difficult time and have been an encouragement to our entire family."

One of the best ways to love others is to pray for them. Jesus is our ultimate example in this. The New Testament tells us about Jesus praying for others on many occasions, and it even shows us that He continues to come to the Father on our behalf. Romans 8:34 says that He "is at the right hand of God and is also interceding for us." Even after showing such selfless love at the cross, the risen and ascended Lord Jesus Christ continues to express His care for us by praying for us still today.

All around us are people who need us to follow Jesus's example and love them with our prayers, inviting God's help and intervention in their lives. We can ask God to help us pray for them, and He will! May our loving Lord strengthen us to generously give the gift of our prayers for others today.

JAMES BANKS

Prayer is a gift to be shared.

The Family of Faith

READ 1 THESSALONIANS 2:6–14

Because we loved you so much, we were delighted to share with you not only the gospel of God but our lives as well. —1 THESSALONIANS 2:8

A singles' class at our church became a close-knit family—offering help whenever it was needed. In the time of sorrow or loss, they were there for each other. When someone needed to move, class members packed boxes, carried furniture, and provided food. Birthdays and holidays were no longer solitary events, because faith and friendship merged into an ongoing relationship of encouragement. Many of those bonds forged during adversity continue to flourish and sustain individuals and families in their faith.

Paul's letter to the followers of Jesus in Thessalonica paints a similar picture of life-giving relationships in God's family. "We were gentle among you, just as a nursing mother cherishes her own children" (1 Thessalonians 2:7 NKJV). "For you remember, [brothers and sisters], our labor and toil . . . that we might not be a burden to any of you" (v. 9 NKJV). "We exhorted, and comforted, and charged every one of you, as a father does his own children" (v. 11 NKJV). Like mothers, fathers, brothers, and sisters, Paul and his associates shared the gospel and their lives with fellow believers who "had become dear" to them (v. 8 NKJV).

In God's family of faith, He provides mothers, fathers, sisters, and brothers for us. The Lord gives His joy as we share our lives together in His grace and love.

DAVID MCCASLAND

The ultimate ground of faith and knowledge is confidence in God. —Charles Hodge

Basin of Love

READ JOHN 13:1–17

After that, he poured water into a basin and began to wash his disciples' feet. —JOHN 13:5

One day in physics class many years ago, our teacher asked us to tell him—without turning around—what color the back wall of the classroom was. None of us could answer, for we hadn't noticed.

Sometimes we miss or overlook the "stuff" of life simply because we can't take it all in. And sometimes we don't see what's been there all along.

It was like that for me as I recently read again the account of Jesus washing His disciples' feet. The story is a familiar one, for it is often read during Passion Week. That our Savior and King would stoop to cleanse the feet of His disciples awes us. In Jesus's day, even Jewish servants were spared this task because it was seen as beneath them. But what I hadn't noticed before was that Jesus, who was both man and God, washed the feet of Judas. Even though He knew Judas would betray Him, as we see in John 13:11, Jesus still humbled himself and washed Judas's feet.

Love poured out in a basin of water—love that He shared even with the one who would betray Him. As we ponder the events that led up to the celebration of Jesus's resurrection, may we too be given the gift of humility so we can extend Jesus's love to our friends and any enemies.

AMY BOUCHER PYE

Because of love, Jesus humbled himself
and washed His disciples' feet.

MARCH
21

River Tree

READ JEREMIAH 17:5–10

They will be like a tree planted by the water
—JEREMIAH 17:8

This was a tree to be envied. Growing on riverfront property, it didn't have to worry about weather reports, withering temperatures, or an uncertain future. Nourished and cooled by the river, it spent its days lifting its branches to the sun, holding the earth with its roots, cleaning the air with its leaves, and offering shade to all who needed refuge from the sun.

By contrast, the prophet Jeremiah pointed to a shrub (Jeremiah 17:6). When the rains stopped and the summer sun turned the ground to dust, the bush shriveled into itself, offering no shade or fruit to anyone.

Why would the prophet compare a flourishing tree to a withering bush? He wanted his people to recall what had happened since their miraculous rescue from the slave yards of Egypt. For forty years in a wilderness, they lived like a tree planted by a river (2:4–6). Yet in the prosperity of their promised land they had forgotten their own story; they were relying on themselves and on gods of their own making (vv. 7–8), even to the point of going back to Egypt looking for help (42:14).

So God, through Jeremiah, lovingly urged the forgetful children of Israel, and now He urges us, to hope and trust in the Lord and to be like the tree—not the bush.

MART DEHAAN

Let's remember in good times what we have learned in days of trouble.

Faith

Judging Origins

READ JUDGES 11:1–8, 29

Then the Spirit of the Lord came on Jephthah. He crossed Gilead and Manasseh, passed through Mizpah of Gilead, and from there he advanced against the Ammonites. —JUDGES 11:29

"Where are you from?" We often use that question to get to know someone better. But for many of us, the answer is complicated. Sometimes we don't want to share all the details.

In Judges, Jephthah might not have wanted to answer that question at all. His half-brothers had chased him out of his hometown of Gilead for his "questionable" origins. "You are the son of another woman," they declared (Judges 11:2). The text says starkly, "His mother was a prostitute" (v. 1).

But Jephthah was a natural leader, and when a hostile tribe picked a fight with Gilead, the people who had sent him packing suddenly wanted him back. "Be our commander," they said (v. 6). Jephthah asked, "Didn't you hate me and drive me from my father's house?" (v. 7). After getting assurances that things would be different, he agreed to lead them. The Scripture tells us, "Then the Spirit of the Lord came on Jephthah" (v. 29). Through faith, he led them to a great victory. The New Testament mentions him in its list of heroes of the faith (Hebrews 11:32).

God so often seems to choose the unlikeliest people to do His work, doesn't He? It doesn't matter where we're from, how we got here, or what we've done. What matters is that we respond in faith to His love.

Tim Gustafson

Many who are first will be last, and many who are last will be first. —Matthew 19:30

Longing for God

READ 1 JOHN 4:13–16

My heart and my flesh cry out for the living God. —PSALM 84:2

One day my daughter was visiting with our one-year-old grandson. I was getting ready to leave the house on an errand, but as soon as I walked out of the room my grandson began to cry. It happened twice, and each time I went back and spent a moment with him. As I headed out the door the third time, his little lip began to quiver again. At that point my daughter said, "Dad, why don't you just take him with you?"

Any grandparent could tell you what happened next. My grandson went along for the ride, just because I love him.

How good it is to know that the longings of our hearts for God are also met with love. The Bible assures us that we can "know and rely on the love God has for us" (1 John 4:16). God doesn't love us because of anything we have or haven't done. His love isn't based on our worthiness at all, but on His goodness and faithfulness. When the world around us is unloving and unkind, we can rely on God's unchanging love as our source of hope and peace.

Our heavenly Father's heart has gone out to us through the gift of His Son and His Spirit. How comforting is the assurance that God loves us with love that never ends!

JAMES BANKS

God longs for us to long for Him.

Hope

Work and Hope

READ 2 THESSALONIANS 3:6–15

Such people we command and urge in the Lord Jesus Christ to settle down and earn the food they eat. —2 THESSALONIANS 3:12

Most of us will work a variety of jobs in our lifetime—some we love, some we would rather not talk about. I had my share of jobs as I made my way through college and grad school—from picking up old appliances to delivering coupon booklets door-to-door to washing dishes to construction to selling clothes in a department store.

Even if we don't enjoy our work, it is better than the alternative (idleness), and it can give our lives real purpose. Our work takes on greater value when we work not just for a paycheck but for the Lord's approval.

A line from English poet Samuel Taylor Coleridge (1772–1834) suggests the connection between work and value. He wrote, "Work without hope draws nectar in a sieve, and hope without an object cannot live." Our work, he suggests, must have hope to maintain its value. But where do we find that hope?

It's an idea found in the Bible. According to Colossians 3:23, we should work "for the Lord" because He is the One who will reward us (v. 24). We are to be known as hard workers who never grow weary in doing good (2 Thessalonians 3:6–15).

It's important that we honor God and be a positive testimony to others with the way we work. That will give our work—no matter what it is—true hope.

DAVE BRANON

Daily work done for God takes on eternal value.

Forecast of Faith

READ PSALM 77:1–15

Then I thought, "To this I will appeal: the years when the Most High stretched out his right hand." —PSALM 77:10

Are you about to lose your faith? Don't give up yet. Remember the author of Psalm 77? He had sunk so low that all hope seemed gone. He was so troubled he couldn't sleep. He was so depressed he couldn't even talk about it. That's what he was—depressed! Down! Blue! He was so low that the fleas of the field had to get on their knees to bite him. But then something happened. He thought how his forefathers had gone through similar troubles before the Lord delivered them, and his faith was renewed.

Looking back can restore hope and give us reason to look ahead. Let me illustrate. After a long and hard winter, the bright and balmy days of spring are suddenly invaded by a renegade polar air mass. You think winter is starting all over again. But nobody concludes that the age-old order of the seasons has come to an abrupt end, or that the solar system has reversed its cycle. Looking back reminds you that late-season storms have happened before and reassures you that spring will come.

So too, the Bible shows us that men and women of God have seen hard times before. It reminds us that many times the sky has been dark and cold just before the Lord responded with the warmth and power of His love.

So don't give up yet. Look back. Then look ahead. The people of God have walked this way before. The forecast of faith is always bright.

MART DEHAAN

Do not judge God's love by His providences but by His promises.

Love

A Loving Father

READ HEBREWS 6:9–20

God is not unjust; he will not forget your work and the love you have shown him as you have helped his people and continue to help them. —HEBREWS 6:10

People around the world are familiar with Mount Rushmore, the South Dakota site where the heads of four American presidents are carved in gigantic scale on a cliff wall. Yet, while millions know of Mount Rushmore, relatively few know the name Doane Robinson—the South Dakota state historian who conceived the idea of the magnificent sculpture and managed the project. The monument is admired and appreciated, but he is the forgotten man behind the masterpiece. His name is largely unrecognized.

Sometimes, in the service of God, we may feel that we have been forgotten or are behind the scenes and not recognized. Ministry can be a life of effort that often goes unappreciated by the very people we are seeking to serve in Jesus's name. The good news, however, is that while people may not know, God does. Hebrews 6:10 says, "For God is not unjust to forget your work and labor of love which you have shown toward His name, in that you have ministered to the saints, and do minister" (NKJV).

What a promise! Our heavenly Father will never forget our service to Him and our labor of love. That is infinitely more important than being applauded by the crowds.

BILL CROWDER

Loving others by serving to please Christ is
a greater reward than public acclaim.

A Blanket for Everyone

READ JOHN 18:15–18, 25–27

Above all, love each other deeply, because love covers over a multitude of sins. —1 PETER 4:8

Linus Van Pelt, better known as simply "Linus," was a mainstay in the *Peanuts* comic strip. Witty and wise, yet insecure, Linus constantly carried a security blanket. We can identify. We have our fears and insecurities too.

The disciple Peter knew something about fear. When Jesus was arrested, Peter displayed courage by following the Lord into the courtyard of the high priest. But then he began to show his fear by lying to protect his identity (John 18:15–26). He spoke disgraceful words that denied his Lord. But Jesus never stopped loving Peter (see John 21:15–19).

Peter's emphasis on love in 1 Peter 4:8 came from one who had experienced the deep love of Jesus. And he, in turn, stressed the importance of love in our relationships with the words "above all." The intensity of the verse continues with the encouragement to "love each other deeply, because love covers over a multitude of sins."

Have you ever needed that kind of "blanket"? I have! After saying or doing something I later regretted, I have felt the chilly draft of guilt and shame. I have needed to be "covered" in the manner that Jesus covered disgraced, shame-filled people in the Gospels.

To followers of Jesus, love is a blanket to be graciously and courageously given away for the comfort and reclamation of others. As recipients of such great love, let us be givers of the same.

ARTHUR JACKSON

God loves you and me—let's love each other.

MARCH
28

Hope

Where to Find Hope

READ ROMANS 5:1–11

And hope does not put us to shame, because God's love has been poured out into our hearts through the Holy Spirit, who has been given to us. —ROMANS 5:5

Elizabeth struggled for a long time with drug addiction, and when she recovered she wanted to help others in return. So she started writing notes and anonymously placing them throughout her city. Elizabeth tucks these notes under car windshield wipers and tacks them on poles in parks. She used to look for signs of hope; now she leaves them for others to find. One of her notes concluded with these words: "Much love. Hope sent."

Hope with love—that's what Jesus gives. He brings us His love with each new day and strengthens us with that hope. His love is not rationed out to us drop by drop but flows out of His heart freely and is poured lavishly into ours: "We know how dearly God loves us, because he has given us the Holy Spirit to fill our hearts with his love" (Romans 5:5 NLT). He desires to use the hard times to develop perseverance and character and bring us a satisfying, hope-filled life (vv. 3–4). And even when we're far from Him, He still loves us (vv. 6–8).

Are you looking for signs of hope? The Lord offers hope with love by inviting us to grow in a relationship with Him. Our hope for a fulfilling life is anchored in His unfailing love.

ANNE CETAS

Hope is the anchor of the soul.

The Power of Demonstration

READ 2 TIMOTHY 3:10–17

All Scripture is God breathed and is useful for teaching, rebuking, correcting and training in righteousness. —2 TIMOTHY 3:16

My attempts at fixing things around the house usually lead to paying someone else to undo the damage I caused while trying to fix the original problem. But recently I successfully repaired a home appliance by watching a YouTube video where a person demonstrated step by step how to do it.

Paul was that kind of teacher for his young protégé Timothy as he traveled with Paul and watched him in action. From prison in Rome, Paul wrote, "You . . . know all about my teaching, my way of life, my purpose, faith, patience, love, endurance, persecutions, sufferings" (2 Timothy 3:10–11). In addition, he urged Timothy to "continue in what you have learned and have become convinced of, because you know those from whom you learned it, and how from infancy you have known the Holy Scriptures" (vv. 14–15).

Paul's life demonstrated the necessity of building our lives on the bedrock of God's Word. He reminded Timothy that the Bible is the powerful, God-given source that we need to teach and to demonstrate to others who want to be Christ-followers.

As we thank the Lord for the people who helped us grow in faith, we are challenged to follow their example of living out the truth as we teach and encourage others.

That's the power of demonstration.

DAVID MCCASLAND

We are called to live out God's Word as we teach and encourage others.

Faith

When God Fills Us

READ PSALM 16:5–11

You make known to me the path of life; you will fill me with joy in your presence, with eternal pleasures at your right hand. —PSALM 16:11

"What had I done?"

It should have been one of the most exciting times of my life. Instead, it was one of the loneliest. I'd just gotten my first "real" job after college, in a city hundreds of miles from where I grew up. But the thrill of that big step quickly faded. I had a tiny apartment. No furniture. I didn't know the city. I didn't know anyone. The job was interesting, but the loneliness felt crushing.

One night, I sat at home with my back against the wall. I opened my Bible and stumbled onto Psalm 16, where verse 11 promises that God will fill us. "Lord," I prayed, "I thought this job was the right thing, but I feel so alone. Please fill me with a sense of Your nearness." I offered variants of that plaintive plea for weeks. Some nights, my sense of loneliness eased, and I had a deep experience of God's presence. Other nights, I still felt achingly isolated.

But as I returned to that verse, anchoring my heart in it night by night, God gradually deepened my faith. I experienced His faithfulness in a way I never had before. And I learned that my task was simply to pour out my heart to Him . . . and humbly await His faithful response, trusting His promise to fill me with joy in His presence.

Adam Holz

Anchor your heart in God.

Loving All

READ LEVITICUS 19:33–34

The foreigner residing among you must be treated as your native-born. Love them as yourself. —LEVITICUS 19:34

I worship in a church located in a large, open field—a rare commodity on the island of Singapore (we're just twenty-five miles long and fifteen miles wide). Some time back, people from abroad who work in my country started gathering on the church property for a picnic every Sunday.

This evoked a range of responses from fellow churchgoers. Some fretted about the mess the visitors would leave behind. But others saw this as a divine opportunity to extend hospitality to a wonderful group of strangers—without even leaving the church grounds!

The Israelites must have faced similar issues in their time. After they settled in their new land, they had to grapple with how to relate to other people groups. But God expressly commanded them to treat foreigners like their own kind, and to love them as themselves (Leviticus 19:34). Many of His laws made special mention of foreigners: they were not to be mistreated or oppressed, and they were to be loved and helped (Exodus 23:9; Deuteronomy 10:19). Centuries later, Jesus would command us to do the same: to love our neighbor as ourselves (Mark 12:31).

May we have God's heart to love others as ourselves, remembering that we too are sojourners on this earth. Yet we have been loved as God's people, treated as His own.

LESLIE KOH

Embracing God's love for us is the key to loving others.

Hope

Hope in the Darkness

READ JEREMIAH 31:16–26

I will refresh the weary and satisfy the faint. —JEREMIAH 31:25

According to legend, Qu Yuan was a wise and patriotic Chinese government official who lived during the time known as the Warring States period (475–246 BC). It has been said that he tried repeatedly to warn his king about an impending threat that would destroy the country, but the king rejected his advice. Eventually, Qu Yuan was exiled. When he learned about the fall of his beloved country to the foe he had warned about, he ended his life.

Qu Yuan's life resembles some aspects of the life of the prophet Jeremiah. He too served kings who scorned his warnings, and his country was ravaged. However, while Qu Yuan gave in to his despair, Jeremiah found genuine hope. Why the difference?

Jeremiah knew the Lord, who offers the only true hope. "There is hope for your descendants," God had assured His prophet. "Your children will return to their own land" (Jeremiah 31:17). Although Jerusalem was destroyed in 586 BC, it was later rebuilt (see Nehemiah 6:15).

At some point, we all find ourselves in situations that can cause us to despair. It could be a bad medical report, a sudden job loss, a shattered family. But when life knocks us down, we can still look up—for God is on the throne! He holds our days in His hands, and He holds us close to His heart.

Poh Fang Chia

The world hopes for the best, but the Lord offers the best hope. —John Wesley

From Bleak to Beautiful

READ JOB 42:10–17

The LORD blessed the latter part of Job's life more than the former part. —JOB 42:12

Spring is the time of year when God reminds us that things are not always as they seem. Over the course of a few short weeks, what appears hopelessly dead comes to life. Bleak woodlands are transformed into colorful landscapes. Trees whose naked arms reached to heaven all winter, as if pleading to be clothed, suddenly are adorned with lacy green gowns. Flowers that faded and fell to the ground in surrender to the cold rise slowly from the earth in defiance of death.

In Scripture, we read about some apparently hopeless situations. One example is that of a wealthy man named Job whom God described as having integrity (Job 2:3). Disaster struck and Job lost everything important to him. In misery, he said, "My days . . . come to an end without hope" (7:6). What appeared to Job and his friends as evidence that God had turned against him was just the opposite. God was so confident of Job's integrity that He trusted him in this battle with Satan. Later, Job's hope and life were renewed.

The faithful arrival of spring every year comforts me when I'm in a situation that seems hopeless. With God, there is no such thing. No matter how bleak the landscape of life may look, God can transform it into a glorious garden of color and fragrance.

JULIE ACKERMAN LINK

With God, there is hope even in the hopeless situation.

APRIL
3

Love

How God Shows His Love

READ JOHN 13:1–17

"I have set you an example that you should do as I have done for you." —JOHN 13:15

Martha, a twenty-six-year-old woman with ALS (amyotrophic lateral sclerosis), needed help. When a group of ladies from Evanston, Illinois, heard about her, they jumped into action. They began to give round-the-clock nursing care. They bathed her, fed her, prayed for her, and witnessed to her. Martha, who had not received Christ as her Savior and couldn't understand how a loving God could let her get ALS, saw His love in these women and eventually became a Christian. She is with the Lord today because sixteen women, following Jesus's example, personified God's love.

The love of God was visibly demonstrated in Jesus when He was here on Earth. In stooping to wash the feet of His disciples, He mirrored the submissive step He took when He left heaven and became a man. He healed the sick and endured bitter hatred as His reward. He died like a criminal on a Roman cross. His endurance and these acts of kindness reflect God's love, for Jesus said, "Anyone who has seen me has seen the Father" (John 14:9).

Jesus is no longer with us in His physical body—He now sits at God's right hand in heaven. So, if God's love is to be embodied today, it must be done through Christians—like you. Like me.

HERB VANDER LUGT

My life helps paint my neighbor's picture of God.

Hope Anyway

READ PSALM 34:15–18

My comfort in my suffering is this. Your promise preserves my life. —PSALM 119:50

Among the hundreds of articles I've written for *Our Daily Bread* since 1988, a few stick in my mind. One such article is from the mid-1990s when I told of a time our three girls were away at camp or on mission trips, so six-year-old Steve and I had some guy time.

As we were enjoying an excursion to the airport, Steve turned to me and said, "It's not as much fun without Melissa," his eight-year-old sister and sidekick. Neither of us knew then how poignant those words would turn out to be. Life indeed has not been "as much fun" for the years since Mell died in a car accident as a teenager. The passage of time may dull the ache, but nothing takes the pain away completely. Time cannot heal that wound. But here's something that can help: listening to, meditating on, and savoring the solace promised by the God of all comfort.

Listen: "Because of the LORD's great love we are not consumed, for his compassions never fail" (Lamentations 3:22).

Meditate: "In the day of trouble he will keep me safe in his dwelling" (Psalm 27:5).

Savor: "My comfort in my suffering is this: Your promise preserves my life" (Psalm 119:50).

Life can never be the same again when someone we love is gone. But God's promises bring hope and comfort.

DAVE BRANON

God's Word is the true source of comfort.

Faith

Charade of the Cuckoo

READ 1 PETER 5:6–11

Submit yourselves, then, to God. Resist the devil, and he will flee from you. —JAMES 4:7

First Peter 5:6–11 reminds us that Satan is serious. He's not merely playing a spirited game of Monopoly with Christians. He is capable of gaining cruel advantage of us. If the devil does make us spiritual prisoners of war, it is not primarily because we have been overpowered by the sinister forces of evil. Instead, our defeat can be attributed to the fact that we have been outmaneuvered and subtly led away from a position of reliance on God. We have been duped by the sly methods of the enemy.

Nature provides a fitting illustration of Satan's tactics. Observers tell us that in the spring of the year the cuckoo bird can be seen mimicking the flight of the sparrow hawk. Gliding and soaring like a natural predator, this impostor frightens songbirds and distracts them to the point that they leave their nests unattended. Mrs. Cuckoo then moves in and devours an unguarded egg, leaving one of her own in its place.

Similarly, the devil tries to distract, deceive, and unsettle the follower of Jesus. Sometimes it's through circumstances; sometimes, through a cloud of gloom and depression.

We should never allow ourselves to be thrown into a panic by the alarming antics of the adversary. Let us rely on the truth of the Word. Then, by faith rather than fear, we can resist the devil as we submit to God.

MART DEHAAN

When Satan attacks, strike back with the Sword of the Spirit.

Loving the Unlovely

READ JOHN 8:1–11

God demonstrates his own love for us in this: While we were still sinners, Christ died for us. —ROMANS 5:8

An inner-city mission worker wanted to show Christ's love to others, but she found it difficult to give genuine affection to one particular person. One day the sickly and unkempt woman to whom she had been witnessing was sentenced to jail. When the Christian worker saw her sobbing bitterly, she was filled with compassion. Quickly going to her side, she tenderly put her arm around her. Never having felt such love, the distressed woman was deeply moved, and later she accepted Jesus as her Savior.

After being released from prison, the woman was nursed back to health by the mission worker. Not only had a needy sinner been rescued, but a Christian had been brought into a deeper experience of Christlike compassion.

God doesn't love us because we're lovable but because of His grace. We freely receive His undeserved favor through the Savior, who loved us "while we were still sinners" (Romans 5:8). We are to reflect this new relationship with Christ in our daily lives by showing His compassion to those who are difficult to love.

As one who has been saved by God's grace, are you showing His love to the unlovely?

HENRY BOSCH

Loving the lost is the first step in leading the lost to Christ.

Hope

A Reason for Hope

READ LAMENTATIONS 3:19–33

[The Lord's compassions] are new every morning; great is your faithfulness. —LAMENTATIONS 3:23

It's one of the saddest stories of the Bible, yet it inspired one of the most hopeful hymns of the twentieth century.

The prophet Jeremiah witnessed unimaginable horrors when the Babylonians invaded Jerusalem. Solomon's temple was reduced to ruins, and with it went not only the center of worship but also the heart of the community. The people were left with no food, no rest, no peace, no leader. But in the midst of suffering and grief, one of their prophets found a reason for hope. "Because of the LORD's great love we are not consumed," wrote Jeremiah, "for his compassions never fail. They are new every morning; great is your faithfulness" (Lamentations 3:22–23).

Jeremiah's hope came from his personal experience of the Lord's faithfulness and from his knowledge of God's promises in the past. Without these, he would have been unable to comfort his people.

This hope of Lamentations 3 is echoed in a hymn by Thomas Chisholm (1866–1960). Although he suffered sickness and setbacks throughout his life, he wrote "Great Is Thy Faithfulness." This song reminds us that even in times of great fear, tragic loss, and intense suffering we can find comfort and confidence as we trust in God's great faithfulness.

JULIE ACKERMAN LINK

The best reason for hope is God's faithfulness.

Sand in Your Shoes

READ PROVERBS 4:14–27

Catch for us the foxes, the little foxes that ruin the vineyards, our vineyards that are in bloom. —SONG OF SONGS 2:15

Imagine walking from New York City to San Francisco. It's been done.

When asked to tell of his biggest hurdle, one man who did it mentioned a rather surprising difficulty he endured. He said that the toughest part of the trip wasn't traversing the steep slopes of the mountains or crossing hot, dry, barren stretches of desert. Instead, he said, "The thing that came the closest to defeating me was the sand in my shoes."

When I read his comment, I was reminded of the Christian life. While we often triumph over major obstacles, too often we are defeated by something insignificant. Faced with a threatening spiritual foe, we rise up and become overcomers in the strength of the Lord and His might. But then we let an unkind word, some small setback, or a minor misunderstanding get us down. We begin to feel so sorry for ourselves that we yield to discouragement. In despair we give up the fight and fall short of our goal—just because of a little "sand in our shoes."

Sir Francis Drake, the sixteenth-century English explorer who had sailed around the world, was crossing the Thames River when a violent storm threatened to sink his ship. His cry was: "Shall I who have endured the storms of oceans be drowned in a ditch?"

Similarly, we can ask: "Shall I, who have come so far by faith, be downed by 'sand in my shoes'?" The answer? An emphatic "No!"

RICHARD DEHAAN

We stumble over pebbles, not mountains.

APRIL
9

Hope

True Hope

READ ROMANS 5:1–11

The Spirit himself testifies with our spirit that we are God's children. —ROMANS 8:16

Not long ago I visited the Empire State Building with a friend. The line looked short—just down the block and around the corner. Yet as we entered the building, we discovered the line of people stretching through the lobby, up the stairs, and into another room. Every new turn revealed more distance to go.

Attractions and theme parks carefully route their crowds to make the lines seem shorter. Yet disappointment can lurk "just around the bend."

Sometimes life's disappointments are much more severe. The job we hoped for doesn't materialize; friends we counted on let us down; the romantic relationship we longed for fails to work out. But into these heartbreaks, God's Word speaks a refreshing truth about our hope in Him. The apostle Paul wrote, "Suffering produces perseverance; perseverance, character; and character, hope. And hope does not put us to shame [or disappoint NKJV], because God's love has been poured out into our hearts through the Holy Spirit, who has been given to us" (Romans 5:3–5).

As we place our trust in Him through His Spirit, God whispers the truth that we are unconditionally loved and will one day be with Him—regardless of the obstacles we face. In a world that may often disappoint us, how good it is to know that God gives genuine hope.

JAMES BANKS

In Christ, the hopeless find hope.

New Beginnings

READ ISAIAH 43:14–21

See, I am doing a new thing! Now it springs up; do you not perceive it? —ISAIAH 43:19

New beginnings are possible. Just ask Brayan, a young man who joined a gang in elementary school. Brayan ran away when he was twelve years old, and for three years he was lost in gang and drug life. Although he left the gang and returned home, it was difficult for him; he had been expelled from school for selling drugs. When he enrolled in a new high school, however, a teacher inspired and encouraged him to write about his experiences rather than repeat them. He embraced the challenge and is now experiencing a fresh start.

God, through the prophet Isaiah, encouraged Jewish exiles (taken from their home country by the Babylonians) to think about a new beginning as well. God said, "Forget the former things; do not dwell on the past" (Isaiah 43:18). He told them to stop dwelling on their punishment and even on His display of power through the original exodus from Egypt. He wanted their attention to be focused on God, who would give them a new beginning by taking them home from Babylon through a new exodus (v. 19).

With God, new beginnings are possible in our hearts. He can help us let go of the past and start clinging to Him. A relationship with Him through trust in Jesus provides new hope.

MARVIN WILLIAMS

Let God have your life; He can do more with it than you can.

Neighbor Love

READ LUKE 10:29–37

He answered, "'Love the Lord your God with all your heart and with all your soul and with all your strength and with all your mind'; and, 'Love your neighbor as yourself.'" —LUKE 10:27

It would have been simpler just to buy a new hair dryer. But determined to save a buck, I decided to fix it myself. In order to loosen the screw buried deep in the handle, I took out the ultimate handyman's helper—my pocket knife. As I put pressure on the knife to turn the screw, the blade folded back—on my finger.

I learned a lesson that day: I love myself. And I am urgent about meeting my needs. There was no thought of, "Well, I don't really have time to stop the bleeding now. I'll get to it later." Also, there was a tenderness about how the need was met. I instructed my first-aid team (my wife and kids) to wash my finger gently and then to put the bandage on in a way that would avoid having the hairs on my finger pulled up when it was removed. My thoughts, words, and actions were driven by my love for myself.

To love "your neighbor as yourself" (Luke 10:27) requires the same urgent kind of love. It's a love that notices the need of another person and won't rest until it's been met. It's a gentle, tender love that thinks and acts carefully. It's the same sacrificial and compassionate love that a nameless Samaritan had for a fallen traveler. It's the kind of love God wants to share with your neighbors through you.

JOE STOWELL

You cannot touch your neighbor's heart with anything less than your own.

Father's on Deck

READ MATTHEW 8:23–27

He replied, "You of little faith, why are you so afraid?" Then he got up and rebuked the winds and the waves, and it was completely calm. —MATTHEW 8:26

Many years ago, a seagoing captain commanded a passenger ship that was sailing from Liverpool, England, to New York City. His family was on board with him. One night when everyone was asleep, a squall unexpectedly swept over the waters and tossed the ship violently, awakening the passengers. They were terribly afraid because of the storm.

The captain's eight-year-old girl was also awakened by the chaos. "What's the matter?" cried the frightened child. Her mother told her that a sudden storm had struck the ship. "Is Father on deck?" she asked. "Yes, your father is on deck," came the encouraging answer. Hearing this, the little girl snuggled back into her bed and in a few moments was sound asleep. The winds still blew and the waves still rolled, but her fears were calmed because her father was at the helm.

We too have the assurance of our Father's presence at the controls—our heavenly Father. Although the squalls of life may strike, we know that He is sovereign in our lives, and He will uphold us with His right hand. We may not dodge the storm, and the winds may still blow. But the Master of wind and wave is on board. We can trust Him. He will either calm the waves or quiet our hearts.

PAUL VAN GORDER

We need not nervously pace the deck if the Captain of our salvation is at the helm.

Hope

The Blessing Is Coming

READ GALATIANS 6:7–10

Let us not become weary in doing good, for at the proper time we will reap a harvest if we do not give up. —GALATIANS 6:9

A friend and I went for a walk with her grandkids. While pushing the stroller, she commented that her steps were being wasted—they weren't being counted on her wristband activity tracker because she wasn't swinging her arm. I reminded her that those steps were still helping her physical health. "Yeah," she laughed. "But I really want that electronic gold star!"

I understand how she feels! Working toward something without immediate results is disheartening. But rewards aren't always immediate or immediately visible.

When that's the case, it's easy to feel that the good things we do are useless, even helping a friend or being kind to a stranger. Paul explained to the church in Galatia, however, that "a man reaps what he sows" (Galatians 6:7). But we must "not become weary in doing good, for at the proper time we will reap a harvest" (v. 9). Doing good isn't the way to gain salvation, and the text doesn't specify whether what we reap will be now or in heaven. However, we can know for sure that there will be "a harvest of blessing" (6:9 NLT).

Doing good is difficult, especially when we don't see or know what the "harvest" will be. But as with my friend who still gained the physical benefit from walking, it's worth continuing to do good, because the blessing is coming!

JULIE SCHWAB

Not all rewards are immediate or visible.

Motivated by Love

READ 2 CORINTHIANS 5:11–17

For Christ's love compels us, because we are convinced that one died for all, and therefore all died. —2 CORINTHIANS 5:14

In the 1920s, Bobby Jones dominated the golfing world, despite being an amateur. In one film about his life, *Bobby Jones: Stroke of Genius*, there is a scene where a professional golfer asks Bobby when he is going to quit being an amateur and grab for the money like everyone else does. Jones answers by explaining that the word *amateur* comes from the Latin *amo*—"to love." His answer was clear: He played golf because he loved the game.

Our motives, why we do what we do, make all the difference. This certainly applies to those who are followers of Jesus Christ. In his letter to the Corinthian church, Paul gives us an example of this. Throughout the epistle he defended his conduct, character, and calling as an apostle of Christ. In response to those who questioned his motives for ministry, Paul said, "Christ's love compels us, because we are convinced that one died for all, and therefore all died. And he died for all, that those who live should no longer live for themselves but for him who died for them and was raised again" (2 Corinthians 5:14–15).

Christ's love is the greatest of all motivators. It causes those who follow Him to live for Him, not for themselves.

BILL CROWDER

We are shaped and fashioned by what we love most.

Faith

Turning the Other Cheek

READ MATTHEW 5:38–48

But I tell you, do not resist an evil person. If anyone slaps you on the right cheek, turn to them the other cheek also. —MATTHEW 5:39

This story goes back a few years, but its point is still vital.

Dr. Overton Stephens was one day severely berated by a fellow doctor for something he had said a few years earlier. Dr. Stephens, a follower of Jesus, couldn't recall the incident and felt himself becoming angry because of the accusation.

Recalling Jesus's suggestion to "turn the other cheek," Dr. Stephens allowed the irate man to continue his criticism. When the diatribe ended in a sharp denunciation of Christians in general, Stephens knew that a deeper hostility had prompted this personal attack.

After the other physician finished, Stephens calmly replied, "George, thank you for being honest with me. You gave me quite a tongue lashing, but I can see that some of my thoughtless words have disturbed you. I am truly sorry and hope you will forgive me."

Stunned, the man realized how wrong he had been about Dr. Stephens. He extended his hand and apologized for the cutting words. He gained a new respect for the Christian faith.

When we are being personally maligned, it's hard not to retaliate. But let's try turning the other cheek—and see how the atmosphere changes.

HERB VANDER LUGT

Turning the other cheek may result in turning another person to Christ!

Loving Is Doing

READ LUKE 10:30–37

Let no debt remain outstanding, except the continuing debt to love one another. —ROMANS 13:8

Eminent psychologist Erich Fromm said that love is "an action, not a passion." This is borne out in Christian experience. For instance, we may say we love our wife, our husband, our sweetheart, or our neighbor, but if that love is indeed real, our actions will demonstrate it.

In his book *Mere Christianity*. C. S. Lewis wrote, "Do not waste your time bothering whether you 'love' your neighbor; act as if you did. As soon as we do this, we find one of the great secrets. When you are behaving as if you loved someone, you will presently come to love him."

Many years ago, when I was a student in a Bible institute, one of the young men living in our dorm was a guy I simply didn't like. I thought he was arrogant. He had few friends. One night after an intramural basketball game, that unpopular student and I happened to walk back to the dorm together. I tried my best to show him Christian friendship; in fact, I took him to the snack shop and bought him a milkshake. As we talked, he told me of his father's serious illness and his family's poverty. I began to appreciate this misunderstood dorm mate. Years later I learned that just before that night he had been ready to quit school. Eventually, he became a successful pastor.

Loving is doing. Jesus demonstrated that when He died for us. Is there someone to whom you should show love?

DAVID EGNER

He who loves much, does much.

Hope

Hope Restored

READ JOHN 5:1–8

When Jesus saw him lying there . . . , he asked him, "Do you want to get well?" —JOHN 5:6

Does the sun rise in the east? Is the sky blue? Is the ocean salty? Is the atomic weight of cobalt 58.9? Okay, that last one you might know only if you're a science geek or tend to dabble in trivia, but the other questions have an obvious answer: Yes. In fact, questions like these are usually mixed with a hint of sarcasm.

If we're not careful, our modern—sometimes jaded—ears can hear a bit of sarcasm in Jesus's question to a man who couldn't walk: "Do you want to get well?" (John 5:6). The obvious answer would seem to be, "Are you kidding me?! I've been wanting help for thirty-eight years!" But there's no sarcasm present, that's the furthest thing from the truth. Jesus's voice is always filled with compassion, and His questions are always posed for our good.

Jesus knew the man wanted to get well. He also knew it had probably been a long time since anyone had made an offer to care. Before the divine miracle, Jesus's intent was to restore in him a hope that had grown cold. He did this by asking a rather obvious question, and then giving ways to respond: "Get up! Pick up your mat and walk" (v. 8). We're like the man on the mat, each of us with places in our lives where hope has withered. He sees us and compassionately invites us to believe in hope again, to believe in Him.

JOHN BLASE

Jesus came to bring hope in the darkest of circumstances.

How Long?

READ LUKE 19:41–44

Behold, I stand at the door and knock. If anyone hears My voice and opens the door, I will come in to him and dine with him, and he with Me. —REVELATION 3:20 NKJV

It took years before she finally said yes. A Welshman had fallen in love with one of his neighbors and wanted to marry her. But they had quarreled, and she refused to forgive. Shy and reluctant to face the offended woman, the persistent suitor slipped a love letter under her door every week.

At last, after forty-two years, he summoned up courage, knocked on her door, and asked her to become his wife. To his surprise and delight, she consented. So they were married at the age of seventy-four!

God is also a persistent lover. Century after century He sent prophets as His messengers beseeching the stubborn, alienated people of Israel to live with Him, a faithful covenant-keeper. But all those overtures were sinfully refused. Then at Bethlehem, God himself came in the Person of Jesus Christ. Now, having opened up the way for reconciliation by His redeeming sacrifice at Calvary, He stands at the door of everyone's heart, knocking and asking that sinners personally accept Him as Savior.

If we have answered yes, let's rejoice that we are His. If that door stays shut, however, we must realize that time may run out. Don't remain forever self-alienated from the Lover of your soul. Trust Him today.

VERNON GROUNDS

God always knocks loud enough for a willing soul to hear.

A Living Faith

READ COLOSSIANS 3:5–10

Put to death, therefore, whatever belongs to your earthly nature: sexual immorality, impurity, lust, evil desires and greed, which is idolatry. —COLOSSIANS 3:5

Walking down a street in Long Beach, California, I met a man who asked what I had to show for myself in life. When I referred to my confidence in Jesus, he became very excited. He said that he also knew Christ as his Savior and quoted a couple of Bible verses that promised eternal salvation. As we parted, he reminded me of our commission to preach the Word.

But I had a problem accepting his admonition, for the poor fellow was roaring drunk! With slurred speech he bounced several "praise the Lords" off the brick and concrete around us, drawing stares from passersby that made me feel uncomfortable. Actually, his inebriated condition shouted a loud protest to the sober truths that had echoed through the streets.

Walking back to my motel room, I was struck with the stark reality of how much Christian credibility is lost when our behavior reveals that we are controlled by the flesh rather than the Spirit. We can't expect men to believe a message that is contradicted by our actions.

How important it is for us to bury every word and deed that obscures the indwelling Christ! Only then can we be sure of offering "dying proof" of a living faith.

MART DEHAAN

No one is more confusing than the person who gives good advice while setting a bad example.

Ripples of Hope

READ 1 PETER 1:3–9

In his great mercy he has given us new birth into a living hope through the resurrection of Jesus Christ. —1 PETER 1:3

In 1966, US Senator Robert Kennedy made an influential visit to South Africa. There he offered words of hope to opponents of apartheid in his famous Ripple of Hope speech at the University of Cape Town. In his speech, he declared, "Each time a man stands up for an ideal, or acts to improve the lot of others, or strikes out against injustice, he sends forth a tiny ripple of hope, and crossing each other from a million different centers of energy and daring, those ripples build a current which can sweep down the mightiest walls of oppression and resistance."

At times in this world, hope seems scarce. Yet there is an ultimate hope readily available for the follower of Christ. Peter wrote, "Praise be to the God and Father of our Lord Jesus Christ! In his great mercy he has given us new birth into a living hope through the resurrection of Jesus Christ from the dead" (1 Peter 1:3).

Through the certainty of Christ's resurrection, the child of God has a hope that is more than a ripple. It is an overwhelming current of confidence in the faithfulness of the One who conquered death for us. Jesus, in His victory over death—our greatest enemy—can infuse hope into the most hopeless of situations.

BILL CROWDER

In Christ the hopeless find hope.

Love

Love in Action

READ 1 JOHN 4:7–16

"My command is this: Love each other as I have loved you." —JOHN 15:12

"Sometimes love sure hurts!" The mother and father were expressing the difficulties and heartaches of guiding their children through their teen years. "Maybe if we didn't love them quite so much it wouldn't be so hard," the husband added.

Even though love brings pain and sorrow, what would life be without it? In his book *The Four Loves*, C. S. Lewis wrote:

"To love at all is to be vulnerable. Love anything and your heart will be wrung and possibly be broken. If you want to make sure of keeping it intact, you must give your heart to no one, not even an animal. Wrap it carefully around with hobbies and little luxuries; avoid all entanglements; lock it up safe in the casket or coffin of your selfishness. . . . The only place outside heaven where you can be perfectly safe from all the dangers . . . of love is hell."

To love is to take risks, to expose our hearts. Sometimes it hurts! It hurt Christ, but He kept on loving, even at the cost of His life. He commanded us, "Love each another as I have loved you" (John 15:12).

We must keep loving that spouse, that teenager, that neighbor, that coworker. It is Christlike—and it's better than locking your heart in a coffin of self-centeredness.

DAVID EGNER

Nothing costs as much as loving except not loving.

Love in the Concrete

READ 2 CORINTHIANS 9:1–15

Each of you should give what you have decided in your heart to give, not reluctantly or under compulsion, for God loves a cheerful giver. —2 CORINTHIANS 9:7

Love in the concrete is not the expression "Blake loves Megan" inscribed on a sidewalk when the cement was still wet. Rather, it is actively doing good for others. We tend to love in the abstract, to express the sentiment, but to go no further.

Russian writer Dostoevsky portrays the contrast between abstract and concrete love in his book *The Brothers Karamazov*. One of the brothers, the highly intellectual Ivan, professes to love mankind and is so disturbed by the sorrow and suffering in the world that he takes a negative stance toward God. Yet he takes no practical steps to help anyone! The godly monk Zossima, on the other hand, doesn't talk much about loving or the problem of evil. But he is continually helping people.

Looking at pictures of starving people or seeing terminally ill children brings disturbing questions to my mind. I love people and wish such conditions didn't exist. And I sometimes wonder why God permits them. But when this inner struggle occurs, I must make a choice. I can either start doubting God's goodness, or I can trust God and start doing what I can to help people by praying, showing kindness, and giving. If I do the latter, I will be following the teaching and example of the apostle Paul in today's Scripture lesson—loving in the concrete.

HERB VANDER LUGT

Love is Christianity in action.

Hope

A Song in the Night

READ PSALM 42:1–11

If we hope for what we do not yet have, we wait for it patiently. —ROMANS 8:25

My father's life was one of longing. He longed for wholeness, even as Parkinson's disease gradually crippled more and more of his mind and body. He longed for peace but was tormented by the deep pain of depression. He longed to feel loved and cherished but often felt utterly alone.

He found himself less alone when he read Psalm 42, his favorite psalm. Like him, the psalmist knew a desperate longing, an unquenched thirst for healing (vv. 1–2). Like him, the psalmist knew a sadness that seemed never to go away (v. 3), leaving times of pure joy merely a distant memory (v. 6). Like my dad, as waves of chaos and pain swept over him (v. 7), the psalmist felt abandoned by God and asked, "Why?" (v. 9).

As the words of the psalm washed over him, assuring him he was not alone, my father felt the beginnings of a quiet peace enter in alongside his pain. He heard a tender voice surrounding him, a voice assuring him that even though he had no answers, even though the waves still crashed over him, still he was dearly loved (v. 8).

And somehow hearing that quiet song of love in the night was enough. Enough for my dad to quietly cling to glimmers of hope, love, and joy. And enough for him to wait patiently for the day when all his longings would finally be satisfied (vv. 5, 11).

MONICA BRANDS

While we wait for the morning, we can rest in God's song of love in the night.

Longing for Home

READ HEBREWS 11:8–16

They were longing for a better country—
a heavenly one. —HEBREWS 11:16

My wife walked into the room and found me poking my head inside the cabinet of our grandfather clock. "What are you doing?" she asked. "This clock smells just like my parents' house," I answered sheepishly, closing the door. "I guess you could say I was going home for a moment."

The sense of smell can evoke powerful memories. We had moved the clock across the country from my parents' house nearly twenty years earlier, but the aroma of the wood inside the cabinet still took me back to my childhood.

The writer of Hebrews tells of others who were longing for home in a different way. Instead of looking backward, they were looking ahead with faith to their home in heaven. Even though what they hoped for seemed a long way off, they trusted that God was faithful to keep His promise to bring them to a place where they would be with Him forever (Hebrews 11:13–16).

Philippians 3:20 reminds us that "our citizenship is in heaven," and we are to "eagerly await a Savior from there, the Lord Jesus Christ." Looking forward to seeing Jesus and receiving everything God has promised us through Him helps us keep our focus. The past or the present can never compare with what's ahead of us!

JAMES BANKS

The best home of all is our home in heaven.

Faith

A Personal Matter

READ LUKE 9:18–26

"But what about you?" [Jesus] asked.
"Who do you say I am?"
Peter answered, "God's Messiah." —LUKE 9:20

In Luke 9 Jesus asked His disciples what other people thought of Him. He inquired, "Who do the crowds say I am?" (v. 18). Did they see Him as a good man, a mighty prophet, a sincere individual but intent on upsetting traditional teachings? Or did they believe He was truly the Son of God? Certainly Jesus knew the thoughts of the multitude far better than anyone. He specifically directed this question to the disciples, however, because He was leading up to something far more important. After receiving their reply, He came right to the point. I can imagine Him looking each disciple straight in the eye and saying, "Who do *you* say I am?" What He really wanted was their personal response.

Faith in Christ is an individual matter. While it may be interesting to consider the opinions of others about Jesus, it's what *you* say about Him that really counts. Your confession regarding the Savior will determine your eternal destiny. The Bible says, "Everyone who believes that Jesus is the Christ [the Messiah] is born of God" (1 John 5:1). No one is assured of heaven unless he or she can truly say, "You are the Messiah, the Son of the living God" (Matthew 16:16).

Have you placed your trust in Him? If not, accept Him today! Remember, faith in Christ is a personal matter!

RICHARD DEHAAN

Christ is the unavoidable One; what you do
with Him determines your destiny.

Imitation Faith

READ ISAIAH 1:1–7

The Lord says. "These people . . . honor me with their lips, but their hearts are far from me." —ISAIAH 29:13

Tourists throughout the centuries have visited the famous Acropolis, the ancient hilltop religious citadel in Athens. Thousands of sightseers from all over the world have picked up marble chunks as souvenirs.

Why hasn't the supply of pieces been exhausted long ago? The answer is very simple. Every few months a truckload of marble fragments from a quarry several miles away is scattered around the whole Acropolis area. So tourists go home happy with what they think are authentic pieces of ancient history.

We can be deceived by other kinds of imitations. Religious language and music, religious objects and services may fool us into imagining that we are experiencing a firsthand relationship with God when in reality we are simply going through empty routines.

During the time of the prophet Isaiah, many of the people of Israel were merely going through the motions. That is why God told them, "Stop bringing meaningless offerings! Your incense is detestable to me. . . . Your New Moons and your appointed festivals I hate with all my being" (Isaiah 1:13–14).

The possibility of religious deception prompts personal soul-searching. Our pious practices may be only imitations of the true heartfelt faith that the Lord desires.

Vernon Grounds

A hypocrite has God in his mouth
and the world in his heart.

Hope for a Mudder

READ JAMES 1:2–4

Suffering produces perseverance; perseverance, character; and character, hope. —ROMANS 5:3–4

When my husband built a covered porch on the front of our house, he anticipated that someday a bird might try to build a nest there. So he built the top of the corner post on a slant. Later we laughed smugly when we saw robins trying their best to claim squatting rights to a new home. Piles of grass on the porch revealed their wasted efforts. But after two days of steady rain, we saw that a nest had indeed appeared in the very spot we thought was impossible. Because of the rain, Mrs. Robin was able to mix up a batch of mud mortar. Weaving it with twigs and grass, our determined feathered friend had built herself a new nest. She had persevered.

Perseverance is inspiring! Trying to live a Christ-honoring life while experiencing hardship can leave us frustrated and discouraged. But when we depend on God to help us through our difficulties, we are empowered to keep going even when we can't always see the resolution of our problems. Galatians 6:9 reminds us not to "become weary in doing good" and encourages us not to give up.

Is our loving God using a seemingly insurmountable challenge in your life to produce perseverance? Let Him produce in you character—and through character, hope (Romans 5:3–4).

CINDY HESS KASPER

When the world says, "Give up," hope whispers, "Try it one more time!"

Reason to Hope

READ LAMENTATIONS 3:19–26

The LORD is good to those whose hope is in him, to the one who seeks him. —LAMENTATIONS 3:25

Sorrow was gripping the hearts of the citizens of Jerusalem (Lamentations 1). The glorious city was in ruins, and the people were facing exile. God's majestic Zion had fallen to the Babylonians.

The destruction of Jerusalem in 586 BC was the result of God's judgment on an unrepentant people. Because we too can find ourselves wondering how to return to fellowship with God after failing Him, the lessons learned by those downcast citizens are worth heeding.

For the defeated people of the Holy City—and for us—the hope of restoration is given in Lamentations 3. It begins, "This I recall to my mind and therefore I have hope" (v. 21).

We have hope because of God's character, which is marked by these traits: His mercy and compassion (v. 22), faithfulness (v. 23), goodness (v. 25), and salvation (v. 26).

Although we cannot understand completely the sadness of the displaced Jerusalemites, we do know how empty life becomes when our sin cuts us off from fellowship with God. Yet we can be restored because He will forgive us when we repent of our sin. His compassions are "new every morning" (v. 23). He alone gives the refreshment of hope, and therefore we too can proclaim, "Great is Your faithfulness."

DAVE BRANON

No one is hopeless whose hope is in God.

Faith

Faith of a Child

READ MATTHEW 18:1–5

And he said: "Truly I tell you, unless you change and become like little children, you will never enter the kingdom of heaven." —MATTHEW 18:3

One Sunday I heard Mike talk about his relationship with his two fathers—the one who raised him as a child and his Father in heaven.

First, he described his childhood trust toward his earthly father as "simple and uncomplicated." He expected his dad to fix broken things and to give advice. He dreaded displeasing him, however, because he often forgot that his father's love and forgiveness always followed.

Mike continued, "Some years ago I made a mess of things and hurt a lot of people. Because of my guilt, I ended a happy, simple relationship with my heavenly Father. I forgot that I could ask Him to fix what I had broken and seek His advice."

Years passed. Eventually Mike became desperate for God, yet he wondered what to do. His pastor said simply, "Say you're sorry to God and mean it!"

Instead, Mike asked complicated questions, like: "How does this work?" and "What if . . .?"

Finally, his pastor prayed, "Please, God, give Mike the faith of a child!" Mike later testified joyfully, "The Lord did!"

That day Mike found closeness with his heavenly Father. The key for him and for us is to practice the simple and uncomplicated faith of a child.

JOANIE YODER

Faith shines brightest in a childlike heart.

Love Letters

READ EPHESIANS 4:25–5:2

Walk in the way of love, just as Christ loved us and gave himself up for us as a fragrant offering and sacrifice to God. —EPHESIANS 5:2

To "walk in the way of love" means that we continually do the little acts of kindness that can make life bearable and better for another person.

One practical way to express our love costs only the price of a postage stamp—plus paper, ink, and a little thought.

All of us have felt the nudge to write a letter—an unexpected note that could brighten another person's day. Perhaps it is a note of appreciation, an expression of concern, or a compliment for a task well done. Too often the letter goes unwritten and the impulse is unexpressed. We convince ourselves that we don't have time or that our letter won't matter.

A young minister cherished a note he received from a busy architect in his congregation. The letter said simply, "Your sermon met me where I was on Sunday—at the crossroads of confusion and hurt. Thanks for preaching it!" Those twenty words met the pastor where he lived—at the intersection of discouragement and pain—and encouraged him to keep on in the ministry. The note took less than five minutes to write.

Can you think of someone who needs a word of encouragement, thanks, or a reminder that you are praying for him or her? Perhaps this is a good day to "walk in the way of love" to the mailbox.

HADDON ROBINSON

It takes only a moment to be kind, but
the result can last a lifetime.

Love

Long Shadows of Love

READ PSALM 100

The LORD *is good and his love endures forever; his faithfulness continues through all generations.* —PSALM 100:5

Several years ago, my wife and I stayed in a rustic bed-and-breakfast in the remote Yorkshire Dales of England. We were there with four other couples, all British, whom we had never met before. Sitting in the living room with our after-dinner coffees, the conversation turned to occupations with the question "What do you do?" At the time, I was serving as the president of Moody Bible Institute in Chicago, and I assumed that no one there knew of MBI or its founder, D. L. Moody.

When I mentioned the name of the school, their response was immediate and surprising. "Of Moody and Sankey . . . that Moody?" Another guest added, "We have a Sankey hymnal and our family often gathers around the piano to sing from it." I was amazed! The evangelist Dwight Moody and his musician Ira Sankey had held meetings in the British Isles more than one hundred and twenty years earlier, and their influence was still being felt.

I left the room that night thinking of the ways our lives can cast long shadows of love and influence for God—a praying mother's influence on her children, an encouraging coworker's words, the support and challenge of a teacher or a mentor, the loving but corrective words of a friend. It's a high privilege to play a role in the wonderful promise that "His love . . . continues through all generations" (Psalm 100:5).

JOE STOWELL

Only what's done for Christ will last.

Faithful to the Finish

READ HEBREWS 12:1–4

Therefore, since we are surrounded by such a great cloud of witnesses, let us throw off everything that hinders and the sin that so easily entangles. And let us run with perseverance the race marked out for us. —HEBREWS 12:1

After running thirty-two kilometers (twenty miles) of the Kielder Marathon in Great Britain, a runner dropped out and rode a bus to a wooded area near the finish line. Then he re-entered the race and claimed third prize. When officials questioned him, he stated that he stopped running because he was tired.

As we run the race of the Christian faith, many of us can relate to the exhaustion of a worn-out athlete. The book of Hebrews encourages us to "run with endurance the race marked out for us" (12:1). Running with endurance requires that we lay aside the sin that stands in our way and shed the weights that hold us back. We may even have to press on through persecution (2 Timothy 3:12).

To prevent weariness and discouragement in our souls (Hebrews 12:3), the Bible urges us to focus on Christ. When we pay more attention to Him than to our struggles, we will notice Him running alongside us—supporting us when we stumble (2 Corinthians 12:9) and encouraging us with His example (1 Peter 2:21–24). Keeping our eyes on "the pioneer and perfecter of our faith" (Hebrews 12:2) will help us stay close to the source of our strength and remain faithful to the finish.

JENNIFER BENSON SCHULDT

We can finish strong when we focus on Christ.

Hope

Living in Tents

READ GENESIS 12:4–9

From there he went on toward the hills east of Bethel and pitched his tent. —GENESIS 12:8

Growing up in Minnesota, a place known for its many beautiful lakes, I loved to go camping to enjoy the wonders of God's creation. But sleeping in a flimsy tent wasn't my favorite part of the experience—especially when a rainy night and a leaky tent resulted in a soggy sleeping bag.

I marvel to think that one of the heroes of our faith spent a hundred years in tents. When he was seventy-five years old, Abraham heard God's call to leave his country so the Lord could make him into a new nation (Genesis 12:1–2). Abraham obeyed, trusting that God would follow through on His promise. And for the rest of his life, until he died at 175 (25:7), he lived away from his home country in tents.

We may not have the same call as Abraham did to live nomadically, but even as we love and serve this world and the people in it, we may long for a deeper experience of home, of being rooted here on earth. Like Abraham, when the wind whips our flimsy covering or the rain soaks through, we can look with faith for the city to come, whose "architect and builder is God" (Hebrews 11:10). And like Abraham, we can find hope that God is working to renew His creation, preparing a "better country—a heavenly one" to come (v. 16).

AMY BOUCHER PYE

God gives us a solid foundation for our lives.

MAY
4

A Brief Message

READ PSALM 117

For great is his love toward us, and the faithfulness of the Lord endures forever. Praise the Lord. —PSALM 117:2

I counted once and discovered that Abraham Lincoln's Gettysburg Address contains fewer than three hundred words. This means, among other things, that words don't have to be many to be memorable.

That's one reason I like Psalm 117. Brevity is its hallmark. The psalmist said all he had to say in thirty words (actually just seventeen words in the Hebrew text).

"Praise the Lord, all you nations; extol him, all you peoples. For great is his love toward us, and the faithfulness of the Lord endures forever. Praise the Lord."

Ah, that's the good news! Contained in this hallelujah psalm is a message to all nations of the world that God's "great love"—His covenant love—is "great . . . toward us" (v. 2).

Think about what God's love means. God loved us before we were born; He will love us after we die. Not one thing can separate us from the love of God that is in Jesus our Lord (Romans 8:39). His heart is an inexhaustible and irrepressible fountain of love!

As I read this brief psalm of praise to God, I can think of no greater encouragement for our journey than its reminder of God's great love. Praise the Lord!

David Roper

What we know about God should lead us to give joyful praise to Him.

Hope

When the Woods Wake Up

READ JOHN 11:14–27

Jesus said . . . , "I am the resurrection and the life. He who believes in Me, though he may die, he shall live." —JOHN 11:25 NKJV

Through cold, snowy winters, the hope of spring sustains those of us who live in Michigan. May is the month when that hope is rewarded. The transformation is remarkable. Limbs that look lifeless on May 1 turn into branches that wave green leafy greetings by month's end. Although the change each day is imperceptible, by the end of the month the woods in my yard have changed from gray to green.

God has built into creation a cycle of rest and renewal. What looks like death to us is rest to God. And just as rest is preparation for renewal, death is preparation for resurrection.

I love watching the woods awaken every spring, for it reminds me that death is a temporary condition and that its purpose is to prepare for new life, a new beginning, for something even better. "Unless a kernel of wheat falls to the ground and dies, it remains only a single seed. But if it dies, it produces many seeds" (John 12:24).

While pollen is a springtime nuisance when it coats my furniture and makes people sneeze, it reminds me that God is in the business of keeping things alive. And after the pain of death, He promises a glorious resurrection for those who believe in His Son.

JULIE ACKERMAN LINK

Every new leaf of springtime is a reminder
of our promised resurrection.

The Open Door

READ LUKE 15:11–24

"I am the gate; whoever enters through me will be saved. They will come in and go out, and find pasture." —JOHN 10:9

Canadian Bible teacher Walter Hughes (1890–1875) told about a Scottish girl who had strayed far from the godly teaching of her parents. After one evening of partying in the city of Edinburgh, she decided to commit suicide.

She had a longing, however, to visit her childhood home one last time. Making her way through the darkness, she arrived at the humble cottage where her mother lived alone now. Pushing open the gate, she walked through the garden, hoping for one last look at the old house.

The sight before her both startled and frightened her. The front door was wide open! Thinking something was wrong, she called out, "Mother, are you all right?" The Scottish woman quickly appeared and cried, "Maggie, it is many a long day since you went away, but always the prayer in my heart has been, 'Lord, send her home.' And I said, 'Whether she comes by night or day, I want her to see an open door and know she is welcome.' "

That mother's message to her daughter is the same for each person—no matter who they are or what they've done. Jesus offers a loving, open-armed reception for all. He who said, "I am the gate," (John 10:9) gives this gracious invitation, "Come to me, all you who are weary and burdened, and I will give you rest" (Matthew 11:28). If you've turned your back on the Savior—come "home." By faith enter the open door!

RICHARD DEHAAN

A man can go to hell in his own way; but he must go to heaven in God's way—through Christ the Door!

Love

Rooted Love

READ HEBREWS 13:15–25

Do not forget to do good and to share with others, for with such sacrifices God is pleased. —HEBREWS 13:16

When I think of all the wonders of God's magnificent creation, I am especially awed by the giant Sequoia tree. These amazing behemoths of the forest can grow to around three hundred feet tall with a diameter that exceeds forty feet. They can live more than three thousand years and are even fire resistant. In fact, forest fires pop the sequoia cones open, distributing their seeds on the forest floor that has been fertilized by the ashes. Perhaps the most amazing fact is that these trees can grow in just three feet of soil and withstand high winds. Their strength lies in the fact that their roots intertwine with other Sequoias, providing mutual strength and shared resources.

God's plan for us is like that. Our ability to stand tall in spite of the buffeting winds of life is directly related to the love and support we receive from God and one another. And then, as the writer of Hebrews says, we are to "do good and to share" (13:16). Think of how tough it would be to withstand adversity if others were not sharing the roots of their strength with us.

There is great power in the entwining gifts of encouraging words, interceding prayers, weeping together, holding each other, and sometimes just sitting with one another and sharing the presence of our love.

JOE STOWELL

Let the roots of God's love in your life be entwined with others who need your support.

Does God Love Me?

READ 1 JOHN 4:7–19

We love because he first loved us. —1 JOHN 4:19

It's not easy to understand the depth of God's love for us. Because of our pride and fear, we fail to grasp how undeserving we are and how free His love is.

At times I struggle with pride, so I tend to believe that I have earned any love I have received. Pride tells me that I am loved only when I am lovable, respectable, and worthy.

At other times I feel the tug of fear. Deep down inside, I know that I don't deserve the love I get. My motives are never pure, and I fear I will be rejected if they are exposed. So even while I am basking in acceptance, I live with the fear of being unmasked, revealing that I am much less than what others think me to be.

When I consider my relationship with God, therefore, I tend to feel that His affection for me is based on my performance. When I do well, He loves me; but if I foul up, then I expect only His scorn.

Yet God does not love us because we deserve it. He loves us in spite of what we are. First John 4:10 states, "This is love: not that we loved God, but that he loved us and sent his Son." Because of what Jesus Christ has done for us, we know we are always loved by God. That simple truth should shatter our pride and dispel our fear.

HADDON ROBINSON

Looking for God's love? Look to Jesus Christ.

Hope

More than a Hero

READ JOHN 1:15, 9–14

We have seen his glory, the glory of the one and only Son, who came from the Father, full of grace and truth. —JOHN 1:14

A few years ago, as Star Wars fans around the world eagerly awaited the release of Episode 8, *The Last Jedi*, people continued to analyze the remarkable success of these films dating back to 1977. Frank Pallotta, media reporter for *CNNMoney*, said that Star Wars connects with many who long for "a new hope and a force of good at a time when the world needs heroes."

At the time of Jesus's birth, the people of Israel were oppressed and longing for their long-promised Messiah. Many anticipated a hero to deliver them from Roman tyranny, but Jesus did not come as a political or military hero. Instead, He came as a baby to the town of Bethlehem. As a result, many missed who He was. The apostle John wrote, "He came to that which was his own, but his own did not receive him" (John 1:11).

More than a hero, Jesus came as our Savior. He was born to bring God's light into the darkness and to give His life so that everyone who receives Him could be forgiven and freed from the power of sin. John called Him "the one and only Son, who came from the Father, full of grace and truth" (v. 14).

"To all who did receive him, to those who believed in his name, he gave the right to become children of God" (v. 12). Indeed, Jesus is the one true hope the world needs.

DAVID MCCASLAND

At Bethlehem, God demonstrated that to love is to give.

MAY
10

Ruth's Story

READ ROMANS 10:1–13

"Everyone who calls on the name of the Lord will be saved." —ROMANS 10:13

Ruth could not tell her story without tears. In her mid-eighties and unable to get around much anymore, Ruth did not appear to be a central figure in our church's life. She depended on others for rides, and because she lived alone she didn't have a huge circle of influence.

But when she told us her story of salvation—as she did often—Ruth stood out as a remarkable example of God's grace. Back when she was in her thirties, a friend invited her to go to a meeting one night. Ruth didn't know she was going to hear a preacher. "I wouldn't have gone if I knew," she said. She already had "religion," and it wasn't doing her any good. But go she did. And she heard the good news about Jesus that night.

More than fifty years later, she cried tears of joy when she talked of how Jesus transformed her life and took away her destructive habits. That evening, she became a child of God. Her story never grew old.

It doesn't matter if our story is similar to Ruth's or not. What does matter is that we take the simple step of putting our faith in Jesus and His death and resurrection. The apostle Paul said, "If you declare with your mouth, 'Jesus is Lord,' and believe in your heart that God raised him from the dead, you will be saved" (Romans 10:9).

That's what Ruth did. You can do that too. Jesus redeems, transforms, and gives us new life.

DAVE BRANON

Belonging to Christ is not rehabilitation; it's re-creation.

Hope

He Knows Us

READ PSALM 139:1–14

You have searched me, LORD, and you know me. You know when I sit and when I rise. —PSALM 139:1–2

Did God know about me as I drove at night on a one hundred-mile journey to my village? Given the condition I was in, the answer was not simple. My temperature ran high and my head ached. I prayed, "Lord, I know you are with me, but I'm in pain!"

Tired and weak, I parked by the road near a small village. Ten minutes later, I heard a voice. "Hello! Do you need any help?" It was a man with his companions from the community. Their presence felt good. When they told me the name of their village, *Naa mi n'yala* (meaning, "The King knows about me!"), I was amazed. I had passed this community dozens of times without stopping. This time, the Lord used its name to remind me that, indeed, He, the King, was with me while I was alone on that road in my ailing condition. Encouraged, I pressed on toward the nearest clinic.

God knows us thoroughly as we go about our everyday chores, at different locations and situations, no matter our condition (Psalm 139:1–4, 7–12). He does not abandon us or forget us; nor is He so busy that He neglects us. Even when we are in trouble or in difficult circumstances—"darkness" and "night" (vv. 11–12)—we are not hidden from His presence. This truth gives us such hope and assurance that we can praise the Lord who has carefully created us and leads us through life (v. 14).

LAWRENCE DARMANI

No matter where we are, God knows about us.

Courage to Be Faithful

READ 1 PETER 3:3–18

It should be that of your inner self, the unfading beauty of a gentle and quiet spirit, which is of great worth in God's sight. —1 PETER 3:4

Fear is Hadassah's constant companion. Hadassah, a young Jewish girl living in the first century, is a fictional character in Francine Rivers' book *A Voice in the Wind*. After Hadassah becomes a slave in a Roman household, she fears persecution for her faith in Christ. She knows that Christians are despised, and many are sent to their execution or thrown to the lions in the arena. Will she have the courage to stand for the truth when she is tested?

When her worst fear becomes reality, her mistress and other Roman officials who hate Christianity confront her. She has two choices: recant her faith in Christ or be taken to the arena. Then, as she proclaims Jesus as the Christ, her fear falls away and she becomes bold even in the face of death.

The Bible reminds us that sometimes we will suffer for doing what is right—whether for sharing the gospel or for living godly lives that are against today's values. We are told not to be frightened (1 Peter 3:14), but to "revere Christ as Lord" in our hearts (v. 15). Hadassah's main battle took place in her heart. When she finally made up her mind to choose Jesus, she found the courage to be faithful.

When we make the decision to honor Christ, He will help us to be bold and to overcome our fears in the midst of opposition.

Keila Ochoa

Let us be bold as we witness for God.

No Outsiders

READ DEUTERONOMY 10:12–22

And now, Israel, what does the Lord *your God ask of you but to fear the* Lord *your God, to walk in obedience to him, to love him, to serve the* Lord *your God with all your heart and with all your soul.* —DEUTERONOMY 10:12

In the remote region of Ghana where I lived as a boy, "Chop time, no friend" was a common proverb. Locals considered it impolite to visit at "chop time" (mealtime) because food was often scarce. The maxim applied to neighbors and outsiders alike.

But in the Philippines, where I also lived for a time, even if you visit unannounced at mealtime, your hosts will insist on sharing with you regardless of whether they have enough for themselves. Cultures differ for their own good reasons.

As the Israelites left Egypt, Moses took up the topic of Israel's treatment of outsiders. God "loves the foreigner residing among you," he said, "giving them food and clothing. And you are to love those who are foreigners, for you yourselves were foreigners in Egypt" (Deuteronomy 10:18–19).

Israel served the "God of gods and Lord of lords, the great God, mighty and awesome" (v. 17). One powerful way they were to show their identification with God was by loving foreigners—those from outside their culture.

What might this small picture of God's character mean for us today? How can we show His love to the marginalized and the needy in our world?

Tim Gustafson

In Christ, there are no outsiders.

A Call for Help

READ ACTS 2:14–21

Everyone who calls on the name of the Lord will be saved. —ACTS 2:21

After five deaths and fifty-one injuries in elevator accidents in 2016, New York City launched an ad campaign to educate people on how to stay calm and be safe. The worst cases were people who tried to save themselves when something went wrong. The best plan of action, authorities say, is simply, "Ring, relax, and wait." New York building authorities made a commitment to respond promptly to protect people from injury and extract them from their predicament.

In the book of Acts, we read a sermon Peter preached that addressed the error of trying to save ourselves. Luke, who wrote the book, records some remarkable events in which believers in Christ were speaking in languages they did not know (Acts 2:1–12). Peter got up to explain to his Jewish brothers and sisters that what they were witnessing was the fulfillment of an ancient prophecy (Joel 2:28–32)—the outpouring of the Spirit and a day of salvation. The blessing of the Holy Spirit was now visibly seen in those who called on Jesus for rescue from sin and its effects. Then Peter told them how this salvation is available for anyone (v. 21). Our access to God comes not through keeping the Law but through trusting Jesus as Lord and Messiah.

If we are trapped in sin, we cannot save ourselves. Our only hope for being rescued is acknowledging and trusting Jesus as Lord and Messiah.

MARVIN WILLIAMS

Rescue comes to those who call on Jesus for help.

MAY
15

Faith

Rooted

READ 2 CHRONICLES 24:15–22

Joash did what was right in the eyes of the L*ORD* *all the years of Jehoiada the priest.* —2 CHRONICLES 24:2

Joash, the king of Judah, must have been confused and frightened when he was told about the evil deeds of his grandmother Athaliah—things that took place when he was a baby. She had murdered his brothers to usurp the power of the throne. During that time, Joash had been safely hidden away by his aunt and uncle for six years (2 Chronicles 22:10–12). As he grew, he enjoyed the love and instruction of his caregivers. When Joash was only seven years old, he was secretly crowned king, and his grandmother was overthrown (23:12–15).

Young King Joash had a wise counselor by his side—Uncle Jehoiada (chapters 22–25). While his uncle was alive, Joash obeyed the Lord by doing right (24:2) and was one of the rare "good kings" of Judah. But once his uncle was no longer there to teach and lead by example, Joash fell away—and his life ended badly (24:15–25). The roots of his faith did not run very deep. He even began to worship idols. Perhaps Joash's "faith" had been more his uncle's than his own.

Others can teach us the principles of their faith, but each of us must come individually to personal faith in Christ. For faith to be real, it must become our own. God will help us walk with Him and become rooted and established in the faith (Colossians 2:6–7).

CINDY HESS KASPER

The faith that continues to the end gives proof that it was genuine in the beginning.

A Warm Welcome

READ 1 PETER 4:7–11

Offer hospitality to one another without grumbling. —1 PETER 4:9

"Who will hug everybody?"

That was one of the questions our friend Steve asked after he got the news that he had cancer and realized he would be away from our church for a while. Steve is the kind of man who makes everyone feel welcome—with a friendly greeting, a warm handshake, and even a "holy hug" for some—to adapt an application from Romans 16:16, which says, "Greet one another with a holy kiss."

And now, as we pray for Steve that God will heal him, he is concerned that as he goes through surgery and treatment—and is away from our church for a time—we will miss out on those welcoming greetings.

Perhaps not all of us are cut out to greet one another as openly as Steve does, but his example of caring for people is a good reminder to us. Notice that Peter says to "offer hospitality to one another without grumbling," or in a way that centers on love (1 Peter 4:9; see Philippians 2:14). While first-century hospitality included offering accommodations to travelers—even that always starts with a welcoming greeting.

As we interact with others in love, whether with a hug or just a friendly smile, we do so "that in all things God may be praised through Jesus Christ" (1 Peter 4:11).

DAVE BRANON

When we practice hospitality,
we share God's goodness.

Hope

Hope in God

READ PSALM 42

Why, my soul, are you downcast? . . . Put your hope in God, for I will yet praise him, my Savior and my God. —PSALM 42:5

Looking at the western shores of Sri Lanka, I found it hard to imagine that a tsunami had struck just a few months earlier. The sea was calm and beautiful, couples were walking in the bright sunshine, and people were going about their business—all giving the scene an ordinary feeling I wasn't prepared for. The impact of the disaster was still there, but it had gone underground into the hearts and minds of the survivors. The trauma itself would not be easily forgotten.

It was catastrophic grief that prompted the psalmist to cry out in anguish: "My tears have been my food day and night, while people say to me all day long, 'Where is your God?' " (Psalm 42:3). The struggle of his heart had likewise been turned inward. While the rest of the world went on with business as usual, he carried in his heart the need for deep and complete healing.

Only as we submit our brokenness to the good and great Shepherd of our hearts can we find the peace that allows us to respond to life: "Why, my soul, are you downcast? . . . Put your hope in God, for I will yet praise him, my Savior and my God" (v. 5).

Hope in God—it's the only solution for the deep traumas of the heart.

BILL CROWDER

A world without Christ would
be a world without hope.

Humble Love

READ PHILIPPIANS 2:1–11

"The greatest among you will be your servant." —MATTHEW 23:11

When Benjamin Franklin was a young man he made a list of twelve virtues he desired to grow in over the course of his life. He showed it to a friend, who suggested he add "humility" to it. Franklin liked the idea. He then added some guidelines to help him with each item on the list. Among Franklin's thoughts about humility, he held up Jesus as an example to emulate.

Jesus shows us the ultimate example of humility. God's Word tells us, "In your relationships with one another, have the same mindset as Christ Jesus: Who, being in very nature God, did not consider equality with God something to be used to his own advantage; rather, he made himself nothing by taking the very nature of a servant" (Philippians 2:5–7).

Jesus demonstrated the greatest humility of all. Though eternally with the Father, He chose to bend beneath a cross in love so that through His death He might lift any who receive Him into the joy of His presence.

We imitate Jesus's humility when we seek to serve our heavenly Father by serving others. Jesus's kindness helps us catch a breathtaking glimpse of the beauty of setting ourselves aside to attend to others' needs.

Aiming for humility isn't easy in our "me first" world. But as we rest securely in our Savior's love, He will give us everything we need to follow Him.

JAMES BANKS

We can serve because we are loved.

MAY
19

Hope

A Word to the Weary

READ ISAIAH 50:4–10

The Sovereign LORD *has given me a well-instructed tongue to know the word that sustains the weary.* —ISAIAH 50:4

The people of Israel were struggling. They had been taken captive by the Assyrians and forced to live in a country far from home. What could the prophet Isaiah give these weary people to help them?

He gave them a prophecy of hope. It was a message from God relating to the promised Messiah. In Isaiah 50:4, the Savior himself described the comfort and consolation He would one day bring: "The Sovereign LORD has given me a well-instructed tongue to know the word that sustains the weary."

These were words of dual comfort—both to the people in exile and to future generations whose lives would be touched by Jesus's compassion. In the Gospels we see how Christ fulfilled the prophecy with "a word in season to him who is weary" (Isaiah 50:4 NKJV). To the crowds who followed Him, Christ proclaimed: "Come to me, all you who are weary and burdened, and I will give you rest" (Matthew 11:28). Words of compassion indeed!

Jesus left us an example of how to minister to people who have grown weary. Do you know someone who needs a timely word of encouragement or the listening ear of a concerned friend? A word of comfort to the weary can go a long way.

DENNIS FISHER

Compassion is needed to heal the hurts of others.

T-Ball Faith

READ LUKE 15:1–7

Nehemiah said, "Go and enjoy choice food and sweet drinks, and send some to those who have nothing prepared. This day is holy to our Lord. Do not grieve, for the joy of the L*ORD* *is your strength."* —NEHEMIAH 8:10

Whoever dreamed up T-ball is a genius: Every kid on the field gets a taste of the fun and joy of the game of baseball before they taste the disappointment of striking out.

In T-ball, a baseball is placed on a rubber tee about waist-high to the five- and six-year-old batters. Players swing until they hit the ball, and then they run. On my first night as a coach, the very first batter hit the ball far into the outfield. Suddenly every player from every position ran to get the ball instead of staying where they were supposed to. When one of them reached it, there was nobody left in the infield for him to throw it to! All the players were standing together—cheering with unrestrained exuberance!

Those who have recently come to know Jesus as Savior know about unrestrained joy. They have been redeemed and freed from sin's penalty—and there is no better feeling! It is so important that even the angels in heaven rejoice! (Luke 15:7). New Christians are in love with God and excited about knowing Him more through the Bible.

Those of us who are longtime Christians may get discouraged with the struggles of life and forget the joy of newfound faith. If so, let's think of those who've recently come to faith and recall their joy. God can use them to inspire us to renew our own commitment to Jesus.

RANDY KILGORE

Restore to me the joy of your salvation. —Psalm 51:12

Love

"Lovable"

READ JEREMIAH 31:1–6

"I have loved you with an everlasting love; I have drawn you with unfailing kindness." —JEREMIAH 31:3

"Lovable!" That exclamation came from my daughter as she got ready one morning. I didn't know what she meant. Then she tapped her shirt, a hand-me-down from a cousin. Across the front was that word: "Lovable." I gave her a big hug, and she smiled with pure joy. "You are lovable!" I echoed. Her smile grew even bigger, if that's possible, as she skipped away, repeating the word over and over again.

I'm hardly a perfect father. But that moment was perfect. In that spontaneous, beautiful interaction, I glimpsed in my girl's radiant face what receiving unconditional love looked like: It was a portrait of delight. She knew the word on her shirt corresponded completely with how her daddy felt about her.

How many of us know in our hearts that we are loved by a Father whose affection for us is limitless? Sometimes we struggle with this truth. The Israelites did. They wondered if their trials meant God no longer loved them. But in Jeremiah 31:3, the prophet reminds them of what God said in the past: "I have loved you with an everlasting love." We too long for such unconditional love. Yet the wounds, disappointments, and mistakes we experience can make us feel anything but lovable. But God opens His arms—the arms of a perfect Father—and invites us to experience and rest in His love.

ADAM HOLZ

No one loves us like our Father.

MAY
22

What Is Love?

READ PSALM 103:1–14

This is love: not that we loved God, but that he loved us and sent his Son as an atoning sacrifice for our sins. —1 JOHN 4:10

When asked, "What is love?" children have some great answers. Noelle, age seven, said, "Love is when you tell a guy you like his shirt, then he wears it every day." Rebecca, who is eight, answered, "Since my grandmother got arthritis, she can't bend over and polish her toenails anymore. So my grandfather does it for her all the time, even after his hands got arthritis too. That's love." Jessica, also eight, concluded, "You really shouldn't say 'I love you' unless you mean it. But if you mean it, you should say it a lot. People forget."

Sometimes we need to be reminded that God loves us. We focus on the difficulties of life and wonder, *Where's the love*? But if we pause and consider all that God has done for us, we remember how much we are loved by God, who is love (1 John 4:8–10).

Psalm 103 lists the "benefits" God showers on us in love: He forgives our sin (v. 3), satisfies us with good things (v. 5), and executes righteousness and justice (v. 6). He is slow to anger and He abounds in mercy (v. 8). He doesn't deal with us as our sins deserve (v. 10), and He has removed our sin as far as the east is from the west (v. 12). He has not forgotten us!

What is love? God is love, and He's pouring out that love on you and me.

Anne Cetas

The death of Christ is the measure of God's love for you.

MAY
23

Hope

Don't Give Up

READ GALATIANS 6:1–10

Let us not become weary in doing good, for at the proper time we will reap a harvest if we do not give up. —GALATIANS 6:9

Bob Foster, my mentor and friend for more than fifty years, never gave up on me. His unchanging friendship and encouragement, even during my darkest times, helped carry me through.

We often find ourselves determined to reach out and help someone we know who is in great need. But when we fail to see improvement right away, our resolve can weaken and we may eventually give up. We discover that what we hoped would be an immediate change has become an ongoing process.

The apostle Paul urges us to be patient in helping one another through the stumbles and struggles of life. When he writes, "Carry each other's burdens" and so "fulfill the law of Christ" (Galatians 6:2), he is comparing our task to the work, time, and waiting it takes for a farmer to see a harvest.

How long should we keep praying and reaching out to those we love? "Let us not become weary in doing good, for at the proper time we will reap a harvest if we do not give up" (v. 9). How many times should we reach out? "As we have opportunity, let us do good to all people, especially to those who belong to the family of believers" (v. 10).

The Lord encourages us today to trust Him, to remain faithful to others, to keep on praying, and to not give up!

DAVID MCCASLAND

In prayer we call on God "who is able to do immeasurably more than all we ask or imagine." —Ephesians 3:20

Who's Going to Heaven?

READ ROMANS 3:21–28

For we maintain that a person is justified by faith apart from the works of the law. —ROMANS 3:28

A poll for *U.S. News & World Report* asked 1,000 adults their opinion about who would likely make it into heaven. At the top of that list, to no one's surprise, was a well-known religious figure. Several celebrities were also listed. But it was surprising to me that of the people being surveyed, eighty-seven percent thought they themselves were likely to get into heaven.

I can't help but wonder what qualifications for admission into heaven they had in mind. People have many erroneous ideas about what God requires.

Is it virtuous character—more good than bad? Giving generous contributions to deserving charities? Following an orthodox creed? Attending church and being involved in religious activities? Commendable as these qualities may be, they miss the one thing God requires for entrance into heaven—faith in the finished work of Jesus Christ on the cross (John 1:12; 1 Timothy 2:5–6). Nothing we can do—as good as it is—can substitute trusting in Jesus's sacrificial death for our sin.

Are you confident that you're headed for heaven? You can be—but only if you're trusting in Jesus.

VERNON GROUNDS

Jesus took our place on the cross to give us a place in heaven.

Love

"I Love You, Daddy"

READ PSALM 116

I love the L*ORD, for he heard my voice; he heard my cry for mercy.* —PSALM 116:1

The value of voicing our love and affection to others was emphasized to me by something my daughter Katie said and did when she was just two years old. Although by that time Katie had learned the mechanics of saying "I love you" by mimicking Mom and Dad as we spoke to her, her words had begun to take on new, special meaning.

One evening while we were playing together, she ran to me without prompting, put her little arms tightly around my neck and said, "I love you, Daddy!" That moment was precious to me and stayed with me through the years. Her words went straight to my heart because they were sincere, unrehearsed, and pure.

As I reflected on that incident from so long ago, I was reminded that the Lord desires the same kind of voluntary response from each of His spiritual children. As we contemplate what God does for us, we will begin to love and appreciate Him more and more. He gives us new life. He showers us with His favor. He disciplines us in love. He provides us with spiritual gifts to serve Him. And He's building an eternal home for us.

When we realize that all these blessings are an expression of His love, we will be eager to show our own love for Him. Then we'll be ready to say "Jesus, I love you!" Has He heard you tell Him that recently?

KURT DEHAAN

God's Word tells us of His love; our words tell Him of our love.

Hope

The Warmth of the Sun

READ PSALM 6

I am worn out from my groaning. All night long I flood my bed with weeping and drench my couch with tears. —PSALM 6:6

On a November day in 1963, Brian Wilson and Mike Love of the Beach Boys wrote a song quite unlike the band's typically upbeat tunes. It was a mournful song about love that's been lost. Mike said later, "As hard as that kind of loss is, the one good that comes from it is having had the experience of being in love in the first place." They titled it "The Warmth of the Sun."

Sorrow serving as a catalyst for songwriting is nothing new. Some of David's most moving psalms were penned in times of deep personal loss, including Psalm 6. Though we aren't told the events that prompted its writing, the lyrics are filled with grief, "I am worn out from my groaning. All night long I flood my bed with weeping . . . . My eyes grow weak with sorrow" (vv. 6–7).

But that's not where the song ends. David knew pain and loss, but he also knew God's comfort. And so he wrote, "The Lord has heard my cry for mercy; the Lord accepts my prayer" (v. 9). In his grief, David not only found a song but he also found reason to trust God, whose faithfulness bridges all of life's hard seasons.

In the warmth of God's presence, our sorrows gain a hopeful perspective.

Bill Crowder

A song of sadness can turn our hearts to the God whose joy for us is forever.

Faith

Bad Faith, Good Faith

READ ROMANS 4:18–25

He did not waver through unbelief regarding the promise of God, but was strengthened in his faith and gave glory to God. —ROMANS 4:20

"You gotta have faith," people say. But what does that mean? Is any and every faith good faith?

"Believe in yourself and all that you are," wrote one positive thinker a century ago. "Know that there is something inside you that is greater than any obstacle." As nice as that may sound, it falls to pieces when it crashes into reality. We need a faith in something bigger than ourselves.

God promised Abram he would have a multitude of descendants (Genesis 15:4–5), but he faced a huge obstacle—he was old and childless. When he and Sarah got tired of waiting for God to make good on His promise, they tried to overcome that obstacle on their own. As a result, they fractured their family and created a lot of unnecessary dissension (see Genesis 16 and 21:8–21).

Nothing Abraham did in his own strength worked. But ultimately he became known as a man of tremendous faith. Paul wrote of him, "Against all hope, Abraham in hope believed and so became the father of many nations, just as it had been said to him, 'So shall your offspring be' " (Romans 4:18). This faith, said Paul, "was credited to him as righteousness" (v. 22).

Abraham's faith was in something far bigger than himself—the one and only God. It's the object of our faith that makes all the difference.

Tim Gustafson

Our faith is good if it's in the right Person.

A Wonderful Explosion

READ JOHN 13:31–35

"A new command I give you: Love one another. As I have loved you, so you must love one another." —JOHN 13:34

In the book *Kisses from Katie*, Katie Davis recounts the joy of moving to Uganda and adopting several Ugandan girls. One day, one of her daughters asked, "Mommy, if I let Jesus come into my heart, will I explode?" At first, Katie said no. When Jesus enters our heart, it is a spiritual event.

However, after she thought more about the question, Katie explained that when we decide to give our lives and hearts to Jesus "we will explode with love, with compassion, with hurt for those who are hurting, and with joy for those who rejoice." In essence, knowing Christ results in a deep care for the people in our world.

The Bible challenges us to "rejoice with those who rejoice; mourn with those who mourn" (Romans 12:15). We can consistently display this loving response because of the Holy Spirit's work in our hearts. When we receive Christ, the Holy Spirit comes to live inside us. The apostle Paul described it this way, "When you believed [in Christ,] you were marked in him with a seal, the promised Holy Spirit" (Ephesians 1:13).

Caring for others—with God's supernatural assistance—shows the world that we are His followers (John 13:35). It also reminds us of His love for us. Jesus said, "As I have loved you, so you must love one another" (v. 34).

JENNIFER BENSON SCHULDT

Love given reflects love received.

Faith

A "New Man"

READ COLOSSIANS 1:3–14

If you continue in your faith, established and firm, and do not move from the hope held out in the gospel. This is the gospel that you heard and that has been proclaimed to every creature under heaven, and of which I, Paul, have become a servant. —COLOSSIANS 1:23

As a group of teenagers visited a home for the elderly in Montego Bay, Jamaica, one young woman noticed a lonely looking man at the end of the room. He appeared to have little left in this world but a bed to sleep on—a bed from which he could not move because of his disability.

The teen began to share the story of God's love and read some Bible passages to him. "As I shared with him," she would say later, "I started to feel his eagerness to hear more." She explained the wonder of Jesus's sacrificial death for us. "It was hard for this man, who had no hope and no family," she recalled, "to understand that Someone he's never met would love him enough to die on the cross for his sins."

She told him about the promise of heaven (including a new body) for all who believe. He asked her, "Will you dance with me up there?" He was beginning to imagine himself free of his crippling limitations.

When he said he wanted to trust Jesus as his Savior, she helped him pray a prayer of forgiveness and faith. When she asked him if she could get a picture with him, he replied, "If you help me sit up. I'm a new man."

Praise God for the life-changing, hope-giving, available-to-all gospel of Jesus Christ! It offers new life for all who trust Him (Colossians 1:5, 23).

DAVE BRANON

Jesus offers new life.

The Friendly Skies of Faith

READ LUKE 17:3–10

The apostles said to the Lord, "Increase our faith!" —LUKE 17:5

Millions of people are afraid to travel by air. Many of them know very well what the statistics say—that they are safer in an airplane than in the family car or the bathtub. But that doesn't matter. Researchers say that a conscious fear of crashing is usually not the problem. Instead, at the root of their anxiety is the fear that once they leave the ground they will lose control of their lives.

A similar crisis of faith occurs when a person puts himself in the care of God. He too is carried a long way from what the world considers "solid ground." Trusting an invisible Lord can be frightening, especially for a new Christian.

Jesus's disciples expressed their concern when He told them that they would have to rise to levels of forgiveness and mercy previously unknown to them. Yet He responded to their lack of faith by pointing out that it takes only a small amount of obedient trust in Him to put the power of heaven at their disposal.

That's the key to our journey through life. When we learn what Christ wants from us, we must take the first step of obedience. He will then give us the strength to do what He wants us to do.

Lord, increase our faith.

MART DEHAAN

A little faith can lift you above your fears.

Hope

A Double Promise

READ ISAIAH 25:1–9

Lord, you are my God; I will exalt you and praise your name, for in perfect faithfulness you have done wonderful things, things planned long ago. —ISAIAH 25:1

Since she suffered cancer several years ago, Ruth has been unable to eat, drink, or even swallow properly. She has also lost a lot of her physical strength, and numerous operations and treatments have left her a shadow of what she used to be.

Yet Ruth is still able to praise God; her faith remains strong, and her joy is infectious. She relies on God daily, and she holds on to the hope that she will recover fully one day. She prays for healing and is confident that God will answer—sooner or later. What an awesome faith!

Ruth explained that what keeps her faith strong is the secure knowledge that God will not only fulfill His promises in His time but will also sustain her until that happens. This was the same hope that God's people, the Israelites, had as they waited for Him to complete His plans (Isaiah 25:1), deliver them from their enemies (v. 2), wipe away their tears, remove their disgrace, and "swallow up death forever" (v. 8).

In the meantime, God gave His people refuge and shelter (v. 4) as they waited. He comforted them in their ordeals, gave them strength to endure, and gave them assurance that He was there with them.

This is the double promise we have—the hope of deliverance one day, plus the provision of His comfort, strength, and shelter throughout our lives.

Leslie Koh

Trusting God's faithfulness can dispel our fearfulness.

Love That Will Not Let Me Go

READ 1 JOHN 4:7–21

Dear friends, since God so loved us, we also ought to love one another. —1 JOHN 4:11

Love is the centerpiece of thriving relationships. Scripture makes it clear that we need to be people who love—love God with all our hearts, love our neighbor as ourselves, and love our enemies. But it's hard to love when we don't feel loved. Neglected children, spouses who feel ignored by their mates, and parents who are alienated from their children all know the heartache of a life that lacks love.

So, for everyone who longs to be loved, welcome to the pleasure of knowing that you are richly loved by God. Think of the profound impact of His love that was poured out for you at the cross. Meditate on the fact that if you've trusted in Him, His love covers your faults and failures and that you are clothed with His spotless righteousness (Romans 3:22–24). Revel in the fact that nothing can separate you from His love (8:39). Embrace His loving provision of a future secured for you where you will be eternally loved (John 3:16).

When John tells us that we "ought to love one another," he calls us "dear friends" (1 John 4:11). Once we embrace how wonderfully loved we are by God, it will be much easier to be the loving people God calls us to be—even toward those who don't show us love.

JOE STOWELL

Embracing God's love for us is the key to loving others.

Hope

On the Winning Side

READ REVELATION 21:1–8

For everyone born of God overcomes the world. This is the victory that has overcome the world, even our faith. —1 JOHN 5:4

It was the first game of the Little League baseball season, and Mikey was playing outfield. After chasing a long hit and hustling the ball back into the infield, someone who just arrived at the game yelled over to him and asked him how his team was doing. Mikey told the spectator that his team was doing well, but they were trailing 17-0. "Are you ready to give up?" the man asked. Just before the next pitch, Mikey yelled back his reply: "We aren't beat—we haven't even been up to bat yet!"

As we make our way through life and all of its negative influences and temptations, doesn't it feel sometimes like we are behind by seventeen runs? But if we do feel that way, there is hope. We know that God will have the final word in life's struggle between good and evil. We know that someday we will be delivered not only from the penalty of sin but also from its presence and power. This encourages us to press on

An old Christian gentleman who was known for his optimistic outlook was asked the secret of his triumphant attitude. He replied, "I've read the last book of the Bible, so I know how the story ends. I'm on the winning side."

Hope is vital in the battle with sin. All power rests in our heavenly Father. We can draw on His unlimited resources. In the power of the indwelling Spirit, resist temptation. Obey God's Word. Remember, we win!

RICHARD DEHAAN

The best time to prove you're a real winner is when it looks like you're losing.

Hope for Worriers

READ PSALM 23

The LORD is my shepherd, I lack nothing. —PSALM 23:1

Everyone worries occasionally, but I was once a "professional worrier." My daily preoccupation was mulling over my worries, one by one.

Then one day I had to face an uncomfortable medical test, and I was frantic with fear. Finally I decided that during the test I would focus on the first five words of Psalm 23, "The LORD is my shepherd." This exercise in meditation not only calmed me but it also helped me gain several fresh insights. Later, as I slowly meditated through the entire psalm, the Lord gave me more insights. Eventually I was able to share at conferences what the Lord had taught me.

If you're a worrier, there's hope for you too! Rick Warren, author of *The Purpose Driven Life*, wrote: "When you think about a problem over and over in your mind, that's called worry. When you think about God's Word over and over in your mind, that's meditation. If you know how to worry, you already know how to meditate!"

The more we meditate on God's Word, the less we need to worry. In Psalm 23, David meditated on his great Shepherd instead of worrying. Later, God chose him to be the shepherd of His people (Psalm 78:70–72). God uses those who can honestly say, "The Lord is my shepherd."

JOANIE YODER

The more we think about God's Word, the less we'll think about our worries.

Faith

The Empty Bed

READ MATTHEW 28:16–20

Go and make disciples of all nations. —MATTHEW 28:19

I was eager to return to St. James Infirmary in Montego Bay, Jamaica, and reconnect with Rendell, who two years earlier had learned about Jesus's love for him. Evie, a teenager in the high school choir I travel with each spring, had read Scripture with Rendell and explained the gospel, and he personally received Jesus as his Savior.

When I entered the men's section of the home and looked toward Rendell's bed, however, I found it was empty. I went to the nurse's station and was told what I didn't want to hear. He had passed away—just five days before we arrived.

Through tears, I texted Evie the sad news. Her response was simple: "Rendell is celebrating with Jesus." Later she said, "It's a good thing we told him about Jesus when we did."

Her words reminded me of the importance of being ready to lovingly share with others the hope we have in Christ. No, it's not always easy to proclaim the gospel message about the One who will be with us always (Matthew 28:20), but when we think about the difference it made for us and for people like Rendell, perhaps we'll be encouraged to be even more ready to "make disciples" wherever we go (v. 19).

I'll never forget the sadness of that empty bed—but also the joy of knowing what a difference one faithful teen made in Rendell's forever life.

DAVE BRANON

God, we know that people need You. Help us to overcome our fear of telling others about You.

Helpful Love

READ JOHN 1:9–14

The Word became flesh and made his dwelling among us. We have seen his glory, the glory of the one and only Son, who came from the Father, full of grace and truth. —JOHN 1:14

At the end of my mother's earthly journey, she and Dad were still very much in love and shared a strong faith in Christ. My mother had developed dementia and began to lose memories of even her family. Yet Dad would regularly visit her at the assisted living home and find ways to accommodate her diminished capacities.

For instance, he would take her some saltwater taffy, unwrap a piece, and place it in her mouth—something she could not do for herself. Then as she slowly chewed the candy, Dad would quietly sit with her and hold her hand. When their time together was over, Dad, beaming with a wide smile, would say, "I feel such peace and joy spending time with her."

Though touched by Dad's great joy in helping Mom, I was more affected by the reality that he was depicting God's grace. Jesus was willing to humble himself to connect with us in our weaknesses. In reflecting on Christ's incarnation, John wrote, "The Word became flesh and made his dwelling among us" (1:14). Taking on human limitations, He did countless acts of compassion to accommodate us in our weakness.

Do you know anyone who might benefit from Jesus's helpful, accommodating love that could flow through you to them today?

DENNIS FISHER

To be a channel of blessing, let Christ's love flow through you.

Unchanging Love

READ JAMES 1:12–20

Every good and perfect gift is from above, coming down from the Father of the heavenly lights, who does not change like shifting shadows. —JAMES 1:17

At a wedding I attended, the bride's grandfather quoted from memory a moving selection of Scripture about the relationship of husband and wife. Then a friend of the couple read "Sonnet 116" by William Shakespeare. The minister conducting the ceremony used a phrase from that sonnet to illustrate the kind of love that should characterize a Christian marriage: "Love is not love which alters when it alteration finds." The poet is saying that true love does not change with circumstances.

The minister noted the many changes this couple would experience during their life together, including health and the inevitable effects of age. Then he challenged them to cultivate the true biblical love that neither falters nor fails in spite of the alterations that would surely come their way.

As I witnessed the joy and excitement of this young couple, a verse came to mind from James: "Every good gift and every perfect gift is from above, coming down from the Father of the heavenly lights, who does not change like shifting shadows" (1:17). God never changes, and neither does His love for us. We are recipients of a perfect love from our heavenly Father, who has loved us "with an everlasting love" (Jeremiah 31:3).

We are called to accept God's unfailing love, to allow it to shape our lives, and to extend it to others.

DAVID MCCASLAND

God's love still stands when all else has fallen.

Little Lies and Kittens

READ ROMANS 5:12–21

Just as sin ruled over all people and brought them to death, now God's wonderful grace rules instead. —ROMANS 5:21 NLT

Mom noticed four-year-old Elias as he scurried away from the newborn kittens. She had told him not to touch them. "Did you touch the kitties, Elias?" she asked. "No!" he said earnestly. So Mom had another question: "Were they soft?"

"Yes," he volunteered, "and the black one mewed."

With a toddler, we smile at such duplicity. But Elias's disobedience underscores our human condition. No one has to teach a four-year-old to lie. "For I was born a sinner," wrote David in his classic confession, "yes, from the moment my mother conceived me" (Psalm 51:5 NLT). The apostle Paul said: "When Adam sinned, sin entered the world. Adam's sin brought death, so death spread to everyone, for everyone sinned" (Romans 5:12 NLT). That depressing news applies equally to kings, four-year-olds, and you and me.

But there's plenty of hope! "God's law was given so that all people could see how sinful they were," wrote Paul. "But as people sinned more and more, God's wonderful grace became more abundant" (Romans 5:20 NLT).

God is not waiting for us to blow it so He can pounce on us. He is in the business of grace, forgiveness, and restoration. We need only recognize that our sin is neither cute nor excusable and come to Him in faith and repentance.

TIM GUSTAFSON

There is now no condemnation for those who are in Christ Jesus. —Romans 8:1

Faith

Lack Nothing

READ MARK 6:7–12

God is able to bless you abundantly, so that . . . you will abound in every good work. —2 CORINTHIANS 9:8

Imagine going on a trip without luggage. No basic necessities. No change of clothing. No money or credit cards. Sounds both unwise and terrifying, doesn't it?

But that's exactly what Jesus told His twelve disciples to do when He sent them out on their first mission to preach and heal. "Take nothing for the journey except a staff," said Jesus. "No bread, no bag, no money in your belts. Wear sandals but not an extra shirt" (Mark 6:8–9).

Yet later on when Jesus was preparing them for their work after He was gone, He told His disciples, "If you have a purse, take it, and also a bag; and if you don't have a sword, sell your cloak and buy one" (Luke 22:36).

So, what's the point here? It's about trusting God to supply.

When Jesus referred back to that first trip, He asked the disciples, "When I sent you without purse, bag or sandals, did you lack anything?" And they answered, "Nothing" (v. 35). The disciples had everything they needed to carry out what God had called them to do. He was able to supply them with the power to do His work (Mark 6:7).

Do we trust God to supply our needs? Are we also taking personal responsibility and planning? Let's have faith that He will give us what we need to carry out His work.

Poh Fang Chia

God's will done in God's way will never lack God's supply.
—Hudson Taylor, founder of China Inland Mission

The Defeat of Death

READ 1 THESSALONIANS 4:15–18

But thanks be to God! He gives us the victory through our Lord Jesus Christ. —1 CORINTHIANS 15:57

One of the greatest tests of our trust in the gospel of Jesus Christ is how we react in the face of death. When we attend a memorial service for a departed friend who loved the Lord Jesus, we gather to honor a believer whose stalwart trust has richly blessed the lives of those who knew him. The words spoken are more an expression of praise to God than a tribute to an admired fellow pilgrim. The service is a God-glorifying testimony to our Savior's victory over death and the grave (1 Corinthians 15:54–57).

How different from the funeral service of Charles Bradlaugh, a belligerent British atheist. Writer Arthur Porritt recalls: "No prayer was said at the grave. Indeed, not a single word was uttered. The remains, placed in a light coffin, were lowered into the earth in a quite unceremonious fashion as if carrion were being hustled out of sight. . . . I came away heart-frozen. It only then dawned on me that loss of faith in the continuity of human personality after death gives death an appalling victory."

Christians, however, believe in a face-to-face fellowship with our Lord after death and the eventual resurrection of our bodies (1 Corinthians 15:42–55; 1 Thessalonians 4:15–18). Even despite the pain and the loss, because of our faith we can rejoice in victory over death.

Vernon Grounds

Because Christ is alive, we too shall live.

A Modest Proposal

READ PHILIPPIANS 2:1–11

And being found in appearance as a man, he humbled himself by becoming obedient to death— even death on a cross! —PHILIPPIANS 2:8

As a college student, I heard countless engagement stories. My starry-eyed friends told about glitzy restaurants, mountaintop sunsets, and rides in horse-drawn carriages. I also recall one story about a young man who simply washed his girlfriend's feet. His "modest proposal" proved he understood that humility is vital for a lifelong commitment.

The apostle Paul also understood the significance of humility and how it holds us together. This is especially important in marriage. Paul said to reject "me-first" urges: "Do nothing out of selfish ambition" (Philippians 2:3). Instead, we should value our spouses more than ourselves and look out for their interests.

Humility in action means serving our spouse, and no act of service is too small or too great. After all, Jesus "humbled himself by becoming obedient to death—even death on a cross!" (v. 8). His selflessness showed His love for us.

What can you do today to humbly serve the one you love? Maybe it's as simple as leaving Brussels sprouts off the dinner menu or as difficult as helping him or her through a long illness. Whatever it is, placing our spouse's needs before our own confirms our commitment to each other through Christlike humility.

JENNIFER BENSON SCHULDT

If you think it's possible to love your spouse too much, you probably haven't loved enough.

Sonrise

READ MALACHI 4:1–6

The sun of righteousness will rise with healing in its rays. —MALACHI 4:2

My state's name, "Idaho," according to one legend, comes from a Shoshone Indian word, *ee-dah-how*. When translated into English, it means something like, "Behold! The sun rising over the mountain." I often think of that when the sun breaks over the eastern peaks and spills light and life into our valley.

Also, I think of Malachi's promise: "The sun of righteousness will rise with healing in its rays" (Malachi 4:2). This is God's irrevocable promise that our Lord Jesus will come again and all creation "will be liberated from its bondage to decay and brought into the freedom and glory of the children of God" (Romans 8:21).

Each new sunrise is a reminder of that eternal morning when "the sun of righteousness" will arise with healing in His wings. Then everything that has been made will be made over and made irrevocably right. There will be no throbbing backs or knees, no financial struggles, no losses, no aging. Malachi says that when Jesus returns we will "go out and frolic like well-fed calves" (4:2). This is my highest imagination and my hope.

Jesus said, "Yes, I am coming soon" (Revelation 22:20). *Even so, come, Lord Jesus!*

David Roper

You have reason for optimism if you're looking for Christ's return.

Love

The Real Prize

READ EPHESIANS 5:22–33

Husbands, love your wives, just as Christ loved the church and gave himself up for her. —EPHESIANS 5:25

I've been amazed at the impact that my wife, Martie, has had on the lives of our kids. Very few roles demand the kind of unconditional, self-sacrificing perseverance and commitment as that of motherhood. I know for certain that my character and faith have been shaped and molded by my mom, Corabelle. Let's face it, where would we be without our wives and mothers?

It reminds me of one of my favorite memories in sports history. Phil Mickelson walked up the eighteenth fairway at the Masters Golf Tournament in 2010 after his final putt to clinch one of golf's most coveted prizes for the third time. But it wasn't his victory leap on the green that had an impact on me. It was when he made a beeline through the crowd to his wife, who was battling life-threatening cancer. They embraced, and the camera caught a tear running down Phil's cheek as he held his wife close for a long time.

Our wives need to experience the kind of sacrificial, selfless love that has been shown to us by the Lover of our souls. As Paul put it, "Husbands, love your wives, just as Christ also loved the church and gave himself up for her" (Ephesians 5:25). Prizes come and go, but it's the people you love—and who love you—that matter most.

JOE STOWELL

Life is not about the prizes we win,
but the people we love.

Faith

JUNE
13

Growing in the Wind

READ MARK 4:36–41

Who is this? Even the wind and the waves obey him! —MARK 4:41

Imagine a world without wind. Lakes would be calm. Falling leaves wouldn't blow in the streets. But in still air, who would expect trees to suddenly fall over? That's what happened in a three-acre glass dome built in the Arizona desert. Trees growing inside a huge windless bubble called Biosphere 2 grew faster than normal until suddenly collapsing under their own weight. Project researchers eventually came up with an explanation. These trees needed wind stress to grow strong.

Jesus let His disciples experience gale-force winds to strengthen their faith (Mark 4:36–41). During a night crossing of familiar waters, a sudden storm proved too much even for these seasoned fishermen. Wind and waves were swamping their boat while an exhausted Jesus slept in the stern. In a panic they woke Him. Didn't it bother their Teacher that they were about to die? What was He thinking? Then they began to find out. Jesus told the wind and waves to be quiet—and asked His friends why they still had no faith in Him.

If the wind had not blown, these disciples would never have asked, "Who is this? Even the winds and the waves obey him!" (Mark 4:41).

Today, life in a protective bubble might sound good. But how strong would our faith be if we couldn't discover for ourselves His reassuring "be still" when the winds of circumstance howl?

MART DEHAAN

God never sleeps.

Love

A Loving Father

READ PSALM 103:7–13

As a father has compassion on his children, so the Lord *has compassion on those who fear him.* —PSALM 103:13

The parents were obviously weary from dragging their two energetic preschoolers through airports and airplanes, and now their final flight was delayed. As I watched the two boys running around the crowded gate area, I wondered how Mom and Dad were going to keep the little guys settled down for our half-hour flight into Grand Rapids. When we finally boarded, I noticed that the father and one of the sons were in the seats behind me. Then I heard the weary father say to his son, "Why don't you let me read one of your storybooks to you." During the entire flight, this loving father softly and patiently read to his son, keeping him calm and focused.

In one of his psalms David declares, "As a father has compassion on his children, so the Lord has compassion on those who fear him" (Psalm 103:13). This tender word *compassion* gives us a picture of how deeply our heavenly Father loves His children, and it reminds us what a great gift it is to be able to look to God and cry, "Abba, Father" (Romans 8:15).

God longs for us to listen again to the story of His love for us when we are restless on our own journey through life. Our heavenly Father is always near, ready to encourage us with His Word.

Bill Crowder

God's great love for His child is
one of His greatest gifts.

JUNE
15

Small but Significant

READ 2 CORINTHIANS 1:8–11

On him we have set our hope that he will continue to deliver us, as you help us by your prayers. —2 CORINTHIANS 1:10–11

The day started out like any other, but it ended as a nightmare. Esther (not her real name) and several hundred women were kidnapped from their boarding school by a religious militant group. A month later all were released—except for Esther, who refused to deny Christ. As my friend and I read about her and others who are being persecuted for their faith, our hearts were moved. We wanted to do something. But what?

When writing to the Corinthian church, the apostle Paul shared about the trouble he experienced in the province of Asia. The persecution was so severe that he and his companions "despaired of life itself" (2 Corinthians 1:8). However, Paul was helped by the prayers of believers (v. 11). Though the Corinthian church was many miles away from the apostle, their prayers mattered and God heard them. Herein lies an amazing mystery: the sovereign One has chosen to use our prayers to accomplish His purpose. What a privilege!

Today we can continue to remember our brothers and sisters in Christ who are suffering for their faith. There's something we can do. We can pray for those who are marginalized, oppressed, beaten, tortured, and sometimes even killed for their belief in Christ. Let's pray for them to experience God's comfort and encouragement and to be strengthened with hope as they stand firmly with Jesus.

POH FANG CHIA

In prayer, we cast ourselves at the feet of divine power.

Hope

False Hope

READ EPHESIANS 2:1–10

For it is by grace you have been saved, through faith—and this is not from yourselves, it is the gift of God—not by works. —EPHESIANS 2:8–9

The name of a pretty Bavarian town in Germany shares the name of a place of horror—Dachau. A museum on the grounds of this infamous Nazi concentration camp attracts many World War II history buffs.

As you look around, it would be hard to miss the misleading words welded to an iron gate: *Arbeit Macht Frei.* This phrase—Work Makes You Free—was just a cruel lie to give false hope to those who entered this place of death.

Many people today have false hope that they can earn a place in heaven by working at being good or by doing good things. God's standard of perfection, however, requires a totally sinless life. Clearly, there's no way any of us can ever be "good enough." It is only through the sacrifice of the sinless Savior that we are made righteous. God made Jesus "who had no sin to be sin for us, so that in him we might become the righteousness of God" (2 Corinthians 5:21). Eternal life is given because of God's gift of grace—not because of our good works (Ephesians 2:8–9).

Don't let Satan trick you by giving you false hope that your good works will save you. It is only through Jesus's work on the cross that you can have real freedom.

Cindy Hess Kasper

We are not saved by good works,
but by God's work.

The Snake and the Tricycle

READ LUKE 1:1–4

With this in mind, since I myself have carefully investigated everything from the beginning, I too decided to write an orderly account for you, most excellent Theophilus. —LUKE 1:3

For years, I retold a story from the time our family lived in Ghana and my brother and I were toddlers. As I recalled it, he had parked our old iron tricycle on a small cobra. The trike was too heavy for the snake, which remained trapped under the front wheel.

But after my mother passed away, we discovered a long-lost letter from her recounting the incident. In reality, I had parked the tricycle on the snake, and my brother had run to tell Mom. Her eyewitness account, written close to the actual event, revealed the reality.

The historian Luke understood the importance of accurate records. He explained how the story of Jesus was "handed down to us by those who from the first were eyewitnesses" (Luke 1:2). "I too decided to write an orderly account for you," he wrote to Theophilus, "so that you may know the certainty of the things you have been taught" (vv. 3–4). The result was the gospel of Luke. Then, in his introduction to the book of Acts, Luke said of Jesus, "After his suffering, he presented himself to them and gave many convincing proofs that he was alive" (Acts 1:3).

Our faith is not based on hearsay or wishful thinking. It is rooted in the well-documented life of Jesus, who came to give us peace with God. His Story stands.

TIM GUSTAFSON

Genuine faith is rooted in reason.

Love Means Giving

READ ROMANS 5:1–8

This is love: not that we loved God, but that he loved us and sent his Son as an atoning sacrifice for our sins. —1 JOHN 4:10

Love's highest expression is found in giving. This was most perfectly displayed when God gave His only Son to save the world (John 3:16). Our love for Him should motivate us to prove the reality of our love through giving (2 Corinthians 8:8–9). We do this by first presenting our bodies "a living sacrifice, holy, acceptable to God," which is our "true and proper worship" (Romans 12:1).

In his book *Man Alive*, John Whittle told about a widow whose only son told her he was obeying the call of God to go to the mission field. Although the woman had been a Christian for many years, her son's decision upset her because she had assumed that as she grew older he would be there when she needed him. Then one day something happened that changed her outlook. As she read John 3, the familiar words of verse 16 caught her attention in new way. The thought came to her mind that, as Whittle expressed it, "God was giving her the privilege of doing in her small way what He had done." Her entire perspective was changed. She was willing to "give up" her son to go to the mission field because of God's love for her. Together they were able to see themselves as partners in the Lord's service.

The apostle Paul said that "Christ's love compels us" (2 Corinthians 5:14). That means we will love by giving ourselves to Him and to others.

RICHARD DEHAAN

A selfish heart loves for what it can get;
a Christlike heart loves for what it can give.

JUNE
19

A Little Piece of Heaven

READ EXODUS 25:1–9

Don't you know that you yourselves are God's temple and that God's Spirit dwells in your midst? —1 CORINTHIANS 3:16

One day not long ago, my wife met a woman who needed a ride. She sensed that this could be from God, so she agreed to take her to her destination. During the ride, the woman revealed to my wife that she was a believer, but she struggled with drug addiction. My wife listened to and talked with this hurting woman. As she gave her hope for a better tomorrow, I believe that in some small way the woman experienced a little piece of heaven on earth.

When God instructed Moses to build the tabernacle according to His specifications, it was so that God's people would sense His presence. I like to think of it as a little piece of heaven on earth. The temple was a physical example of God's presence on earth also (1 Kings 5–8). The purpose of these holy places was for God to dwell among His people. This was God's plan when Jesus, the perfect temple, "made his dwelling among us" (John 1:14).

When Jesus ascended to heaven, He sent the Holy Spirit to indwell His followers (John 14:16–17), so that we would be God's tabernacles and temples in the world (1 Corinthians 3:16; 6:19). As God's representatives of His presence, let's find ways to bring the peace and hope of heaven to others on earth.

MARVIN WILLIAMS

A Christian who is willing to do little things for others can do great things for the Lord.

Faith

God's Plan, Not Ours

READ 1 SAMUEL 4:1–21

I will say of the L*ORD*, *"He is my refuge and my fortress, my God, in whom I trust."* —PSALM 91:2

Everybody was wrong about the ark of the covenant (an item in the tabernacle that represented the throne of God). After losing a battle to the Philistines, Israel sent messengers to Shiloh to ask that the ark be hauled to Ebenezer, the site of their army camp.

When the ark arrived, the Israelites celebrated so loudly the enemy heard them all the way over in Aphek. The ark's arrival caused the Philistines to fear and the Israelites to have courage.

They were both wrong. First, the Israelites took the ark into battle and were again clobbered by the Philistines, who captured the ark. Then, while the ark was in their possession, the Philistines got sick and their false gods were destroyed.

We can understand the Philistines' error—they were idol-worshipers. But the Israelites should have known better. They failed to consult God about using the ark. While they knew that the ark was earlier carried in battle (Joshua 6), they didn't consider that God's plan, not the ark's involvement, allowed Israel to defeat Jericho.

No matter our resources, we will fail unless we use them according to God's plan. Let's study the Word, pray for God's direction, and trust His leading (Psalm 91:2) before we step out in any venture of faith.

DAVE BRANON

We see in part; God sees the whole.

Hope

Finding Hope

READ PSALM 42:1–11

Why, my soul, are you downcast? . . . Put your hope in God, for I will yet praise him. —PSALM 42:5

A study conducted by researchers at the University of Minnesota found that almost fifteen percent of American teenagers felt it was "highly likely" that they would die before their thirty-fifth birthday. Those with this pessimistic outlook were more likely to engage in reckless behavior. Dr. Iris Borowsky, author of the study published in *Pediatrics* magazine, said: "These youth may take risks because they feel hopeless and figure that not much is at stake."

No one is immune to feelings of despair. The Psalms express repeated pleas for help when life seems dark. "Why are you in despair, O my soul? And why have you become disturbed within me? Hope in God, for I shall again praise Him for the help of His presence" (Psalm 42:5 NASB). In a defiant step of faith, the psalmist tells himself not to forget about God, who will never forsake him.

Curtis Almquist has written: "Hope is fueled by the presence of God. . . . [It] is also fueled by the future of God in our lives." We can say with the psalmist, "I will yet praise him" (v. 5).

No follower of Christ should feel reluctant to seek counsel for depression. Nor should we feel that faith and prayer are too simplistic to help. There is always hope in God!

DAVID MCCASLAND

Hope for the Christian is a certainty—
because its basis is Christ.

Love

Love in the Sky

READ ROMANS 6:1–11

Now if we died with Christ, we believe that we will also live with him. —ROMANS 6:8

My husband and I were at a public swimming pool when the people around us started staring into the sky. A small plane was emitting smoke in the form of letters. As we watched, the pilot spelled out the letters: "I L-O-V-E." People began speculating: Maybe it was to be a marriage proposal. Perhaps a romantic man is standing nearby on a balcony with his girlfriend and will soon pop the Will-you-marry-me? question. We kept gazing upward: "I L-O-V-E Y-O-U J-E-." I heard young girls guessing: "I bet it will be Jen or maybe Jessica." He kept spelling. No. It was: "J-E-S-U-S." The pilot was declaring love for Jesus for many people to see.

A friend of mine often ends his prayers with "I love you, Lord." He says, "I can't help but say 'I love you' after all He's done for me." In Romans 6:1–11, our Bible text for today, the apostle Paul tells us some of what Jesus has done for us that deserves our love: He was crucified, buried, and raised to life. Because of that, those of us who have put our faith in Jesus now have a new life (v. 4). We no longer have to be controlled by sin or fear of death (vv. 6, 9), and one day we too will be resurrected to live with Him forever (v. 8).

No wonder we say, "I love you, Jesus!"

Anne Cetas

To show His love, Jesus died for us;
to show our love, we live for Him.

Still in God's Hands

READ JOB 1:6–22

In all this, Job did not sin by charging God with wrongdoing. —JOB 1:22

During my first year of seminary, I listened as a new friend described her life. Abandoned by her husband, she was raising two small children alone. Earning just over minimum wage, she had little chance of escaping the poverty and dangers she described in her neighborhood.

As a father, I was moved by her concern for her children and asked, "How do you handle all of this?" She seemed surprised by my question and replied, "We are doing all we can do, and I must leave them in God's hands." Her trust in God in the midst of trials reminded me of Job's trust (1:6–22).

A year later, she phoned and asked if I would come be with her at the funeral home. Her son had been killed in a drive-by shooting. I asked God for words to comfort her and for the wisdom not to try to explain the unexplainable.

Standing with her that day, however, I marveled as again and again she comforted others—her confidence in God unshaken by this terrible blow. Turning to me as we parted, her final words were a poignant reminder of the depth of her faith: "My boy is still in God's hands." Like Job, she "did not sin by charging God with wrongdoing" (v. 22).

We too can develop an unshakable faith as we daily live in fellowship with the Lord.

RANDY KILGORE

Nothing can shake those who are secure in God's hands.

Love

Love Is for Losers

READ 1 CORINTHIANS 13

And now these three remain: faith, hope and love. But the greatest of these is love. —1 CORINTHIANS 13:13

You can learn a lot about a person by what his or her T-shirt says. Recently, one of these messages caught my attention as I walked through a local shopping mall. A young woman wore a bright red T-shirt that said, "Love Is for Losers." Maybe she thought it was clever or provocative, even funny. Or perhaps she had been hurt by a relationship and had pulled away from others rather than risk being hurt again. Either way, the T-shirt got me thinking.

Is love for losers? The fact is, when we love, we take risks. People could very well hurt us, disappoint us, or even leave us. Love can lead to loss.

The Bible, though, challenges us to higher ground in loving others. In 1 Corinthians 13, Paul describes what it means to live out God's kind of love. The person who exercises godly love doesn't do so for personal benefit or gain but rather "always protects, always trusts, always hopes, always perseveres" (13:7). Why? Because godly love endures beyond life's hurts by pulling us relentlessly toward the never-diminishing care of the Father.

So, perhaps love is for losers—for it is in times of loss and disappointment that we need God's love the most. Even in our struggles, we know that "love never fails" (1 Corinthians 13:8).

BILL CROWDER

God's love never fails.

From Mourning to Dancing

READ ISAIAH 61:1–4

He has sent me . . . to bestow on [those who grieve] a crown of beauty instead of ashes, the oil of joy instead of mourning. —ISAIAH 61:1, 3

"We're cutting your job." A decade ago those words sent me reeling when the company I worked for eliminated my position. At the time, I felt shattered, partly because my identity was so intertwined with my role as editor. Recently I felt a similar sadness when I heard that my freelance job was ending. But this time I didn't feel rocked at my foundation, because over the years I have seen God's faithfulness and how He can turn my mourning to joy.

Although we live in a fallen world where we experience pain and disappointment, the Lord can move us from despair to rejoicing—as we see in Isaiah's prophecy about the coming of Jesus (Isaiah 61:1–3). The Lord gives us hope when we feel hopeless; He helps us to forgive when we think we can't; He teaches us that our identity is in Him and not in what we do. He gives us courage to face an unknown future. When we wear the rags of "ashes," He gently gives us a coat of praise.

When we face loss, we shouldn't run from the sadness, but neither do we want to become bitter or hardened. When we think about God's faithfulness over the years, we know that He's willing and able to turn our grief to dancing once again—to give us sufficient grace in this life and full joy in heaven.

AMY BOUCHER PYE

God can bring times of growth
out of our times of heartache.

Faith

"Mower" Faith

READ GENESIS 24:10–28

Then [Abraham's servant] prayed, "Lord, God of my master Abraham, make me successful today, and show kindness to my master Abraham." —GENESIS 24:12

The fifth-grader watched her father struggling under the hot sun to cut the grass on the family's sizable yard. When he was finally done, she said to him, "Daddy, I wish we had a riding lawn mower. I'm going to buy you one." She did more than make what seemed like an impossible promise. She began praying for a riding mower for her dad. And she began doing odd jobs to earn money.

In Genesis 24, we read the account of Abraham's servant seeking a bride for Isaac. He had the seemingly impossible task of finding a woman from a family hundreds of miles away. Plus, she had to be willing to return with him to Canaan to marry Isaac. He prayed specifically, did everything he could, and waited on the Lord. When he arrived at Nahor, he found Rebekah, the woman who would marry Isaac.

The girl saved $50, but that was clearly not enough. One day, though, she and her mom saw a riding mower for sale. Unbelievably, the sign said $50. And the mower worked! Two seemingly impossible requests. Two faithful believers in prayer and action. It's a formula for great results.

Not all prayers are answered affirmatively, of course, but that isn't our concern. Our job is to see the need, ask God in His mercy to help us, and then do what we can. We all need a little "mower" faith.

Dave Branon

A living faith is a working faith.

Because I Love Him

READ REVELATION 22:12–21

He who testifies to these things says, "Yes, I am coming soon." Amen. Come, Lord Jesus. —REVELATION 22:20

The day before my husband was to return home from a business trip, my son said, "Mom! I want Daddy to come home." I asked him why, expecting him to say something about the presents his daddy usually brings back or that he missed playing ball with him. But with solemn seriousness he answered, "I want him to come back because I love him!"

His answer made me think about our Lord and His promise to come back. "I am coming soon," Jesus says (Revelation 22:20). I long for His return, but why do I want Him to come back? Is it because I will be in His presence, away from sickness and death? Is it because I am tired of living in a difficult world? Or is it because when I've loved Him so much of my life, when He has shared my tears and my laughter, when He has been more real than anybody else, I want to be with Him forever?

I'm glad my son misses his daddy when he's away. It would be terrible if he didn't care at all about his return or if he thought it would interfere with his plans. How do we feel about our Lord's return? Let us long for that day passionately, and earnestly say, "Lord, come back! We love you."

Keila Ochoa

Look forward eagerly for the Lord's appearing.

Loving Perfectly

READ 1 CORINTHIANS 13:4–8

[Love] always protects, always trusts, always hopes, always perseveres. Love never fails. —1 CORINTHIANS 13:7–8

Her voice shook as she shared the problems she was having with her daughter. Worried about her teenager's questionable friends, this concerned mum confiscated her daughter's mobile phone and chaperoned her everywhere. Their relationship seemed only to go from bad to worse.

When I spoke with the daughter, I discovered that she loves her mum dearly but is suffocating under a smothering love. She longs to break free.

As imperfect beings, we all struggle in our relationships. Whether we are a parent or child, single or married, we grapple with expressing love the right way, saying and doing the right thing at the right time. We grow in love throughout our lifetime.

In 1 Corinthians 13 the apostle Paul outlines what perfect love looks like. His standard sounds wonderful, but putting that love into practice can be absolutely daunting. Thankfully, we have Jesus as our example. As He interacted with people with varying needs and issues, He showed us what perfect love looks like in action. As we walk with Him, keeping ourselves in His love and steeping our mind in His Word, we'll reflect more and more of His likeness.

We'll still make mistakes, but God is able to redeem them and cause good to come out of every situation, for His love "always protects" and it "never fails" (vv. 7–8).

POH FANG CHIA

To show His love, Jesus died for us;
to show our love, we live for Him.

JUNE
29

The God of Victory

READ 2 CORINTHIANS 2:14–17

Do not be overcome by evil, but overcome evil with good. —ROMANS 12:21

In Greek mythology, Nike was the goddess of victory. Nike fought on the side of the Olympian gods, gaining a victory over the mighty Titans. As a result, she became a symbol of winning. But Nike's alleged powers were not just limited to warfare. She also became a favorite goddess of athletes who wanted to win in competitive sports. The Romans adopted her into their worship and gave her the Latin name Victoria.

In the Greco-Roman world where Paul taught, victory was highly valued. So when he expressed Christian truth, he used words his audience could understand. In his letters, he described Christ as the One who leads us in a military procession of triumph (2 Corinthians 2:14–17), and he compared the Christian life to someone training for the biennial Isthmian Games—an athletic competition held in Corinth (1 Corinthians 9:24–27).

Paul also used the word for victory in reference to our struggles with those who intentionally hurt us. "Overcome [be a victor over] evil with good" (Romans 12:21). This may mean returning kindness for spite or respectfully setting limits on evil behavior. In either case, an attitude of love cannot be generated in our own strength. But in Christ, we have divine power that ancient pagans could only hope for. Jesus Christ is the genuine God of victory.

DENNIS FISHER

God will give us the victory when
we join Him in the fight.

JUNE
30

Hope

Flying Machines

READ PSALM 6

I am worn out from my groaning. All night long I flood my bed with weeping and drench my couch with tears. —PSALM 6:6

Recording artist James Taylor exploded onto the music scene in early 1970 with the song "Fire and Rain." In it, he talked about the disappointments of life, referring to them as flying machines that ended up in pieces on the ground. That was a reference to Taylor's original band Flying Machine, whose attempt at breaking into the recording industry had failed badly, causing him to wonder if his dreams of a musical career would ever come true. The reality of crushed expectations had taken their toll, leaving Taylor with a sense of loss and hopelessness.

The psalmist David also experienced hopeless despair as he struggled with his own failures, the attacks of others, and the disappointments of life. In Psalm 6:6 he said, "I am worn out from my groaning. All night long I flood my bed with weeping and drench my couch with tears." The depth of his sorrow and loss drove him to heartache—but in that grief he turned to the God of all comfort. David's own crushed and broken "flying machines" gave way to the assurance of God's care, prompting him to say, "The LORD has heard my cry for mercy; the LORD accepts my prayer" (v. 9).

In our own seasons of disappointment, we too can find comfort in God, who cares for our broken hearts.

BILL CROWDER

God's whisper of comfort quiets the noise of our trials.

Childlike Faith

READ MATTHEW 8:5–10

Jesus replied, "What is impossible with man is possible with God." —LUKE 18:27

On the way home from a family camping trip, six-year-old Tanya and her dad were the only ones still awake in the car. As Tanya looked at the full moon through the car window, she asked, "Daddy, do you think I can touch the moon if I stand on my tiptoes?"

"No, I don't think so," he said, smiling.

"Can you reach it?"

"No, I don't think I can either."

She was quiet for a moment, then she said confidently, "Daddy, maybe if you hold me up on your shoulders?"

Faith? Yes—the childlike faith that daddies can do anything. True faith, though, has the written promise of God for its foundation. In Hebrews 11:1, we read, "Faith is confidence in what we hope for and assurance about what we do not see." Jesus talked a lot about faith, and throughout the Gospels we read of His response to those who had great faith.

When a paralyzed man's friends brought him to Jesus, He "saw their faith," forgave the man of his sins, and healed him (Matthew 9:2–6). When the centurion asked Jesus to "say the word, and my servant will be healed" (8:8), Jesus "was amazed" and said, "I have not found anyone in Israel with such great faith" (8:10).

When we have faith in God, we will find that all things are possible.

CINDY HESS KASPER

A childlike faith unlocks the door
to the kingdom of heaven.

Love

Going First

READ 1 JOHN 4:7–21

We love because he first loved us.
—1 JOHN 4:19

We worked patiently to help our son heal and adjust to his new life with our family. Trauma from his early days in an orphanage was fueling some negative behaviors. While I had enormous compassion for the hardships he experienced in his early days, I felt myself begin to withdraw from him emotionally because of those behaviors. Ashamed, I shared my struggle with his therapist. Her gentle reply hit home: "He needs you to go first . . . to show him he's worthy of love before he'll be able to act like it."

John pushes the recipients of his letter to an incredible depth of love, citing God's love as both the source and the reason for loving one another (1 John 4:7, 11). I admit I often fail to show such love to others, whether strangers, friends, or my own children. Yet John's words spark in me renewed desire and ability to do so: God went first. He sent His Son to demonstrate the fullness of His love for each of us. I'm so thankful He doesn't respond as we all are prone to do by withdrawing His heart from us.

Although our sinful actions don't invite God's love, He is unwavering in offering it to us (Romans 5:8). His "go-first" love compels us to love one another in response to, and as a reflection of, that love.

KIRSTEN HOLMBERG

God loved us first so we can love others.

JULY
3

Rescue from Despair

READ JUDGES 13:1–7

He will take the lead in delivering Israel from the hands of the Philistines. —JUDGES 13:5

When a powerful typhoon swept through the city of Tacloban, Philippines, an estimated 10,000 people died, and many who survived found themselves homeless and jobless. Necessities became scarce. Three months later, while the town was still struggling to dig itself out from the destruction, a baby was born on a roadside near Tacloban amid torrents of rain and strong wind. Although the weather brought back painful memories, residents worked together to find a midwife and transport the mother and newborn to a clinic. The baby survived, thrived, and became a symbol of hope during a time of despair.

Forty years of Philistine oppression marked a grim period in Israel's national history. During this time, an angel informed an Israelite woman that she would give birth to a special son (Judges 13:3). According to the angel, the baby would be a Nazirite—a man set apart to God—and would "begin to deliver Israel out of the hand of the Philistines" (v. 5 NKJV). The infant, Samson, was a gift of hope born in a troubled time.

Trouble is unavoidable, yet Jesus has the power to rescue us from despair. Christ was born "to shine on those living in darkness and in the shadow of death, to guide our feet into the path of peace" (Luke 1:76–79).

JENNIFER BENSON SCHULDT

Jesus is the hope that calms life's storms.

Dangerous Freedom

READ GALATIANS 5:1–6; 16–21

You, my brothers and sisters, were called to be free. But do not use your freedom to indulge the flesh; rather, serve one another humbly in love. —GALATIANS 5:13

Freedom is dangerous in the hands of those who don't know how to use it. That's why criminals are confined in prisons with barbed wire, steel bars, and concrete barriers. Or consider a campfire that is allowed to spread in a dry forest. It quickly becomes a blazing inferno. Unchecked freedom can create chaos.

Nowhere is this more evident than in the Christian life. Believers are free from the law's curse, its penalty, and its guilt-producing power. Fear, anxiety, and guilt are replaced by peace, forgiveness, and liberty. Who could be freer than one who is free in the depths of his soul? But here is where we could fail. It is possible to use freedom's luxury to live selfishly or to claim ownership of what God has merely entrusted to us.

The proper use of freedom is "faith working through love" to serve one another (Galatians 5:6, 13). When we rely on the Spirit and use our energies to love God and help others, we can always use our liberty to build up, not to tear down.

Freedom without limits can be dangerous. Instead, let's "serve one another humbly in love."

DENNIS DEHAAN

Freedom doesn't give us the right to do what we please, but to do what pleases God.

Do You Love Me?

READ JOHN 21:15–25

Jesus did many other things as well. If every one of them were written down, I suppose that even the whole world would not have room for the books that would be written. —JOHN 21:25

Occasionally it is fun to think back to the days when our now-adult children were little. Like the time our Jennie's four-year-old legs were propelling her toward the front door. Suddenly she hit the brakes, wheeled around and called out with a sense of childish urgency, "Mom!"

It was the kind of call that could have meant anything from, "I need you to tie my shoes" to "I'm going to paint my braids the same color Dad is painting the fence." Instead, she unexpectedly called out, "Mom, I love you." Then she was off and running again. She could melt a parent's heart!

Imagine that same scene but with different circumstances. Suppose Jennie had just been told for the third time to come to the supper table. Watch her stop and say, "I love you," only to spin around and run out the front door. In that setting the words would not have warmed anyone's heart.

Our Lord also looks for an "I love you" from His children that is backed up by action. When Jesus asked Peter, "Do you love me?" (John 21:15, 16, 17) He was not satisfied with a casual, "Sure, Lord, you know I do!" Each time He responded to His disciple's reply by saying in effect, "If you love Me, care for those I care for. Peter, if you love Me, follow Me."

May our words delight the Father's heart because they come from obedient children.

MART DEHAAN

The best proof of love for God is love for one another.

JULY
6

Hope

Such a Hope

READ ROMANS 8:18–27

We have this hope as an anchor of the soul, firm and secure. It enters the inner sanctuary behind the curtain. —HEBREWS 6:19

Two women. One a former coworker I had known for twenty years. The other, the wife of a former student from my days as a schoolteacher. Both dedicated moms of two young children. Both missionaries. Both incredibly in love with Jesus Christ.

Then suddenly, within the space of a month—both were dead. The first, Sharon Fasick, died in a car accident, attracting little attention though deeply affecting family and friends. The second, Roni Bowers, died with her daughter Charity when their plane was shot down over the jungles of Peru—a situation that thrust her story into the international spotlight.

Their deaths filled many people with inexpressible sorrow. But there was something else—hope. Both women's husbands had the confident expectation that they would see their wives again in heaven. What happened after they died demonstrates that the Christian faith works. Both men, Jeff Fasick and Jim Bowers, have spoken about the peace God has given them. They have testified that this kind of hope has allowed them to continue on in the midst of the unspeakable pain.

Paul said that our present sufferings "are not worth comparing with the glory that will be revealed in us" (Romans 8:18). Such a hope comes only from Christ.

DAVE BRANON

The hope of heaven is God's solution for sorrow.

To Have One You Must Be One

READ JOHN 15:9–17

A man who has friends must himself be friendly, but there is a friend who sticks closer than a brother. —PROVERBS 18:24 NKJV

In a book by Scottish pastor Henry Durbanville (1878–1964), he underscored the importance of friends as a means of overcoming loneliness. Durbanville included the following quotes: Ralph Waldo Emerson said, "A friend may well be reckoned the masterpiece of nature." A small boy defined a friend as "Someone who knows all about you and likes you just the same." And an old Arab saying goes like this: "A friend is one to whom we may pour out all the contents of our hearts, chaff and grain together, knowing that the gentlest of hands will take and sift it, keep what is worth keeping, and with the breath of kindness blow the rest away." Durbanville also made this observation, which has been attributed to numerous sources: "A friend is the first person to come in when the whole world goes out."

Solomon wrote in Proverbs 17:17, "A friend loves at all times." We can't improve on that definition. To have someone who remains true to us under all circumstances is indeed one of life's choicest blessings. Proverbs 18:24 notes that "a man who has friends must himself be friendly." The implication is clear: Friendliness must begin with us. We must take the initiative in developing relationships with others.

Let us be to others what we desire for ourselves. When it comes to friends, to have one you must be one!

RICHARD DEHAAN

Friendship is a treasure ship anyone can launch.

Faith

Anchors in the Storm

READ JOSHUA 1:1–9

"Have I not commanded you? Be strong and courageous. Do not be afraid; do not be discouraged, for the LORD *your God will be with you wherever you go."* —JOSHUA 1:9

When Matt and Jessica tried to navigate their sailboat into a Florida inlet during a hurricane, the craft ran aground. As the waves crashed around them, they quickly dropped anchor. It held the sailboat in place until they could be rescued. They said that if they had not put down the anchor, "We would have lost our boat for sure." Without the anchor, the relentless waves would have smashed the vessel onto the shore.

We need anchors that hold us secure in our spiritual lives as well. When God called Joshua to lead His people after Moses's death, He gave him anchors of promise he could rely on in troubled times. The Lord said to him, "I will be with you. I will never leave you nor forsake you. . . . The LORD your God will be with you wherever you go" (Joshua 1:5, 9). God also gave Joshua and His people the "Book of the Law" to study and observe (vv. 7–8). That, and God's presence, were anchors the Israelites could rely on as they faced many challenges.

When we're in the middle of suffering or when doubts start threatening our faith, what are our anchors? We could start with Joshua 1:5. Although our faith may feel weak, if it's anchored in God's promises and presence, He will safely hold us.

ANNE CETAS

When we feel the stress of the storm, we learn the strength of the anchor.

He Feels and Understands

READ HEBREWS 4:9–16

For we do not have a high priest who is unable to empathize with our weaknesses, but we have one who has been tempted in every way, just as we are—yet he did not sin. —HEBREWS 4:15

A man put up a sign in his yard that read: "Puppies for Sale." Among those who inquired was a young boy. "Please, Mister," he said, "I'd like to buy one of your puppies if they don't cost too much." "Well, son, they're $25." The boy looked crushed. "I've only got two dollars and five cents."

"Could I see them anyway?" "Of course. Maybe we can work something out," said the man. The lad's eyes danced at the sight of those five little balls of fur. "I heard that one has a bad leg," he said. "Yes, I'm afraid she'll be crippled for life." "Well, that's the puppy I want. Could I pay for her a little at a time?" The man responded, "But she'll always have a limp." Smiling bravely, the boy pulled up one pant leg, revealing a brace. "I don't walk good either." Then, looking at the puppy sympathetically, he continued, "I guess she'll need a lot of love and help. I sure did. It's not so easy being disabled." "Here, take her," said the man. "I know you'll give her a good home. And just forget the money."

That story can illustrate our Savior's sympathetic understanding of our human condition. Christ knows all about our weaknesses. Having suffered himself, He can identify compassionately with us.

Jesus is touched by your distress and grief. His arms of love will enfold you and carry you through every heartache and trial.

HENRY BOSCH

God's heart is touched whenever His child's heart is tried.

JULY
10

Hope

Let Us . . .

READ HEBREWS 10:19–25

Let us consider how we may spur one another on toward love and good deeds. —HEBREWS 10:24

While standing in line for a popular attraction at Disneyland, I noticed that most people were talking and smiling instead of complaining about the long wait. It made me ponder what made waiting in that line an enjoyable experience. The key seemed to be that very few people were there by themselves. Instead, friends, families, groups, and couples were sharing the experience, which was far different from standing in line alone.

The Christian life is meant to be lived that way—in company with others and not alone. In Hebrews 10:19–25 the writer urges us to live in community with other followers of Jesus. "Let us draw near to God with a sincere heart and with the full assurance that faith brings . . . . Let us hold unswervingly to the hope we profess, for he who promised is faithful. And let us consider how we may spur one another on toward love and good deeds, not giving up meeting together" (vv. 22–25). In community we reassure and reinforce each other by "encouraging one another" (v. 25).

Even our most difficult days can become a meaningful part of our journey of faith when others share them with us. Instead of facing life alone, let's travel together.

David McCasland

Life in Christ is meant to be a shared experience.

Tennis and Parenting

READ EPHESIANS 6:1–9

Fathers, do not exasperate your children; instead, bring them up in the training and instruction of the Lord. —EPHESIANS 6:4

What do tennis and parenting have in common? At first glance, not much. One is a game; the other is anything but a game. But there are certain similarities in the way the two tasks are carried out.

Tennis can be played two ways: with sportsmanship and graciousness, or with temper tantrums, "bashing" the officials, and bitter excuses.

Parents have similar options. They can concentrate on developing grace, self-control, and skill. Or they can make excuses by saying, "These kids are bringing out the worst in me. I know I shouldn't yell and scream, but I can't help it."

Like successful tennis players, parents need a good coach—one who understands parenting's fine points, one who is experienced in self-control and unconditional love. We need Christ, the master teacher. Success is possible only when we seek His help and rely on Him. He said, "I am the vine, you are the branches. . . . apart from me you can do nothing" (John 15:5).

No, parenting isn't easy. Some tough shots may be fired at us. We may not win in straight sets. But Christ will help us to respond to our children with love and grace.

Mart DeHaan

To win your children, serve with grace and respond with love.

Faith

Eyes of Faith

READ JOHN 4:46–54

For we live by faith, not by sight.
—2 CORINTHIANS 5:7

God sometimes answers our prayers in marvelous ways, but He does not want us to become preoccupied with the miraculous. That's why Jesus gently rebuked the nobleman who begged Him to come and heal his son (John 4:48). But in response to the father's repeated appeal He said, "Go, your son will live (v. 50). The father came to "believe" on the basis of Jesus's word alone. The reality of his faith is seen in the fact that he obeyed Christ's simple command and "departed."

Upon returning home, the nobleman discovered that his son had been healed "at one in the afternoon" on the previous day. From his servants he learned exactly what had taken place and when. His son was made well at the same instant that Jesus said, "Your son will live" (vv. 50–53).

At times we are amazed by God's perfect timing and miraculous intervention when He answers our prayers. We must be careful, though, not to become so preoccupied with the miracle that we forget the One who performed it. We need to remain focused on Christ, whether a miracle takes place or not.

Sooner or later we will be called upon to trust God as we endure sickness, grief, or disappointment. That's when "we live by faith, not by sight" (2 Corinthians 5:7).

Herb Vander Lugt

Believing is seeing what our eyes cannot see.

Can't Die But Once

READ MATTHEW 6:26–32

"Do not be afraid of those who kill the body but cannot kill the soul." —MATTHEW 10:28

Born into slavery and badly treated as a young girl, Harriet Tubman (c. 1822–1913) found a shining ray of hope in the Bible stories her mother told. The account of Israel's escape from slavery under Pharaoh showed her a God who desired freedom for His people.

Harriet found freedom when she slipped over the Maryland state line and out of slavery. She couldn't remain content, however, knowing so many were still trapped in captivity. So she led more than a dozen rescue missions to free those still in slavery, dismissing the personal danger. "I can't die but once," she said.

Harriet knew the truth of the statement: "Do not be afraid of those who kill the body but cannot kill the soul" (Matthew 10:28). Jesus spoke those words as He sent His disciples on their first mission. He knew they would face danger, and not everyone would receive them warmly. So why expose the disciples to the risk? The answer is found in the previous chapter. "When he saw the crowds, [Jesus] had compassion on them, because they were harassed and helpless, like sheep without a shepherd" (9:36).

When Harriet Tubman couldn't forget those still trapped in slavery, she showed us a picture of Christ, who did not forget us when we were trapped in our sins. Her courageous example inspires us to remember those who remain without hope in the world.

TIM GUSTAFSON

True freedom is found in knowing and serving Christ.

Love

Knowing and Loving

READ JOHN 10:7–16

"My sheep listen to my voice; I know them, and they follow me." —JOHN 10:27

"Jesus loves me, this I know, for the Bible tells me so" is the message of one of Christian music's most enduring songs, particularly for children. Written by Anna B. Warner in the 1800s, this lyric tenderly affirms our relationship with Him—we are loved.

Someone gave my wife a plaque for our home that gives these words a fresh twist by flipping that simple idea. It reads, "Jesus knows me, this I love." This provides a different perspective on our relationship with Him—we are known.

In ancient Israel, loving and knowing the sheep distinguished a true shepherd from a hired hand. The shepherd spent so much time with his sheep that he developed an abiding care for and a deep knowledge of his lambs. Little wonder then that Jesus tells His own, "I am the good shepherd; I know my sheep and my sheep know me. . . . My sheep listen to my voice; I know them, and they follow me" (John 10:14, 27).

He knows us and He loves us! We can trust Jesus's purposes for us and rest in the promise of His care because His Father "knows what [we] need before [we] ask him" (Matthew 6:8).

As you deal with the ups and downs of life today, be at rest. You are known and loved by the Shepherd of your heart.

BILL CROWDER

The wonder of it all—just to think that Jesus loves me!

Pure Love

READ 1 CORINTHIANS 6:18–7:9

But if they cannot control themselves, they should marry, for it is better to marry than to burn with passion. —1 CORINTHIANS 7:9

A situation that once was viewed by most people as unacceptable and immoral has become commonplace. According to the National & International Religion Report, before the majority of American marriages take place, the man and woman have already been living together.

The report goes on to point out that this practice has devastating effects. "Marriages that are preceded by living together have fifty percent higher disruption (divorce or separation) rates than marriages without premarital cohabitation."

Even among Christians there is no shortage of those who think they can violate God's moral standards.

The temptations were similar in the first century. That's why Paul had to make it clear to the believers at Corinth that they had no business being involved in sexual immorality. He said that if they found their passions becoming so strong that they could not control their sexual desires, there was an answer. It was not found in an immoral relationship; it was found in marriage.

In a day when immorality continues to devour people, let's do all we can to promote the joys and privileges of love that is honoring to God—the love that is shared in marriage. There is no substitute for pure love.

DAVE BRANON

Saving yourself for marriage will help to save your marriage.

Faith

Unexpected Blessings

READ RUTH 2:11–23

He will renew your life and sustain you in your old age. For your daughter-in-law, who loves you and who is better to you than seven sons, has given him birth. —RUTH 4:15

Naomi and Ruth came together in less-than-ideal circumstances. To escape a famine in Israel, Naomi's family moved to Moab. While living there, her two sons married Moabite women: Orpah and Ruth. Then Naomi's husband and sons died. In that culture, women were dependent on men, which left the three widows in a predicament.

Word came to Naomi that the famine in Israel had ended, so she decided to make the long trek home. Orpah and Ruth started to go with her, but Naomi urged them to return home, saying, "The LORD's hand has turned against me!" (1:13).

Orpah went home, but Ruth continued, affirming her belief in Naomi's God despite Naomi's own fragile faith (1:15–18).

The story, which started in desperately unpleasant circumstances (1:1–5), turned because of undeserved kindnesses: Ruth to Naomi (1:16-17; 2:11–12) and Boaz to Ruth (2:13–14). And it ended in unimaginable blessing: a baby who would be in the lineage of the Messiah (4:16–17).

God makes miracles out of what seems insignificant: fragile faith, a little kindness, and ordinary people.

JULIE ACKERMAN LINK

In all the setbacks of your life as a believer,
God is plotting for your joy. —John Piper

Love Comes First

READ 1 JOHN 4:7–19

We love because [God] first loved us. —1 JOHN 4:19

My friend showed me one of the three decorative plaques that would be part of a wall arrangement she was installing in her living room. "See, I've already got Love," she said, holding up the plaque with that word written on it. "Faith and Hope are on order."

So, Love comes first, I thought. Faith and Hope soon follow!

Love did come first. In fact, it originated with God. First John 4:19 reminds us that "we love because [God] first loved us." God's love, described in 1 Corinthians 13 (known as the "love chapter"), explains a characteristic of real love when it says, "Love never fails" (v. 8).

Faith and hope are essential to the believer as well. It is only because we are justified by faith that "we have peace with God through our Lord Jesus Christ" (Romans 5:1). And hope is described in Hebrews 6 as "an anchor for the soul, firm and secure" (v. 19).

One day we will no longer need faith and hope. Faith will be exchanged for the reality of being with Jesus, and our hope will be realized when we see our Savior face to face. But love is eternal, for love is of God and God is love (1 John 4:7–8). "Now these three remain: faith, hope and love. But the greatest of these is love"—it is first and last (1 Corinthians 13:13).

CINDY HESS KASPER

We love because God first loved us.

Hope

Fresh Mercies

READ LAMENTATIONS 3:21–26

Because your love is better than life, my lips will glorify you. —PSALM 63:3

On a recent airline flight, the landing was a little rough, jostling us left and right as we went down the runway. Some of the passengers were visibly nervous, but the tension broke when two little girls sitting behind me cheered, "Yeah! Let's do that again!"

Children are open to new adventures and see life with humble, wide-eyed wonder. Perhaps this is part of what Jesus had in mind when He said that we have to "receive the kingdom of God like a little child" (Mark 10:15).

Life has its challenges and heartaches. Few knew this better than Jeremiah, who is also called "the weeping prophet." But in the middle of Jeremiah's troubles, God encouraged him with an amazing truth: "The faithful love of the LORD never ends! His mercies never cease. Great is his faithfulness; his mercies begin afresh each morning" (Lamentations 3:22–23 NLT).

God's fresh mercies can break into our lives at any moment. They are always there, and we see them when we live with childlike expectation—watching and waiting for what He alone can do. Jeremiah knew that God's goodness is not defined by our immediate circumstances and that His faithfulness is greater than life's rough places. Look for God's fresh mercies today.

JAMES BANKS

God is greater than anything that happens to us.

The Right Triangle

READ COLOSSIANS 3:16–24

And whatever you do, whether in word or deed, do it all in the name of the Lord Jesus, giving thanks to God the Father through him. —COLOSSIANS 3:17

Although we usually think of a marriage triangle as a dangerous situation, there is one sense in which a third person could create the right triangle.

Viola Walden tells the story of a newly married couple riding a train on their honeymoon. A silver-haired man leaned across the aisle and asked, "Is there a third party going with you on your honeymoon?" The couple looked at him strangely; then he added, "When Sarah and I were married, we invited Jesus to our marriage. One of the first things we did in our new home was to kneel and ask Jesus to make our marriage a love triangle—Sarah, myself, and Jesus. And all three of us have been in love with each other for all fifty years of our married life."

When the Lord Jesus is invited into a marriage to stay, His love fills both heart and home. Notice that before Paul gave instructions to husbands and wives in Colossians 3, he said to do "all in the name of the Lord Jesus" (v. 17). If a couple lives by that principle when difficult times come, Jesus is there to mediate the disagreement. When tough decisions must be made, He is wisdom. When the home experiences grief, He stands by to comfort and cheer. And He is the One who brings genuine happiness.

When a husband and wife are in love with each other and with Jesus, they form the right triangle.

PAUL VAN GORDER

God is the only third party in a marriage that can make it work.

JULY
20

Faith

It's Too Easy

READ ROMANS 4:1–8

To the one who does not work but trusts God who justifies the ungodly, their faith is credited as righteousness. —ROMANS 4:5

I read about an instant cake mix that was a big flop. The instructions said all you had to do was add water and bake. The company couldn't understand why it didn't sell—until their research discovered that the buying public felt uneasy about a mix that required only water. People thought it was too easy. So the company altered the formula and changed the directions to call for adding an egg to the mix in addition to the water. The idea worked, and sales jumped dramatically.

That story reminds me of how some people react to the plan of salvation. To them it sounds too easy and simple to be true, even though the Bible says, "By grace you have been saved, through faith, . . . it is the gift of God—not by works" (Ephesians 2:8–9). They feel that there is something more they must do, something they must add to God's "recipe" for salvation. They think they must perform good works to gain God's favor and earn eternal life. But the Bible is clear—we are saved "not because of righteous things we had done, but because of his mercy" (Titus 3:5).

Unlike the cake-mix manufacturer, God has not changed His "formula" to make salvation more marketable. The gospel we proclaim must be free of works, even though that sounds far too easy.

RICHARD DEHAAN

We are saved by God's mercy, not by our merit—
by Christ's dying, not by our doing.

JULY
21

Arms of Love

READ 1 JOHN 3:16–20

Dear children, let us not love with words or speech but with actions and in truth. —1 JOHN 3:18

Many college students go on summer mission trips. But rarely does one come back with plans to rescue a baby. Several years ago, Mallery Thurlow, a student at Cornerstone University in Grand Rapids, went to Haiti to help distribute food. One day a mother showed up at the distribution center with a very sick infant in her arms. The woman was out of options. The baby needed surgery, but no one would perform it. Without intervention, the baby would die. Mallery took baby Rose into her arms—and into her heart.

After returning to the US, Mallery searched for someone to operate on baby Rose. Most doctors held out little hope. Finally, Rose was granted a visa to leave Haiti, and Mallery went back to get her. Detroit Children's Hospital donated the $100,000 surgery, and it was successful. A little life was saved.

It's unlikely that we will have such a dramatic impact on others. Yet challenged by this student's willingness, we can find ways to provide help. She didn't let circumstances, youth, or inconvenience stop her from saving Rose's life.

Like Mallery, we are called to love "with actions and in truth" (1 John 3:18). Who needs you to be God's arms of love today?

DAVE BRANON

Compassion puts love into action.

Hope

Sharing a Cup of Comfort

READ 2 CORINTHIANS 1:3–11

Our hope for you is firm, because we know that just as you share in our sufferings, so also you share in our comfort. —2 CORINTHIANS 1:7

A friend mailed me some of her homemade pottery. Upon opening the box, I discovered that the precious items had been damaged during their journey. One of the cups had shattered into a few large pieces, a jumble of shards, and clumps of clay dust. After my husband glued the broken mess back together, I displayed the beautifully blemished cup on a shelf.

Like that pieced-together pottery, I have scars that prove I can still stand strong after the difficult times God has brought me through. That cup of comfort reminds me that sharing how the Lord has worked in and through my life can help others during their times of suffering.

The apostle Paul praises God because He is the "Father of compassion and the God of all comfort" (2 Corinthians 1:3). The Lord uses our trials and sufferings to make us more like Him. His comfort in our troubles equips us to encourage others as we share what He did for us during our time of need (v. 4).

As we reflect on Christ's suffering, we can be inspired to persevere in the midst of our own pain, trusting that God uses our experiences to strengthen us and others toward patient endurance (vv. 5–7). Like Paul, we can be comforted in knowing that the Lord redeems our trials for His glory. We can share His cups of comfort and bring reassuring hope to the hurting.

XOCHITL DIXON

God comforts others as we
share how He comforted us.

Sign Language

READ JOHN 1:14–18

May the Lord make your love increase and overflow for each other and for everyone else, just as ours does for you. —1 THESSALONIANS 3:12

A friend of mine pastors a church in a small mountain community not far from Boise, Idaho. The community is nestled in a wooded valley through which a pleasant little stream meanders. Behind the church and alongside the stream is a grove of willows, a length of grass, and a sandy beach. It's an idyllic spot that has long been a place where members of the community gather to picnic.

One day, a man in the congregation expressed concern over the legal implications of "outsiders" using the property. "If someone is injured," he said, "the church might be sued." Although the elders were reluctant to take any action, the man convinced them that they should post a sign on the site informing visitors that this was private property. So the pastor posted a sign. It read: "Warning! Anyone using this beach may, at any moment, be surrounded by people who love you." I read his sign the week after he put it up and was charmed. "Exactly," I thought. "Once again grace has triumphed over law!"

This love for one's neighbor springs from God's kindness, forbearance, and patience with us. It's not the law, but the goodness of God that draws men and women to repentance (Romans 2:4) and to saving faith in His Son Jesus Christ.

DAVID ROPER

Love is the magnet that draws believers together and attracts unbelievers to Christ.

Faith

Unopened Tomorrows

READ MATTHEW 6:25–34

For we live by faith, not by sight. —2 CORINTHIANS 5:7

We often wish we could see what lies around the corner in life. Then we could prepare for it, control it, or avoid it.

A wise person has said, "Though we can't see around corners, God can." How much better and more reassuring that is!

One day my ten-year-old granddaughter Emily and I were boiling eggs for breakfast. As we stared into the boiling water and wondered how long it would take to get the eggs just right, Emily said, "Pity we can't open them up to see how they're doing." I agreed. But that would have spoiled them, so we had to rely on guesswork—with no guarantee of results.

We began talking about other things we would like to see but can't—like tomorrow. Too bad we can't crack tomorrow open, we said, to see if it's the way we would like it. But meddling with tomorrow before its time, like opening a partly cooked egg, would spoil both today and tomorrow.

Because Jesus has promised to care for us every day—and that includes tomorrow—we can live by faith one day at a time (Matthew 6:33–34).

Emily and I decided to leave tomorrow safely in God's hands. Have you?

JOANIE YODER

You're only cooking up trouble when
you stew about tomorrow.

Hope

A City of Smiles

READ REVELATION 21:5

God will wipe away every tear from their eyes; there shall be no more . . . sorrow. —REVELATION 21:4 NKJV

When Mindy Bryant went to Karaganda for a short-term mission trip, she discovered that it lives up to its nickname, "The City Where No One Smiles." She saw hopelessness and hardness on the faces of those who passed by her in this major city in Kazakhstan, which had been part of the former Soviet Union.

Of all the casualties of the communist system, perhaps Karaganda suffered most. Graft and corruption touched all aspects of society. Jobs were few, money was scarce, little food and medicine were available, and stores were empty. No one, including governmental leaders, knew what to do next. It was a city without hope. No wonder it seemed that no one smiled!

But Mindy discovered that there were some people living in Karaganda who did smile. Their faces reflected the joy in their hearts because they had trusted in Jesus Christ. Knowing that they will dwell forever with the Lord in the place He is preparing, they had hope.

What about your city? Perhaps its people have jobs, food, and goods in abundance, yet many probably are not smiling because they do not have hope in Christ. Perhaps the joy in your life and in your words can bring some of them to salvation—giving them something to smile about.

—DAVID EGNER

Hope in the heart puts a smile on the face.

Love

"My Prince"

READ EPHESIANS 5:22–33

Husbands, love your wives, just as Christ loved the church and gave himself up for her. —EPHESIANS 5:25

People around the world reacted with shock several years ago when news broke that Steve Irwin, the "Crocodile Hunter," died while on one of his adventures. His enthusiasm for life and for God's creatures was contagious, making him a favorite personality worldwide.

When his wife Terri was interviewed shortly after Steve's death, her love for him was obvious as she said through her tears, "I've lost my prince." What an affectionate way to memorialize her husband! She saw him as her prince and her best friend.

Too often today the husband-wife relationship is viewed as anything but the tender one Terri and Steve must have shared. We often see bitterness, insults, and animosity presented in the media as the norm. How much more desirable it is to see true love—to see a husband unashamedly cherish his wife, to unselfishly be her "prince."

How can a husband love his wife in a princely way? Try these suggestions: Listen—enjoy those tender times when she can unburden her heart without fear. Love life—find ways to add fun to your marriage. Lead spiritually—guide the way into prayer and intimate fellowship with the Lord.

DAVE BRANON

Marriage thrives in a climate of love and respect.

Pulling Together

READ HEBREWS 10:19–25

Let us consider how we may spur one another on toward love and good deeds. —HEBREWS 10:24

Why do more than five million people a year pay money to run several miles over an obstacle course where they must ascend vertical walls, slog through mud, and climb up inside a vertical pipe with water pouring down on them? Some see obstacle course racing as a personal challenge to push their limit of endurance or conquer their fears. For others, the attraction is teamwork where competitors help and support each other. Writing about this phenomena in *The Washington Post*, Stephanie Kanowitz noted that one competitor called it "a no-judgment zone" where people who are strangers will reach out to help each other finish the race.

The Bible urges us to pursue teamwork as a model of living out our faith in Jesus. "Let us consider how we may spur one another on toward love and good deeds, not giving up meeting together, as some are in the habit of doing, but encouraging one another—and all the more as you see the Day approaching" (Hebrews 10:24–25).

Our goal is not to "finish first" in the race of faith, but to reach out in tangible ways of encouragement by setting an example and lending a helping hand along the way.

Let's spur each other on, be ready to help, and keep pulling together every day.

DAVID MCCASLAND

We run together in the race of life.

Hope

Positive about the Outcome

READ JOHN 11:1–16

Then Thomas (also known as Didymus) said to the rest of the disciples, "Let us also go, that we may die with him." —JOHN 11:16

Before a baseball game one day, a Little League player walked up to his coach and told him he thought they were going to lose. When the coach gently chided him for not having a more positive attitude, the youngster replied, "I'm sorry, Coach, I forgot. I'm positive we're going to lose!" And sure enough, they did.

Thomas, a loyal follower of Jesus, seemed to respond to life in much the same way. When the Savior announced that He was going to the town of Bethany where He would resurrect Lazarus, for example, Thomas expected the worst. Keenly aware of the Jews' hostility toward the Lord, he said, "Let us also go, that we may die with Him" (John 11:16).

If he had just thought about the Master's earlier statement that the death of Lazarus was for God's glory, he might not have been so pessimistic. And even though Thomas witnessed the great miracle of Lazarus being raised from the dead, he later had difficulty believing that Jesus himself had risen from the grave. Only when he saw the Lord with his own eyes did his outlook change.

If we pay careful attention to the words and promises of God and remember that Christ lives and reigns, we can look to the future with hope. Even if things don't go quite our way, we can be positive about the outcome!

—DENNIS DEHAAN

Happiness often depends upon the quality of our thoughts.

Faith

Walking in the Light

READ HEBREWS 12:18–24

In him was life, and that life was the light of all mankind. —JOHN 1:4

Darkness descended on our forest village when the moon disappeared. Lightning slashed the skies, followed by a rainstorm and crackling thunder. Awake and afraid, as a child I imagined all kinds of grisly monsters about to pounce on me! By daybreak, however, the sounds vanished, the sun rose, and calm returned as birds jubilated in the sunshine. The contrast between the frightening darkness of the night and the joy of the daylight was remarkably sharp.

The author of Hebrews recalls the time when the Israelites had an experience at Mount Sinai so dark and stormy they hid in fear (Exodus 20:18–19). For them, God's presence, even in His loving gift of the law, felt dark and terrifying. This was because, as sinful people, the Israelites couldn't live up to God's standards. Their sin caused them to walk in darkness and fear (Hebrews 12:18–21).

But God is light; in Him there's no darkness (1 John 1:5). In Hebrews 12, Mount Sinai represents God's holiness and our old life of disobedience, while the beauty of Mount Zion represents God's grace and the believers' new life in Jesus, "the mediator of a new covenant" (vv. 22–24).

Whoever follows Jesus will "never walk in darkness, but will have the light of life" (John 8:12). Through Him, we can let go of the darkness of our old life and celebrate the joy of walking in the light and beauty of His kingdom.

LAWRENCE DARMANI

The gift of God's love can bring light to any darkness.

Love

Mistaken about God

READ 1 JOHN 4:12–19

So we know and rely on the love God has for us. God is love. Whoever lives in love lives in God, and God in them. —1 JOHN 4:16

Confusion was written on his face. A young man was explaining his concept of God. It was apparent that he did not understand what the Bible teaches about Him. His feeling was, "If God is love, why should I worry about things like judgment?"

A lot of people think of God only in terms of His love. They feel that He is much too loving to judge them for not living by the book—God's Book. So they live with little or no thought about how God might view their actions.

The apostle John wrote, "God is love" (1 John 4:8, 16). But is God love and nothing else? No, God is more than love. Among other things, He is also a God of anger. Psalm 7 tells us, "God is angry with the wicked every day" (v. 11 NKJV).

God's righteous anger should cause us to think soberly about our relationship with Him. A right relationship comes only when we believe in Christ and our sins are forgiven. For those who have taken that step of faith, there is no condemnation (Romans 8:1). But for those who have never turned to Christ, there is plenty to worry about (John 5:24–29).

What the Bible tells us about God's anger is not meant to drive us away from Him. Rather, it's meant to draw us to His love. Don't be mistaken!

MART DEHAAN

To escape God's wrath, embrace His love.

Faith and Riches

READ EPHESIANS 1

I pray that the eyes of your heart may be enlightened in order that you may know the hope to which he has called you, the riches of his glorious inheritance in his holy people. —EPHESIANS 1:18

Let's talk about money for a moment. Do you want to be rich? Do you think your faith will bring you riches? What kind of riches are you looking for?

There's good news and bad news if wealth is what you want. The good news is that God's Word does promise riches to the believer. The "bad" news is that it doesn't have anything to do with money.

Here are some examples of the riches that can be ours as believers in Jesus Christ:

- An understanding of God the Father and the Son, "in whom are hidden all the treasures of wisdom and knowledge" (Colossians 2:2–3).
- Christ, "the hope of glory," living in us (Colossians 1:27).
- Mighty strength in our inner being, "through His Spirit" (Ephesians 3:16).
- Having all our needs met by God (Philippians 4:19).
- The "wisdom and knowledge of God" (Romans 11:33).
- "Redemption through his blood, the forgiveness of sins," which comes from God's grace (Ephesians 1:7).

Yes, God's Word promises us great riches—treasures that we cannot even attempt to purchase with any amount of money. It is these riches that we must seek, enjoy, and use to glorify their source—our heavenly Father.

DAVE BRANON

God's Word promises riches that money cannot buy.

AUGUST
1

Hope

Hope Is for . . .

READ HEBREWS 10:19–25

Let us hold unswervingly to the hope we profess, for he who promised is faithful. —HEBREWS 10:23

Although I try not to be shocked by the things I see these days, I was caught off-balance by the message on the woman's T-shirt as she walked past me in the mall. The bold letters declared: "Hope Is for Suckers." Certainly, being naïve or gullible can be foolish and dangerous. Disappointment and heartache can be the tragic offspring of unfounded optimism. But not allowing oneself to have hope is a sad and cynical way to view life.

Biblical hope is unique; it's a confident trust in God and what He is doing in the world and in our lives. That's something everyone needs! The writer to the Hebrews clearly stated the importance of hope when he wrote, "Let us hold unswervingly to the hope we profess, for he who promised is faithful" (Hebrews 10:23).

Having biblical hope is not foolish, because it has a strong foundation. We hold fast to the hope we have received in Christ because our God is faithful. He can be trusted with anything and everything we will ever face—both for today and forever. Our hope is grounded in the trustworthy character of the God who loves us with an everlasting love.

So, the T-shirt had it wrong. Hope is not for suckers; it's for you and for me!

Bill Crowder

Hope that has its foundation in God will not crumble under the pressures of life.

Is There Hope?

READ MATTHEW 28:1–10

"He is not here; he has risen, just as he said." —MATTHEW 28:6

I sat quietly at the graveside of my father, waiting for the private family burial of my mother to begin. The funeral director carried the urn that held her ashes. My heart felt numb and my head was in a fog. How can I handle losing them both within just three months? In my grief I felt loss and loneliness, and I felt a little hopeless facing a future without them.

Then the pastor read about another graveside. On the first day of the week, early in the morning, women went to Jesus's tomb, carrying spices for His body (Matthew 28:1; Luke 24:1). There they were startled to find an open and empty tomb—and an angel. "Do not be afraid," he said to them (Matthew 28:5). They didn't need to be afraid of the empty tomb or of the angel, because he had good news for them.

Hope stirred when I heard the next words: "He is not here; he has risen, just as he said" (v. 6). Because Jesus had come back to life, death had been conquered! Jesus reminded His followers just a few days before His death: "Because I live, you also will live" (John 14:19).

Even though we grieve at the loss of our loved ones, we find hope through the resurrection of Jesus and His promise that there is life after death.

ANNE CETAS

Because He lives, we live.

AUGUST
3

Love

The Difference Love Makes

READ 1 JOHN 4:7–12

Put on love, which binds them all together in perfect unity. —COLOSSIANS 3:14

If an athletic team is to succeed, there must be a bond of unity among its members. In the words of Hall of Fame football coach Vince Lombardi, "If you're going to play together as a team, you've got to care for one another. You've got to love each other." He added, "The difference between mediocrity and greatness is the feeling these guys have for one another."

Long before football existed, Justin Martyr (c. AD 100–165) gave an eloquent defense of Christianity. In writing to the emperor of Rome, he explained the dramatic transformation Christ brings to believers: "Before we became Christians, . . . we used to value above all else money and possessions; now we bring together all we have and share it with those who are in need. Formerly, we hated and killed one another . . . . Now . . . we all live in peace. We pray for our enemies and seek to win over those who hate us unjustly."

The same Christ-centered change is to be evident in Christians today. Before we can reach out in love to our unsaved friends and neighbors, we must demonstrate God's love to our fellow believers in Christ. It's His commandment to us (1 John 4:20–21), and it's the best way to show the world the difference love makes.

VERNON GROUNDS

Love is the magnet that draws believers together and attracts unbelievers to Christ.

Take Another Look at Jesus

READ HEBREWS 3:1–6

But Christ is faithful as the Son over God's house. And we are his house, if indeed we hold firmly to our confidence and the hope in which we glory. —HEBREWS 3:6

If there ever was a faithful person, it was Brother Justice. He was committed to his marriage, dedicated to his job as a postal worker, and each Sunday stood at his post as a leader in our local church. I visited my childhood church recently, and perched on the upright piano was the same bell that Brother Justice rang to notify us that the time for Bible study was about to end. The bell has endured the test of time. And although Brother Justice has been with the Lord for years, his legacy of faithfulness also endures.

Hebrews 3 brings a faithful servant and a faithful Son to the readers' attention. Although the faithfulness of Moses as God's "servant" is undeniable, Jesus is the one believers are taught to focus on. "Therefore, holy brothers and sisters . . . fix your thoughts on Jesus" (v. 1). Such was the encouragement to all who face temptation (2:18). Their legacy could come only from following Jesus, the faithful One.

What do you do when the winds of temptation are swirling all around you? When you are weary and worn and want to quit? The text invites us to, as one paraphrase renders it, "Take a good hard look at Jesus" (3:1 MSG). Look at Him again—and again and again. As we reexamine Jesus, we find the trustworthy Son of God, who gives us courage to live in His family.

Arthur Jackson

Looking to Jesus can give us courage to face the challenges in our lives.

Love

Listening with Love

READ LUKE 18:9–14

"I tell you that this man, rather than the other, went home justified before God. For all those who exalt themselves will be humbled, and those who humble themselves will be exalted." —LUKE 18:14

One August evening in Vermont, a young missionary spoke at our small church. The country where he and his wife served was in religious turmoil, and it was considered too dangerous for children. In one of his stories, he told us about a heart-wrenching episode when his daughter pleaded with him not to leave her behind at a boarding school.

I was a new dad at that time, having recently been blessed with a daughter, and the story upset me. *How could loving parents leave their daughter alone like that?* I thought to myself. By the time the talk was finished, I was so worked up that I ignored the offer to visit with the missionary. I charged out of the church, saying out loud as I left: "I'm sure glad I'm not like . . ."

In that instant, the Holy Spirit stopped me cold. I couldn't even finish the sentence. Here I was, saying almost word for word what the Pharisee said to God: "I thank you that I am not like other people" (Luke 18:11). How disappointed I was in myself! How disappointed God must have been! Since that evening, I've asked God to help me listen to others with humility and restraint as they pour their hearts out in confession, profession, or pain.

RANDY KILGORE

We don't get closer to God by passing judgment on others.

He Walked in Our Shoes

READ HEBREWS 2:10–18

Because he himself suffered when he was tempted, he is able to help those who are being tempted. —HEBREWS 2:18

To help his staff of young architects understand the needs of those for whom they design housing, David Dillard sends them on "sleepovers." They put on pajamas and spend twenty-four hours in a senior living center in the same conditions as people in their eighties and nineties. They wear earplugs to simulate hearing loss, tape their fingers together to limit manual dexterity, and exchange eyeglasses to replicate vision problems. In an article written by Rodney Brooks in *USA Today*, Dillard says, "The biggest benefit is [that] when I send twenty-seven-year-olds out, they come back with a heart ten times as big. They meet people and understand their plights."

Jesus lived on this earth for thirty-three years and shared in our humanity. He was made like us, "fully human in every way" (Hebrews 2:17), so He knows what it's like to live in a human body on this earth. He understands the struggles we face and comes alongside with understanding and encouragement.

"Because [Jesus] himself suffered when he was tempted, he is able to help those who are being tempted" (v. 18). The Lord could have avoided the cross. Instead, He obeyed His Father. Through His death, He broke the power of Satan and freed us from our fear of death (vv. 14–15).

In every temptation, Jesus walks beside us to give us courage, strength, and hope along the way.

David McCasland

Jesus understands.

Love

The Tree of Love

READ MATTHEW 27:27–35

"He himself bore our sins" in his body on the cross, so that we might die to sins and live for righteousness; "by his wounds you have been healed." —1 PETER 2:24

The corkscrew willow tree stood vigil over our backyard for twenty years. It shaded all four of our children as they played in the yard, and it provided shelter for the neighborhood squirrels. But one spring, the tree didn't awaken from its winter slumber, and it was time to bring it down. Each day for a week I worked on it—first to fell it and then to chop two decades of growth into manageable pieces. It gave me a time to think about trees.

I thought about the first tree—the one on which hung the forbidden fruit that Adam and Eve just couldn't resist (Genesis 3:6). God used that tree to test their loyalty and trust. Then there's the tree in Psalm 1 that reminds us of the fruitfulness of godly living. And in Proverbs 3:18, wisdom is personified as a tree of life.

But it is a transplanted tree that is most important—the crude cross of Calvary that was hewn from a sturdy tree that grew somewhere near Jerusalem. There our Savior hung between heaven and earth to bear every sin of every generation on His shoulders. It stands above all trees as a symbol of love, sacrifice, and salvation.

At Calvary, God's only Son suffered a horrible death on a cross. That's the tree of life for us.

DAVE BRANON

The cross of Christ reveals man's sin at its worst and God's love at its best.

The Real Thing

READ 1 JOHN 2:3–11

But if anyone obeys his word, love for God is truly made complete in them. This is how we know we are in him. —1 JOHN 2:5

A church in Naperville, Illinois, basked in excitement about its brand-new bells in the belfry above its sanctuary. When the church was built many years earlier, the people didn't have the money to purchase bells. However, for the church's twenty-fifth anniversary the people raised funds to purchase three bells to hang in the vacant space. Although they were stunning to look at, there was one problem: the congregation will never hear the bells ring. They aren't real bells.

The apostle John wrote his first epistle to encourage believers not to just look like real Christians but also to prove they are genuine by how they live. The evidence that a person's faith is real is not found in some mystical experience with God. The proof that people truly know and love God is found in submitting to His authority and to His Word. John writes, "But if anyone obeys his word, love for God is truly made complete in them. This is how we know we are in him: Whoever claims to live in him must live as Jesus did" (1 John 2:5–6).

If we claim that we have been transformed by the gospel and intimately know and love God, we should validate it by our obedience to His Word. That's evidence of the real thing.

MARVIN WILLIAMS

Obedience to God is an expression of our love for God.

AUGUST
9

Faith

Seeing to Tomorrow

READ 2 CORINTHIANS 5:1–9

For we live by faith, not by sight.
—2 CORINTHIANS 5:7

I enjoy gazing up at a cloudless blue sky. The sky is a beautiful part of our great Creator's masterpiece, given for us to enjoy. Imagine how much pilots must love the view. They use several aeronautical terms to describe a perfect sky for flying, but my favorite is, "You can see to tomorrow."

"Seeing to tomorrow" is beyond our view. Sometimes we even struggle to see or understand what life is throwing at us today. The Bible tells us, "Why, you do not even know what will happen tomorrow. What is your life? You are a mist that appears for a little while and then vanishes" (James 4:14).

But our limited visibility is not cause for despair. Just the opposite. We trust in the God who sees all of our tomorrows perfectly—and who knows what we need as we face the challenges ahead. The apostle Paul knew this. That's why Paul encourages us with hopeful words, "We live by faith, not by sight" (2 Corinthians 5:7).

When we trust God with our day as well as our unseen tomorrows, we don't need to worry about anything life throws at us. We walk with Him and He knows what is ahead; He is strong enough and wise enough to handle it.

BILL CROWDER

God sees the beginning to the end.

The One Who Understands

READ JOHN 1:1–18

The Word became flesh and made his dwelling among us. —JOHN 1:14

John Babler, a chaplain for the police and fire departments in his Texas community, took an extra step to understand the people he worked with. During a sabbatical from his job, he attended police academy training so he could relate to the situations law enforcement officers face. Through spending time with the other cadets and learning about the intense challenges of the profession, Babler gained a new sense of humility and empathy. He felt that training would make him more effective as he counsels police officers who struggle with emotional stress, fatigue, and loss.

We know that God understands the situations we face, because He sees everything that happens to us. But we also know that He understands because through the person of Jesus Christ, He lived on earth and experienced life as a human being. Here's how John explained it: Jesus "became flesh and made his dwelling among us" (John 1:14). During Jesus's earthly life, He felt the searing heat of the sun, the pain of an empty stomach, and the uncertainty of homelessness. Emotionally, He endured the tension of disagreements, the burn of betrayal, and the ongoing threat of violence.

Jesus experienced the joys of friendship and family love, as well as the worst problems we face here on earth. He provides hope. He is the Wonderful Counselor who patiently listens to our concerns with insight and care (Isaiah 9:6). He is the One who can say, "I've been through that. I understand."

JENNIFER BENSON SCHULDT

God understands the struggles we face.

A Motivating Hope

READ REVELATION 22:16–21

He who testifies to these things says, "Yes, I am coming soon." Amen. Come, Lord Jesus. —REVELATION 22:20

One of the most encouraging teachings in the Bible is the truth that the Lord himself will return to earth.

Three times in Revelation 22 this promise is repeated. As the pages of divine revelation were about to be closed, our Lord called attention to this grand theme, announcing, "Surely I am coming quickly." Think of it! The last words of Jesus twenty centuries ago remind us that He is coming back for us. If such a forceful assurance closes the canon of Scripture, shouldn't this hope be continually in our heart?

The great British preacher F. B. Meyer (1847–1929) once asked his contemporary preacher Dwight L. Moody, "What is the secret of your success?" Moody replied, "For many years I have never given an address without the consciousness that the Lord may come before I have finished." Perhaps this was the secret to Moody's zeal.

In this sinful old world, it's easy to lose the upward look. Yet we must keep the hope of Christ's return on our heart and mind. The apostle Paul talked about this when he said, "For our citizenship is in heaven. And we eagerly await a Savior from there, the Lord Jesus Christ" (Philippians 3:20). May His last words, "Surely I am coming quickly," motivate us to serve Him.

Paul Van Gorder

The hope of glorification keeps before us the need of purification.

Tough to Love

READ ACTS 13:12–23

For about forty years he endured their conduct in the wilderness. —ACTS 13:18

Years ago I was a camp counselor for some rebellious boys. It was challenging to deal with their behavior. They would mistreat the animals at the petting zoo and occasionally fight among themselves. So I adopted a calm and firm approach to leading them. Although they often exasperated me, I always made sure their physical needs were taken care of.

Even though I had a kind and loving exterior, I often felt on the inside that I was just "putting up with them." That caused me to prayerfully reflect on how a loving heavenly Father provides for His rebellious children. In telling the story of the Israelites during the exodus, Paul said, "For about forty years [God] endured their conduct in the wilderness" (Acts 13:18). The Greek word for *endured* most likely means "to patiently provide for people's needs despite an ungrateful response."

Some people may not react favorably to our efforts to show care and concern. When this happens, it may help to remember that God is patient with us. And He has given us His Spirit to help us respond with love to those who are hard to love or who are ungrateful (Galatians 5:22–23).

Give us your patience, Lord, for anyone in our lives who is difficult to love.

DENNIS FISHER

Be as patient with others as God has been with you.

Love

Where Has Love Gone?

READ JEREMIAH 2:1–13

"What fault did your ancestors find in me, that they strayed so far from me?" —JEREMIAH 2:5

New love is exciting! We've all seen it in newly married couples. It doesn't matter if they're twenty or seventy, love makes their faces beautiful and their feet bounce.

It's not only true of marriages. We've seen people who lovingly wash and wax their new sports car—and then do it all over again.

Whether it's a new car or a new relationship, at first we respond with wholehearted devotion. But with the passing of time, excitement often fades. Unrealistic hopes can blind us to the flaws in the object of our affection. When we expect too much from a person or a possession, we set ourselves up for disappointment.

A car, a house, or a spouse may turn out to be less than ideal. But if our relationship with God cools, it's because our communication has broken down and disinterest has set in. It's then that intimacy is lost. It happened with Israel (Jeremiah 2:5–8); it happens with us. But we can't blame God. He never changes. His love for us is unfailing!

If your relationship with the Lord has grown cold, take time to think about who He is and what He has done. Draw near to Him in prayer. Then you won't be left wondering where your love has gone.

MART DEHAAN

To renew your love for Christ,
review Christ's love for you.

Letting Go

READ GENESIS 12:1–9

The Lord had said to Abram, "Go from your country, your people and your father's household to the land I will show you." —GENESIS 12:1

For our wedding anniversary, my husband borrowed a tandem bike so we could enjoy a romantic adventure together. As we began to pedal on our way, I quickly realized that as the rider on the back my vision of the road ahead was eclipsed by my husband's broad shoulders. Also, my handlebars were fixed; they didn't affect the steering of our bike. Only the front handlebars determined our direction; mine served merely as support for my upper body. I had the choice to either be frustrated by my lack of control or to embrace the journey and trust Mike to guide us safely on our route.

When God asked Abram to leave his homeland and family, He didn't offer much information concerning the destination. No geographic coordinates. No description of the new land or its natural resources. Not even an indication of how long it would take to get there. God simply gave the instruction to "go" to the land He would show him. Abram's obedience to God's instruction, despite lacking the details most humans crave, is credited to him as faith (Hebrews 11:8).

If we find ourselves grappling with uncertainty or a lack of control in our lives, let's seek to adopt Abram's example of following and trusting God. The Lord will steer us well.

Kirsten Holmberg

God can be trusted to guide us.

Hope

The Cross of Hope

READ 1 PETER 1:1–8

Praise be to the God and Father of our Lord Jesus Christ! In his great mercy he has given us new birth into a living hope through the resurrection of Jesus Christ from the dead. —1 PETER 1:3

In recounting his experiences as a political prisoner in the old Soviet Union, Aleksandr Solzhenitsyn (1918–2008) told of a moment when he was on the verge of giving up all hope.

He was forced to work twelve hours a day at hard labor while existing on a starvation diet, and he had become gravely ill. The doctors were predicting his death. One afternoon, while shoveling sand under a blazing sun, he simply stopped working. He did so even though he knew the guards would beat him severely—perhaps to death. But he felt that he just couldn't go on. Then he saw another prisoner, a fellow Christian, moving toward him cautiously. With his cane the man quickly drew a cross in the sand and erased it. In that brief moment, Solzhenitsyn felt all of the hope of the gospel flood through his soul. It gave him courage to endure that difficult day and the months of imprisonment that followed.

The apostle Peter explained that Christ suffered for us, leaving us an example (1 Peter 2:21). Our Savior's willing submission to the cross can give us the strength to go on. When we encounter opposition, physical pain, or mental anguish, we may feel like giving up. If so, we need to look to the One who died on Calvary. His suffering will bring us renewed strength and grace. The cross is indeed our cross of hope.

DAVID EGNER

Christ was lifted up that He might lift us up.

Guard Your Brand

READ COLOSSIANS 3:1–14

And over all these virtues put on love, which binds them all together in perfect unity. —COLOSSIANS 3:14

A popular clothing retailer requires that its sales clerks dress like the models in the store windows, which advertise its clothes. This practice is referred to as "guarding their brand." The idea behind it is that shoppers will be more likely to purchase clothes because they will want to look like the people they see wearing them.

In a consumer-oriented culture, it's easy to be seduced into thinking that we can "buy" acceptance by wearing the things that beautiful people wear. Retailers would have us believe that looking good will make us desirable.

Sometimes we even convince ourselves that we can win followers for God by making ourselves attractive to the world. But the Bible is clear about what's really important to God. He wants us to look like Jesus in our character. In a sense, Jesus is our "brand," for we are being conformed to His image (Romans 8:29). We attract others to Christ when we put on His attributes, which include tender mercies, kindness, humility, meekness, longsuffering (Colossians 3:12), and, above all, love (v. 14).

Instead of polishing and protecting our own image, we need to be guarding and reflecting the image of God, which is being perfected in us through Christ.

JULIE ACKERMAN LINK

One of the Spirit's roles is to form
the likeness of Christ in us.

AUGUST
17

Faith

Food in the Cupboard

READ MATTHEW 6:25–34

"Therefore I tell you, do not worry about your life, what you will eat or drink; or about your body, what you will wear. Is not life more than food, and the body more than clothes?" —MATTHEW 6:25

My friend Marcia, the director of the Jamaica Christian School for the Deaf near Montego Bay, illustrated an important way to look at life when things are difficult. In a school newsletter article she titled "A Blessed Start," she pointed out that for the first time in seven years the boarding school began the new year with a surplus. And what was that surplus? Thousands of dollars in the bank? No, that never happens at JCSD. Enough school supplies for the year? That too is beyond rare. It was simply this: A month's supply of food in the cupboard for the children.

When you're responsible for feeding thirty hungry students on a tiny budget, that's huge! She accompanied her note with this verse from 1 Chronicles 16:34, "Oh, give thanks to the LORD, for He is good! For His mercy endures forever" (NKJV).

Year after year Marcia trusts God to provide for the children and staff at her school. She never has much—whether it's water or food or school supplies. Yet she is always grateful for what God sends, and she is faithful to believe that He will continue to provide.

When we have that kind of faith in God's provision, we take our Savior at His word: "Do not worry about tomorrow" (Matthew 6:25, 34).

DAVE BRANON

Worry does not empty tomorrow of its sorrow; it empties today of its strength.
—Corrie ten Boom

Begin the Day with Hope

READ PSALM 3

I lie down and sleep; I wake again, because the Lord *sustains me. I will not fear though tens of thousands assail me on every side.* —PSALM 3:5–6

While we usually wake up each morning anticipating the activities of a new day, sometimes we experience feelings of dread. After a night of fitful sleep, we may feel ill-equipped to face the problems we expect to encounter. Dark, depressing thoughts can quickly overwhelm us.

If anyone had reason to feel like that, it was David when he composed Psalm 3. He and a small band of followers had been driven from the palace in Jerusalem because of a rebellion staged by his son Absalom. They had spent the first night fording the Jordan River, had made camp the next day, and had retired on the second night with the problem still unresolved. Even so, David was able to lie down and go to sleep.

When he awoke in the morning, the thought of the great odds against him came to mind (v. 1), but he didn't entertain it long. Instead, he looked upward in faith to God, backward in gratitude for His mercies, and forward in expectation of His mighty deliverance. Thus he could enter the new day with hope.

Some mornings you and I will wake up to a very difficult day. When this happens, we can either give in to despair or follow the example of David. Faith, gratitude, and expectation will enable us to face the most trying day with strong confidence in God.

Herb Vander Lugt

If the best things are not possible, make the best of the things that are possible.

Love

Realism and Romance

READ EPHESIANS 5:22–33

Husbands, love your wives, just as Christ loved the church and gave himself up for her. . . . However, each one of you also must love his wife as he loves himself, and the wife must respect her husband. —EPHESIANS 5:25, 33

Good marriages have a balance. The practical realities of daily living are enhanced by the joy and spontaneity of continually falling in love with each other.

Realism can help a husband to see that he is taking his wife for granted and is not being sensitive to her feelings. It can cause a wife to see that her critical comments are tearing down her husband's self-respect.

Realism is not enough, however. Romance, often discarded after the wedding, keeps a marriage from growing dull. It can prevent the kind of situation depicted in the cartoon of a couple sitting on the front porch of their home. The husband is saying, "Sometimes, Sarah, when I think of how much you mean to me, I can hardly keep from telling you so."

Paul's words in Ephesians 5 encourage a love between two people that reflects Christ's self-sacrificing devotion to His church. In addition, it's a love filled with kindness and tenderness.

Whether you've have been married half a year or half a century, Christ can help you balance your relationship with realism and romance. Keep drawing on His love and see what it does for your marriage.

DENNIS DEHAAN

The bonds of matrimony aren't worth much unless the interest is kept up.

No Greater Love

READ 1 JOHN 4:7–11

Dear friends, since God so loved us, we also ought to love one another. —1 JOHN 4:11

On our family room wall, in a small shadowbox, hangs a "treasure" that belongs to my wife Carolyn. Oh, we have things more intrinsically valuable on the walls of our home—a handmade quilt from the Blue Ridge Mountains of Kentucky, antique mirrors, oil paintings, and a magnificent dulcimer from an artisan in the backcountry of Idaho.

Carolyn's treasure, though, is far more valuable to her than any other possession, for it contains a gift from our granddaughter Julia. It was a present to her "Nana" on Valentine's Day several years ago when Julia was only six years old—a small, red, clay heart. Inscribed on it in childish scrawl are the words "I Luv U."

The little heart is crudely made, ragged on the edges, and bears a number of thumbprints and smudges, but Carolyn has enshrined it in a frame made especially for that heart. Each day it reminds her of Julia's love.

Is God's love more valuable to you than silver or gold or any other possession? He "sent his one and only Son into the world that [you] might live through him" (1 John 4:9). He did that because He loves you—not because you loved Him. And because of His love, one day you will be with Him in heaven. There is no greater love!

DAVID ROPER

God's eternal love is the source of our eternal life.

Love

A "Yes" of Love

READ 1 JOHN 3:16–24

Let us not love with words or speech but with actions and in truth. —1 JOHN 3:18

On August 21, 2016, my friend Carissa posted photos on social media of a devastating flood in Louisiana. The next morning she included a note from someone in the flooded area pleading for help. Five hours after that, she and her husband, Bobby, sent out a call for others to join them on their 1,000-mile trip to provide help. Less than twenty-four hours later, thirteen people were on their way to serve those whose homes had been severely damaged.

What motivates people to drop everything and drive seventeen hours to move appliances, do demolition work, and provide hope in a place they've never been before? It's love.

Think about this verse, which she posted along with her call for help: "Commit your way to the LORD; trust in him and he will do this" (Psalm 37:5). This is especially true when we follow God's call to help. The apostle John said, "If anyone . . . sees a brother or sister in need but has no pity on them, how can the love of God be in that person?" (1 John 3:17). It may be a daunting task—but we have God's promise of help when we "do what pleases him" (v. 22).

When a need arises, we can honor God by being willing to offer a "yes" of love to what we sense He is asking us to do for others.

DAVE BRANON

We show God's love when we are willing to help others; we show His strength when we take on the task He gives us to do.

AUGUST
22

The "Few Things"

READ MATTHEW 25:14–30

"His master replied, 'Well done, good and faithful servant! You have been faithful with a few things; I will put you in charge of many things. Come and share your master's happiness!' " —MATTHEW 25:23

No two people are alike. Every child born into this world is different physically, emotionally, and intellectually. Even identical twins have slightly different DNA. Some people, because of natural abilities inherited from their parents, have tremendous potential. Others, lacking this hereditary advantage, have little chance of achieving great things. But the key thing for all people is to use the abilities and talents God has given—despite the differences.

It's amazing to see what good has been accomplished by those who faced limiting circumstances. John Milton, despite being blinded in 1652, wrote his masterpiece *Paradise Lost* after the loss of his eyesight forced him into retirement. Isaac Watts had a severe physical deformity, yet he became a preacher and the writer of many great hymns. Fanny Crosby, accidentally blinded at six weeks of age, triumphed over her disability and gave us more than 8,000 hymns. Although these people were deprived in ways that could have caused them to be discouraged, they diligently employed the gifts they did possess, and they accomplished great things.

Our task, whether we are running over with talent or have no special abilities, whether we are basking in the sunlight of blessing or suffering under the cloud of adversity, is to use what we have for the Lord. Let's strive to be faithful over our "few things."

RICHARD DEHAAN

The world would be silent if no birds sang except those that sang best.

AUGUST
23

Love

Seeing God in Familiar Places

READ ISAIAH 6:1–6

The whole earth is full of his glory. —ISAIAH 6:3

Because of where I live, I'm treated to spectacular displays of the magnificent, creative glory of God. Recently, on a drive through the woods, I was struck with a breath-taking display of deep, rich reds and a variety of yellows that decorated the trees of autumn—all artfully arranged against the backdrop of a brilliant blue sky.

And later, as the temperatures plummet and winter blows in, I'll be reminded that no two snowflakes are ever the same as they pile on top of one another to create a rolling landscape of pristine white drifts. After that will come the miracle of spring, when that which seemed hopelessly dead bursts into life with buds and blossoms that will grace the meadows with a multiplicity of colors.

Wherever we look in the world around us, we see evidence that "the whole earth is full of [God's] glory" (Isaiah 6:3). What is amazing is that the creation that surrounds us is damaged by sin (see Romans 8:18–22), yet God has seen fit to grace our fallen landscape with these loving brushstrokes of His creative hand. It serves as a daily reminder that the beauty of His grace covers our sin and that His love for that which is fallen is always available to us.

JOE STOWELL

Never pass up an opportunity to enjoy nature's beauty—it's the handwriting of God.

The Heavenly Alternative

READ 2 CORINTHIANS 5:1–11

We are confident, I say, and would prefer to be away from the body and at home with the Lord. —2 CORINTHIANS 5:8

Recently, I wished a young friend "happy birthday" and asked him how it felt to be a year older. His playful response? "Well, I guess it's better than the alternative!"

We laughed together, but I later stopped to think—is it really? Don't misunderstand me. I'm happy to live as long as the Lord allows me to live and to watch my kids and grandkids grow and experience life. I'm not excited about the inevitability of death. But as a believer, the alternative to getting older is heaven—and that's not bad!

In 2 Corinthians 5, Paul talks about the reality of living with the aches and pains of our physical bodies, our "tents" of flesh. But we should not live in despair about aging. In fact, the apostle calls us to just the opposite. He wrote, "We are confident, I say, and would prefer to be away from the body and at home with the Lord" (v. 8). Confident! Pleased! Why? Because our alternative to earthly life is that we will be present with the Lord—forever! The heavenly perspective of what awaits us can give us confidence for living now.

If you know Christ, His promise can give you strength as you go through today and bright hope as you look ahead to tomorrow. What a great alternative!

BILL CROWDER

Death is gain because it means heaven, holiness, and Him!

AUGUST
25

Faith

Rebuilding

READ NEHEMIAH 2:11–18

Come, let us rebuild the wall of Jerusalem, and we will no longer be in disgrace. —NEHEMIAH 2:17

When Edward Klee returned to Berlin after being away for many years, the city he remembered and loved was no longer there. It had changed dramatically, and so had he. Writing in *Hemispheres* magazine, Klee said, "Returning to a city you once loved tends to be a hit-or-miss proposition . . . . It can be a letdown." Going back to the places of our past may produce a feeling of sorrow and loss. We are not the same person we were then, nor is the place that was so significant in our lives exactly as it was.

Nehemiah had been in exile from the land of Israel for many years when he learned of the desperate plight of his people and the devastation in the city of Jerusalem. He received permission from Artaxerxes, the Persian king, to return and rebuild the walls. After a nighttime reconnaissance to examine the situation (Nehemiah 2:13–15), Nehemiah told the inhabitants of the city, "You see the trouble we are in: Jerusalem lies in ruins, and its gates have been burned with fire. Come, let us rebuild the wall of Jerusalem, and we will no longer be in disgrace" (v. 17).

Nehemiah did not return to reminisce, but to rebuild. It's a powerful lesson for us as we consider the damaged parts of our past that need repair. It is our faith in Christ and His power that enables us to look ahead, move forward, and rebuild.

DAVID MCCASLAND

We cannot change the past, but God is changing us for the future.

Keep On Going

READ EXODUS 10:21–29

By faith [Moses] left Egypt, not fearing the king's anger. —HEBREWS 11:27

Working in the corporate world allowed me to interact with many talented and levelheaded people. However, one project led by an out-of-town supervisor was an exception. Regardless of our team's progress, this manager harshly criticized our work and continually demanded more effort.

These run-ins left me discouraged and fearful. At times, I wanted to quit.

It's possible that Moses felt like quitting when he encountered Pharaoh during the plague of darkness. God had hurled eight other epic disasters at Egypt, and Pharaoh finally exploded, "[Moses,] get out of my sight! Make sure you do not appear before me again! The day you see my face you will die" (Exodus 10:28).

Despite this threat, Moses eventually was used by God to free the Israelites from Pharaoh's control. "[By faith] Moses left the land of Egypt, not fearing the king's anger. He kept right on going because he kept his eyes on the one who is invisible" (Hebrews 11:27 NLT). Moses overcame Pharaoh by believing that God would keep His promise of deliverance (Exodus 3:17).

Today, we can rely on the promise that God is with us in every situation, supporting us through His Holy Spirit. He helps us resist the pressure of intimidation and wrong responses to it by granting us supernatural power, love, and self-control (2 Timothy 1:7). The Spirit provides the courage we need to keep going and to follow God's leading in our lives.

JENNIFER BENSON SCHULDT

God's guidance in the past gives
us courage for the future.

AUGUST
27

Hope

See You in the Morning

READ JOHN 14:1–6

If I go and prepare a place for you, I will come back and take you to be with me that you also may be where I am. —JOHN 14:3

For many years David Fant was a locomotive engineer on the line between Washington, D.C., and Atlanta. He told of one cloudy afternoon when he was at the throttle of a train heading south. He said, "I had been somewhat depressed in spirit all day. The dark, gloomy weather on the outside seemed to correspond to the way I was feeling on the inside. We were running near the Blue Ridge Mountains when I was privileged to witness a most unusual sunset. For a few minutes the sun was bursting from behind the mountains in glorious splendor. Then suddenly it disappeared behind the towering landscape, leaving the heavens painted with a golden glow."

Fant continued, "As that evening sun went down, it seemed to say, 'Good night, I will see you in the morning.' " Immediately Fant's mood changed and great joy filled his heart. To him, that experience became a picture of the dark age through which the Christian sometimes journeys and of the bright hope of the Savior's return.

Ever since the Son "went down" at Calvary and left this earth after His resurrection, the age has been steadily darkening. But before Christ left His disciples, He promised, "I will come again." And Christians in every age have found hope in that prospect.

Yes, we will see Him in the morning!

PAUL VAN GORDER

The bright ray of hope in the darkening skies
is the promised return of the Son.

Helping Love Grow

READ 1 CORINTHIANS 13

[Love] does not dishonor others, it is not self-seeking, it is not easily angered, it keeps no record of wrongs. —1 CORINTHIANS 13:5

A young man told his father, "Dad, I'm going to get married."

"How do you know you're ready to get married, Ron?" asked the father. "Are you in love?"

"I sure am," he replied.

The father then asked, "Ron, how do you know you're in love?"

"Last night as I was kissing my girlfriend goodnight, her dog bit me and I didn't feel the pain until I got home!" Ron has got that loving feeling, but he has a lot of growing to do. Vernon Grounds, a former writer for *Our Daily Bread*, who was married for more than 70 years before his death in 2010, shared these points about how to grow in love:

Ponder God's love in Christ. Take time to reflect on how He gave His life for you. Read about Him in the Gospels, and thank Him.

Pray for the love of God. Ask Him to give you an understanding of His love and to teach you how to live that out in your relationships with your spouse and others (1 Corinthians 13).

Practice the love of God. Give of yourself. A newlywed told me he thinks love is practical. He said, "My responsibility is to make life easier for my spouse." The other, tougher side of love is to challenge each other to act in godly ways.

Love will grow when we ponder love, pray for love, and practice love.

ANNE CETAS

As Christ's love grows in us,
His love flows from us.

Love

Look and Be Quiet

READ LUKE 23:44–49

Look around and see. Is any suffering like my suffering? —LAMENTATIONS 1:12

In the song "Look at Him," Mexican composer Rubén Sotelo describes Jesus at the cross. He invites us to look at Jesus and be quiet, because the type of love Jesus demonstrated at the cross leaves us speechless. By faith we can imagine the scene described in the Gospels. We can imagine the cross and the blood, the nails, and the pain.

When Jesus breathed His last, those who "had gathered to witness this sight . . . beat their breasts and went away" (Luke 23:48). Others "stood at a distance, watching these things" (v. 49). They looked and were quiet. Only one spoke, a centurion, who said, "Surely he was the Son of God" (Matthew 27:54).

Songs and poems have been written to describe this great love. Hundreds of years earlier, Jeremiah wrote about Jerusalem's pain after its devastation. "Is it nothing to you, all you who pass by?" (Lamentations 1:12). He was asking people to look and see; he thought there was no greater suffering than Jerusalem's. However, has there been any suffering like Jesus's suffering?

All of us are passing by the road of the cross. Will we look and see His love? Let us take a moment to ponder Jesus's death; and in the quietness of our hearts, may we whisper to Him our deepest devotion.

KEILA OCHOA

Look at the cross and worship.

True Faith

READ ROMANS 10:1–13

God made him who had no sin to be sin for us, so that in him we might become the righteousness of God. —2 CORINTHIANS 5:21

Some things in life call for us to be absolutely accurate—to do exactly as the directions say. For instance, I can't fill out my tax returns any old way I want. I have to do exactly as the tax code requires, or I'll spend a lot of time explaining myself. Even in a land of liberty, we are bound to follow certain rules.

Following the Bible as the guidebook in our spiritual life is even more vital. Some people may consider these matters to be peripheral and easily ignored, but out of love for God and a desire to honor Him, we want to know and live by the Book He has given us.

That's why it is distressing to learn that according to the Barna Research Group, forty-two percent of Americans think Jesus committed sins. And even twenty-five percent of professing Christians say He was not sinless. Beyond that, sixty-one percent of Americans think there are other ways to salvation besides faith in Christ.

These are dangerous deviations from the absolute truth of Scripture. Our Guidebook, the Bible, is clear—Jesus Christ lived a perfect life, and His sacrificial death is the only way to establish a relationship with God.

We can't afford to make up our own rules. For instance, only those who call "on the name of the Lord will be saved" (Romans 10:13). That's true faith. Any other way leads to eternal death.

DAVE BRANON

To get into heaven, it's who you know that counts.

Hope

An Appropriate Name

READ MATTHEW 1:18–25

You are to give him the name Jesus.
—MATTHEW 1:21

The name of the southeastern Asian nation of Indonesia is formed by combining two Greek words that together mean "island." That name is appropriate, because Indonesia is made up of more than 17,500 islands spanning nearly 750,000 square miles. Indonesia—an appropriate name for a nation of islands.

In the Bible, we find that people were often given names—sometimes at birth, sometimes later—that made a statement about them or their character. Barnabas, whose name means "son of encouragement," continually encouraged those he encountered. Jacob, whose name means "schemer," repeatedly manipulated people and situations for his own selfish ends.

And no one has ever been more appropriately named than Jesus. When the angel of the Lord spoke to Joseph about Mary's soon-to-be-born Son, he told Joseph, "You are to give him the name Jesus, for he will save his people from their sins" (Matthew 1:21).

Jesus means "the Lord saves" and defines both who Jesus is and why He came. He was also called Immanuel, which means "God with us" (1:23). His name reveals our eternal hope!

BILL CROWDER

The name of Jesus is at the heart
of our faith and our hope.

Climate Control

READ 3 JOHN

May the Lord make your love increase and overflow for each other and for everyone else, just as ours does for you. —1 THESSALONIANS 3:12

It's one of the few places on earth where the air is as fresh and clean as it must have been millennia ago. Constant winds keep out pollution and germs, and the climate discourages the growth of native viruses.

It sounds like the healthiest place on earth. So why doesn't anyone want to live there? Because it's just too cold. With temperatures that drop to –100° Fahrenheit, the South Pole is too frigid even for germs.

We have to be careful that our churches don't bear a striking resemblance to that sterile atmosphere. Suppose that the truth of God is preached, Scriptures are meticulously quoted, and error has no chance to survive—but there is no corresponding obedience or love, and the spiritual temperature is sub-zero. What if the poor are given the cold shoulder (James 2:2–6)? Or if those weak in the faith are engaged in icy arguments (Romans 14:1)? Or if brothers in Christ are left out in the cold because they pose a threat to comfortable cliques (3 John 5–10)? No one should be unloved.

The church was formed by the redeeming love of Christ and is designed to be a warm and inviting fellowship! Our desire must not be merely to "keep out the germs," but to let the Lord create a climate where brothers and sisters can open their hearts to His soul-healing love.

MART DEHAAN

The church will always be a
warm shelter in a cold world.

Hope

Looking for Hope?

READ PSALM 42:5–11

Why, my soul, are you downcast? Why so disturbed within me? Put your hope in God, for I will yet praise him, my Savior and my God. —PSALM 42:5

A missionary in India lay burning with the fever of malaria. As the disease sapped her strength, depression dragged her into the depths of despair. She felt so overwhelmed that she asked God to take her to heaven.

Later, while enclosed in this cocoon of discouragement, the sounds of music drifted into her room from another part of the house. A group of Indian Christians were having a worship service. She heard them sing in their dialect, "I have decided to follow Jesus; no turning back, no turning back." The song touched her heart and she began praying. Soon prayer graduated to praise, and God lifted her discouragement. Eventually, her health returned and she continued to serve in that country.

When we face that kind of discouragement, we may echo David's question, "Why, my soul, are you downcast? Why so disturbed within me?" (Psalm 42:5).

That's when we can recall that David had not only the problem but also the solution. "Put your hope in God," he said. The encouragement of God's presence brings praise to our heart and renewed faithfulness to our walk. Then we can say, "I have decided to follow Jesus; no turning back, no turning back." When we trust Jesus, we can find hope.

PAUL VAN GORDER

If you're having trouble coping, trying hoping—in God.

The Twelfth Man

READ HEBREWS 11:32–12:3

Since we are surrounded by such a great cloud of witnesses, let us throw off everything that hinders and the sin that so easily entangles. And let us run with perseverance the race marked out for us. —HEBREWS 12:1

A large sign at Kyle Field, the home the Texas A&M University football team, says "HOME OF THE 12TH MAN." While each team is allowed eleven players on the field, the 12th Man is the symbolic name for the thousands of A&M students who remain standing during the entire game to cheer their team on. The tradition traces its roots to 1922 when the coach called a student from the stands to suit up and be ready to replace an injured player. Although he never entered the game, his willing presence on the sideline greatly encouraged the team.

Hebrews 11 describes heroes of the faith who faced great trials and remained loyal to God as "a great cloud of witnesses" (v. 1). And as this symbolic crowd watches us, we are encouraged to "throw off everything that hinders and the sin that so easily entangles. And let us run with perseverance the race marked out for us" (v. 1).

We are not alone on our journey of faith. The great saints and ordinary people who have been faithful to the Lord encourage us by their example and also by their presence in heaven. They are a spiritual 12th Man standing with us while we are still on the field.

As we fix our eyes on Jesus, "the pioneer and perfecter of faith" (12:2), we are spurred on by all those who followed Him.

David McCasland

Faithful Christians from the past encourage us today.

Love

Relationships Under Repair

READ PHILEMON

Be kind and compassionate to one another, forgiving each other, just as in Christ God forgave you. —EPHESIANS 4:32

Are you easy to get along with? Do you have a good relationship with your spouse or your friends? Then you probably aren't guilty of the following behaviors:

- criticizing instead of praising
- using insensitive words
- neglecting others
- making jokes at another's expense
- not listening
- refusing to admit wrong
- belittling others' opinions

These kinds of behavior will wreck relationships and hinder the healing of past hurts.

For a good example of the way to strengthen relationships, read the apostle Paul's short letter to Philemon, a wealthy resident of Colosse. The subject is Onesimus, Philemon's slave, who had stolen from him and fled to Rome. There Onesimus met Paul, who led him to a saving knowledge of Jesus. The letter is Paul's kind, compassionate appeal to Philemon to accept Onesimus back—now as a brother. It's a great example of love in action.

Although Onesimus deserved Philemon's punishment, Paul called him a "son" (v. 10) and a "beloved brother" (v. 16). He said he would repay what Onesimus had stolen.

Paul knew how to restore a relationship. Do we?

DAVE BRANON

God sometimes puts us in the dark
so that we may see the light.

Signs of Love

READ JOHN 14:15–24

"If you love me, keep my commands."
—JOHN 14:15

School was over for the day, and fourteen-year-old Mandy couldn't wait to get home. Bursting into the kitchen, she exclaimed, "Mother, I'm in love! I tingle whenever I'm near him, and I have butterflies in my stomach when he talks to me."

Mandy's mother listened as her daughter bubbled over about the wonders of being in love, but she wasn't unduly alarmed. She expected that before long the romance would end—and in a few days it did. There's much more to true love than a tingling sensation and butterflies in the stomach.

Likewise, the signs of a genuine love for Jesus must be much more than the good feelings gained from enthusiastic singing and glowing testimonies in public.

I heard of a woman who exuberantly described how much she enjoyed her church and loved Jesus. Yet she refused to speak to her mother-in-law, fought with her sisters, and tried to dominate her husband. If she couldn't show her devotion to Jesus by obeying His command to love others, the happiness she felt at church meant nothing.

When Jesus said, "If you love me, keep my commands" (John 14:15), He was giving us the supreme test of our devotion to Him. Do we pass the test?

HERB VANDER LUGT

One proof of our love for God
is our love for our neighbor.

Hope

Christ the Redeemer

READ JOB 19:23–29

I know that my redeemer lives.
—JOB 19:25

The famous statue *Christ the Redeemer* overlooks the city of Rio de Janeiro. The statue is a model of Christ with His arms extended so that His body forms the shape of a cross. Brazilian architect Heitor da Silva Costa designed the figure. He imagined that the city's residents would see it as the first image to emerge from the darkness at dawn. At dusk, he hoped the city dwellers would view the setting sun as a halo behind the statue's head.

There is value in keeping our eyes on our actual Redeemer each day—during the good times and the difficult times. As Job suffered, he said, "I know that my redeemer lives, and that in the end he will stand on the earth" (Job 19:25).

The cry of Job's heart points us to Jesus—our living Savior who will visit the earth again one day (1 Thessalonians 4:16–18). Keeping our eyes on Jesus means remembering that we have been rescued from our sin. Jesus "gave himself for us to redeem us from all wickedness and to purify for himself a people that are his very own" (Titus 2:14).

All of us who have accepted Jesus as Savior have a reason to be glad. No matter what we endure on earth, we can have hope today and look forward to enjoying eternity with Him.

JENNIFER BENSON SCHULDT

Through His cross and resurrection,
Jesus rescues and redeems.

Renewed Hope

READ 1 KINGS 19:1–18

[Elijah] went a day's journey into the wilderness. He came to a broom bush, sat down under it and prayed that he might die. "I have had enough, LORD," he said. "Take my life; I am no better than my ancestors." —1 KINGS 19:4

People who live without hope can become suicidal. So it was with an Italian prisoner of war being held on a military base in the United States during World War II. He had become despondent after learning that his wife had died in Italy. The camp commander, knowing that the man had been a stonemason, asked him if he could design a chapel for the base. The POW accepted the assignment and even supervised its construction.

Today a unique chapel stands at the Letterkenny Army Depot in Chambersburg, Pennsylvania. The formerly despondent prisoner found renewed hope by using his God-given talents to bless others.

In 1 Kings 19, we read that Elijah was despondent. He was physically and emotionally drained after fleeing from the evil Queen Jezebel. In despair, he asked God to take his life. Instead, the angel of the Lord ministered to his physical needs. Some days later, the Lord spoke to Elijah and told him that his work was not over.

When you are in despair, the first step on the pathway to new hope is to take care of your physical needs. Then listen to God's voice through the Scriptures. The Lord will show you your spiritual condition and tell you what He would have you do to bless others.

DENNIS DEHAAN

God gives hope to us as we give help to others.

Faith

The Greatest Gift

READ JOHN 1:43–51

We have found . . . Jesus of Nazareth, the son of Joseph. —JOHN 1:41, 45

Over the years, my friend Barbara has given me countless encouraging cards and thoughtful presents. After I told her I had received Jesus as my Savior, she handed me the greatest gift she'd ever given me—my first Bible. She said, "You can grow closer to God and mature spiritually by meeting with Him daily, reading Scripture, praying, and trusting and obeying Him." My life changed when Barbara invited me to get to know God better.

Barbara reminds me of the apostle Philip. After Jesus invited Philip to follow Him (John 1:43), the apostle immediately told his friend Nathanael that Jesus was "the one Moses wrote about in the Law, and about whom the prophets also wrote" (v. 45). When Nathanael doubted, Philip didn't argue, criticize, or give up on his friend. He simply invited him to meet Jesus face to face. "Come and see," he said (v. 46).

I can imagine Philip's joy when he heard Nathanael declare Jesus as "the Son of God" and "the king of Israel" (v. 49). What a blessing to know that his friend wouldn't miss out on seeing the "greater things" Jesus promised they would witness (vv. 50–51).

The Holy Spirit initiates our intimate relationship with God and then lives in all who respond in faith. An invitation to know Jesus better is a great gift to receive and give.

XOCHITL DIXON

Knowing Jesus is the greatest gift we can receive;
sharing Him is the greatest gift we can give.

SEPTEMBER
9

Can You Help?

READ JAMES 2:14–20

In the same way, faith by itself, if it is not accompanied by action, is dead. —JAMES 2:17

The administrators of the high school in Barrow, Alaska, were tired of seeing students get into trouble and drop out at a rate of fifty percent. To keep students interested, they started a football team, which offered them a chance to develop personal skills, practice teamwork, and learn life lessons. The problem with football in Barrow, which is farther north than Iceland, is that it's hard to plant a grass field. So they competed on a gravel and dirt field.

Four thousand miles away in Florida, a woman named Cathy Parker heard about the football team and their dangerous field. Feeling that God was prompting her to help and impressed by the positive changes she saw in the students, she went to work. About a year later, the school dedicated its new field, complete with a beautiful artificial-turf playing surface. She had raised thousands of dollars to help some kids she didn't even know.

This is not about football—or money. It is about remembering "to do good and to share" (Hebrews 13:16). The apostle James reminds us that we demonstrate our faith by our actions (2:18). The needs in our world are varied and overwhelming. But when we love our neighbor as ourselves, as Jesus said (Mark 12:31), we reach people with God's love.

DAVE BRANON

Open your heart to God to learn compassion
and open your hand to give help.

Hope

Hope in Suffering

READ 1 PETER 1:3–9

In this [living hope] you greatly rejoice, though now for a little while you may have had to suffer grief in all kinds of trials. —1 PETER 1:6

When I opened my Bible to read Jeremiah 1 through 4, the subhead ascribed to the book startled me: "Hope in Time of Weeping." I almost cried. The timing was perfect, as I was walking through a season of weeping over the death of my mom.

I felt much the same way after hearing my pastor's sermon the day before. The title was "Joy in Suffering," taken from 1 Peter 1:3–9. He gave us an illustration from his own life: the one-year anniversary of his father's death. The sermon was meaningful for many, but for me it was a gift from God. These and other events were indications backed up by His Word that God would not leave me alone in my grief.

Even though the way of sorrow is hard, God sends reminders of His enduring presence. To the Israelites expelled from the Promised Land due to disobedience, God made His presence known by sending prophets like Jeremiah to offer them hope—hope for reconciliation through repentance. And to those He leads through times of testing, He shows His presence through a community of believers who "love one another deeply, from the heart" (1 Peter 1:22). These indications of God's presence during trials on earth affirm God's promise of the living hope awaiting us at the resurrection.

JULIE ACKERMAN LINK

We need never be ashamed of our tears.

Send Tranquility

READ JOHN 14:25–31

The Lord gives strength to his people; the Lord blesses his people with peace. —PSALM 29:11

When Jesus was with His disciples in the upper room shortly before His crucifixion, He knew they would face turmoil and unrest in the days ahead. First, they would experience the distressing events of His betrayal, arrest, execution, and burial. Then, after His resurrection and ascension, long periods of hard work, opposition, ridicule, and persecution would come. So in the quiet of those final moments together, He gave them these words of comfort: "Peace I leave with you; my peace I give you. I do not give to you as the world gives" (John 14:27).

A peaceful heart is still one of mankind's most precious and needed commodities. In his book *A Time to Heal*, former US President Gerald R. Ford repeated a story he had heard some years earlier. During the civil war in Greece in 1948, a villager was planning to emigrate to the United States. Before he left, he asked his weary, beleaguered, poverty-stricken neighbors, "What should I send when I get to America? Should I send money? Food? Clothing?" "No," one of his neighbors replied, "you should send us a ton of tranquility."

If you know Jesus as Savior, trust Him to make good on His promise of peace (John 14:27). Rest by faith in His loving arms. Cast your burden on Him. Let the Prince of Peace bring you tranquility.

David Egner

Peace floods the soul when Christ rules the heart.

A Prayer of Forgiveness

READ LUKE 6:27–36

"Love your enemies, do good to those who hate you, bless those who curse you, pray for those who mistreat you." —LUKE 6:27–28

In 1960, six-year-old Ruby Bridges was the first African-American child to integrate an all-white public elementary school in the American South. Every day for months, federal marshals escorted Ruby past a mob of angry parents shouting curses, threats, and insults at her. Safely inside, she sat in a classroom alone with Barbara Henry, the only teacher willing to instruct her while parents kept their children from attending school with Ruby.

Noted child psychiatrist Robert Coles met with Ruby for several months to help her cope with the fear and stress she experienced. He was amazed by the prayer Ruby said every day as she walked to school and back home. "Please, God, forgive them because they don't know what they're doing" (see Luke 23:34).

These words of Jesus spoken from the cross were stronger than the hatred and insults hurled at Him. In the most agonizing hours of His life, our Lord demonstrated the radical response He taught His followers: "Love your enemies, do good to those who hate you, bless those who curse you, pray for those who mistreat you . . . . Be merciful, just as your Father is merciful" (Luke 6:27–28, 36).

This remarkable approach is possible only as we consider the powerful love Jesus has given us—love stronger than even the deepest hatred. Ruby Bridges helped show us the way.

DAVID MCCASLAND

Bless those who curse you and pray for those who mistreat you.

His Loving Presence

READ HEBREWS 13:1–6

Keep your lives free from the love of money and be content with what you have, because God has said, "Never will I leave you; never will I forsake you." —HEBREWS 13:5

Our hearts sank when we learned that our good friend Cindy had been diagnosed with cancer. Cindy was a vibrant person whose life blessed all who crossed her path. My wife and I rejoiced when she went into remission, but a few months later her cancer returned with a vengeance. In our minds she was too young to die. Her husband told me about her last hours. When she was weak and hardly able to talk, Cindy whispered to him, "Just be with me." What she wanted more than anything in those dark moments was his loving presence.

The writer to the Hebrews comforted his readers by quoting Deuteronomy 31:6, where the people were told that God "will never leave [them] nor forsake [them]" (see Hebrews 13:5). In the darkest moments of life, the assurance of God's loving presence gives us confidence that we are not alone. He gives us the grace to endure, the wisdom to know He is working, and the assurance that Christ can "empathize with our weaknesses" (Hebrews 4:15).

Together let's embrace the blessing of His loving presence so we can confidently say, "The Lord is my helper; I will not be afraid" (13:6).

JOE STOWELL

There is peace in the presence of God.

Hope

Hope Lives

READ 1 PETER 1:3–9

Your faith—of greater worth than gold . . . may result in praise, glory and honor when Jesus Christ is revealed. —1 PETER 1:7

When unspeakable tragedy shatters people's lives, they search for answers. Recently, a mother who had lost a teenager said to me, "I can't figure it out. I don't know if I can believe anymore. I try, but God doesn't make sense to me. What does it all mean?" There are no easy answers to such big concerns. But for those who have trusted Christ, there is hope—whether we are basking in blessings or grinding through grief.

Peter spells this out in his first letter. In glowing terms, he praises God for our "new birth into a living hope" (1 Peter 1:3) through our salvation. That hope can bring joy even in the middle of tragedy. He also assures us of the permanence of this hope (v. 4). He then tells us of the heart-breaking reality that we may "suffer grief in all kinds of trials" (v. 6). Those who have suffered loss turn hopeful hearts toward Peter's next words: Trials come so that "your faith . . . may result in praise, glory and honor when Jesus Christ is revealed" (v. 7).

Trials—seemingly random and inexplicable—can be seen differently in the light of these words. In the midst of tragedy, the power and beauty of our salvation can shine through because of our great Savior. And that may be just enough light to get a troubled person through another day.

DAVE BRANON

The light of salvation shines clearly
even in the darkest night.

What About Depression?

READ 1 KINGS 19:1–18

[Elijah] went a day's journey into the wilderness. He came to a broom bush, sat down under it and prayed that he might die. "I have had enough, Lord," he said. "Take my life; I am no better than my ancestors." —1 KINGS 19:4

Depression is a condition of prolonged sadness, marked by feelings of hopelessness and an inability to think clearly. Depressed persons are apt to think, "I'm worthless. I'm a failure. I can't handle stress. There's no hope. I'll never feel better again."

Some of the most godly people have struggled with these feelings. The Old Testament prophet Elijah is a case in point. After being on the mountaintop, he experienced a great letdown. He had won a stunning victory over the prophets of Baal and had run seventeen miles in the strength of the Lord. But then he learned that Jezebel had vowed to kill him. Fear gripped his heart, and he fled for his life. Finally, physically and emotionally exhausted, he gave in to feelings of worthlessness and despair.

The Lord was gentle, however. He let Elijah rest, He fed him, and He strengthened him. But Elijah's sadness continued. So the Lord assured him of His presence; gave him a companion; Elisha, and a new task to perform.

Our feelings of utter aloneness do not mean that God has abandoned us. Those feelings only block our awareness of His presence.

As we wait helplessly on Him, we may feel hopeless. But we never are. God is there to help us through our down times.

Mart DeHaan

No one is hopeless whose hope is in God.

Faith

Fresh Faith

READ JOHN 20:24–29

Let us hold unswervingly to the hope we profess, for he who promised is faithful. —HEBREWS 10:23

When our son was struggling with heroin addiction, if you had told me God would one day use our experience to encourage other families who face these kinds of battles, I would have had trouble believing it. God has a way of bringing good out of difficult circumstances that isn't always easy to see when you are going through them.

The apostle Thomas also didn't expect God to bring good out of the greatest challenge of his faith—Jesus's crucifixion. Thomas wasn't with the other disciples when Jesus came to them after the resurrection, and in his deep grief he insisted, "Unless I see the nail marks in his hands and put my finger where the nails were . . . I will not believe" (John 20:25). But later, when Jesus appeared to all the disciples together, out of the dust of Thomas's doubts God's Spirit would inspire a striking statement of faith. When Thomas exclaimed, "My Lord and my God!" (v. 28), he was grasping the truth that Jesus was actually God in the flesh, standing right in front of him. It was a bold confession of faith that would encourage and inspire believers in every century that followed.

Our God is able to inspire fresh faith in our hearts, even in moments when we least expect it. We can always look forward to His faithfulness. Nothing is too hard for Him!

JAMES BANKS

God can change our doubts into
bold statements of faith.

SEPTEMBER 17

God's Embrace

READ ROMANS 12:3–11

Be devoted to one another in love. Honor one another above yourselves. —ROMANS 12:10

Soon after her family left for the evening, Carol started to think that her hospital room must be the loneliest place in the world. Nighttime had fallen, her fears about her illness were back, and she felt overwhelming despair as she lay there alone.

Closing her eyes, she began to talk to God: "O Lord, I know I am not really alone. You are here with me. Please calm my heart and give me peace. Let me feel Your arms around me, holding me."

As she prayed, Carol felt her fears beginning to subside. And when she opened her eyes, she looked up to see the warm, sparkling eyes of her friend Marge, who reached out to encircle her in a big hug. Carol felt as if God himself were holding her tightly.

God often uses fellow believers to show us His love. "In Christ we, though many, form one body in Christ. . . . We have different gifts, according to the grace given to each of us" (Romans 12:5–6). We serve others "with the strength God provides, so that in all things God may be praised through Jesus Christ" (1 Peter 4:11).

When we show love and compassion in simple, practical ways, we are a part of God's ministry to His people.

CINDY HESS KASPER

We show our love for God when we love His family.

Misplaced Love

READ PSALM 115

Their idols are silver and gold, made by human hands. —PSALM 115:4

Martin Lindstrom, an author and speaker, thinks that cellphones have become akin to a best friend for many owners. Lindstrom's experiment using fMRI (functional magnetic resonance imaging) helped him discover why. When the subjects saw or heard their phone ringing, their brains fired off neurons in the area associated with feelings of love and compassion. Lindstrom said, "It was as if they were in the presence of a girlfriend, boyfriend, or family member."

Many things vie for our affection and time and attention, and it seems we're always needing to evaluate where we're focusing our lives. Joshua told the people of Israel that they were to give their affection and worship to God alone (Joshua 24:14). This was significant in contrast to the idols worshiped by the nations around them. These idols were made of metal and were only the work of men's hands (Psalm 115:4). They were totally powerless. Therefore, God's people were exhorted to find their security in Him and not in other gods (Judges 10:13–16). Jesus reiterated this in His discussion of the commandments: "Love the Lord your God with all your heart and with all your soul and with all your mind" (Matthew 22:37).

The Lord alone is our help and shield (Psalm 115:9). May we reserve our worship for Him.

—MARVIN WILLIAMS

God is most worthy of our affections.

How to Be Saved

READ EPHESIANS 2:1–10

For it is by grace you have been saved, through faith—and this is not from yourselves, it is the gift of God—not by works, so that no one can boast. —EPHESIANS 2:8–9

As a young man, Allen Stewart was troubled because he wasn't sure where he would spend eternity. A Christian friend talked with him about this and told him he only had to believe on the Lord Jesus. But Allen thought this was far too easy, so he decided to follow his own ideas.

He joined a church, sang in the choir, and became a busy worker, hoping that through these efforts he would gain salvation. Yet nothing he did brought him inner satisfaction and joy. One day as he was reading Jesus's parable of the sower, he was struck by the verse, "Then the devil comes and takes away the word from their hearts, so that they may not believe and be saved" (Luke 8:12). As he pondered the last phrase, the truth suddenly dawned on him. "Will you look at that!" he exclaimed. "Even the devil knows that a man finds forgiveness if he just believes!" He turned from his own works and trusted Jesus—finally finding the peace he had so desperately sought.

Many people stumble over the simplicity of the gospel. Thinking they can win divine approval through their good deeds or religious efforts, they try to establish their own righteousness. But it is Jesus's work, not ours, that is the key to heaven!

HENRY BOSCH

Christ believed is salvation received!

Hope

The Cross and the Crown

READ JOHN 19:21–30

Jesus said . . . , "I am the resurrection and the life. He who believes in Me, though he may die, he shall live." —JOHN 11:25 NKJV

London's magnificent Westminster Abbey has a rich historical background. In the tenth century, Benedictine monks began a tradition of daily worship at this location (although the building was not built until the 1200s) that still continues today. The Abbey is also the burial place of many famous people, and since AD 1066 every English monarch but two has been crowned at the Abbey. In fact, eighteen of those monarchs are also buried there—their rule ending where it began.

No matter how grandiose their burial, world rulers rise and fall; they live and die. But another king, Jesus, though once dead, is no longer buried. In His first coming, Jesus was crowned with thorns and crucified as the "king of the Jews" (John 19:3, 19). Because Jesus rose from the dead in victory, we who are believers in Christ have hope beyond the grave and the assurance that we will live with Him forever. Jesus said, "I am the resurrection and the life. He who believes in Me, though he may die, he shall live. And whoever lives and believes in Me shall never die" (11:25–26 NKJV).

We serve a risen King! May we gladly yield to His rule in our lives now as we look forward to the day when the "Lord God Almighty" will reign for all eternity (Revelation 19:6).

BILL CROWDER

Jesus's resurrection spelled the death of death.

Water, Hope, and God's Love

READ PSALM 112

Even in darkness light dawns for the upright, for those who are gracious and compassionate and righteous. —PSALM 112:4

In the African country where my friend Roxanne serves others, water is a precious commodity. People often have to travel long distances to collect water from small, contaminated creeks—leading to sickness and death. Because of the lack of water, it is difficult for organizations like orphanages and churches to serve the people. But that's beginning to change.

Through Roxanne's leadership and the unselfish gifts of some loving people in established churches, clean water wells are being dug. At least twelve new wells are now operational, allowing churches to be centers of hope and encouragement for their communities. A health center and a home for 700 orphans will also be opened because of access to water.

This is the kind of love that can flow from believers in Christ because we have experienced the love and generosity of God. Paul says in 1 Corinthians 13 that if we don't have love, our voices clang on people's ears and our faith means nothing. And the apostle John says that if we have material possessions, see others in need, and take action, that's evidence that God's love is abiding in us (1 John 3:16).

God desires that we deal "graciously" (Psalm 112:5 NKJV) with those in need, because His heart is gracious toward us.

DAVE BRANON

Kindness is Christianity with its working clothes on.

Love

God's Love Through Me

READ 1 CORINTHIANS 13

Love never fails. But where there are prophecies, they will cease; where there are tongues, they will be stilled; where there is knowledge, it will pass away. —1 CORINTHIANS 13:8

During a devotional session at a conference, our leader asked us to read aloud 1 Corinthians 13:4–8, and substitute the word "Jesus" for "love." It seemed so natural to say, "Jesus is patient, Jesus is kind; Jesus does not envy; Jesus does not boast, is not proud; does not dishonor others, is not self-seeking . . . . Jesus never fails."

Then our leader said, "Read the passage aloud and say your name instead of Jesus." We laughed nervously at the suggestion. "I want you to begin now," the leader said. Quietly, haltingly I said the words that felt so untrue: "David is not self-seeking, is not easily angered, does not delight in evil but rejoices with the truth. David never fails."

The exercise caused me to ask, "How am I hindering God from expressing His love through me?" Do I think that other expressions of faith are more important? Paul declared that from God's perspective, eloquent speech, deep spiritual understanding, lavish generosity, and self-sacrifice are worthless when not accompanied by love (vv. 1–3).

God longs to express His great heart of love for others through us. Will we allow Him to do it?

DAVID MCCASLAND

Living like Christ is loving like God.

Deeply Loved

READ MATTHEW 6:25–34

Look at the birds of the air; they do not sow or reap or store away in barns, and yet your heavenly Father feeds them. Are you not much more valuable than they? —MATTHEW 6:26

Years ago I had an office in Boston that looked out on the Granary Burying Ground where many prominent American heroes are buried. There one can find the gravestones for John Hancock and Samuel Adams, two signers of the Declaration of Independence, and just a few feet beyond that is Paul Revere's marker.

But no one really knows where in this burial ground each body is buried because the stones have been moved many times—sometimes to make the grounds more picturesque and other times so lawn mowers could fit between them. And while the Granary features approximately 2,300 markers, closer to 5,000 people are buried there! Even in death, it seems, some people are not fully known.

There may be times when we feel as if we are like those unmarked residents of the Granary, unknown and unseen. Loneliness can make us feel unseen by others—and maybe even by God. But we must remind ourselves that even though we may feel forgotten by our Creator God, we are not. God not only made us in His image (Genesis 1:26–27) but He also values each of us individually and sent His Son to save us (John 3:16).

Even in our darkest hours, we can rest in the knowledge that we are never alone, for our loving God is with us.

RANDY KILGORE

We are important because God loves us.

Faith

Saddest Words

READ EPHESIANS 2:1–9

Remember that at that time you were separate from Christ, excluded from citizenship in Israel and foreigners to the covenants of the promise, without hope and without God in the world. —EPHESIANS 2:12

Several famous people were asked what they felt was the saddest word in the English language. Here's what some of them said. Poet T. S. Eliot: "The saddest word in the English language is, of course, 'saddest.' " Lyricist Oscar Hammerstein II: "But." Writer John Dos Passos quoted John Keats: "Forlorn! the very word is like a bell." Psychiatrist Karl Menninger: "Unloved." President Harry Truman quoted John Greenleaf Whittier: "For of all sad words of tongue or pen, the saddest are these: 'It might have been!' " Aleksandra Tolstoi: "The saddest word in all languages, which has brought the world to its present condition, is 'atheism.' "

Let's focus on the word Keats used so dramatically—"forlorn." It is the English form of the Dutch word *verloren*, which means "lost." But the Word of God, through the apostle Paul, gives what we could consider the ultimate description or being "forlorn," ". . . separate from Christ, . . . foreigners to the covenants of promise, without hope and without God in the world" (Ephesians 2:12).

The truly "forlorn" of this world face an eternity of being lost—of being without God. Don't take a chance on being forlorn forever. Trust Jesus today. You'll know the true meaning of a new word: *redeemed*. And that's one of the greatest words in our language.

PAUL VAN GORDER

No one is hopeless whose hope is in God.

Fast Feet

READ PHILIPPIANS 4:10–19

The Sovereign Lord is my strength; he makes my feet like the feet of a deer, he enables me to tread on the heights. —HABAKKUK 3:19

While in Chile for a Bible conference, I was resting at the hotel when I noticed a rugby match on TV. Although I don't fully understand rugby, I enjoy it and admire the courage it takes to play such a dangerous sport.

During the match, one of the French players was injured and had to be taken to the sidelines. As the trainers attended to him, the camera showed a closeup of his shoes. With a black marker the player had written the words: "Habakkuk 3:19" and "Jesus is the way." Those expressions of faith and hope were a strong testimony of that young athlete's priorities and values.

The verse cited on that rugby player's shoes is not just one of heavenly hope and persevering faith. It is one of practical value—especially to an athlete dependent on speed for success. It says, "The Sovereign Lord is my strength; he makes my feet like the feet of a deer, he enables me to tread on the heights."

In all of life, we need the strength and supply of our God. He alone can give us "feet" that are swift and strong. He alone can equip us for all of the uncertainties of life, for He alone is our strength. With Paul, we can be assured: "My God will meet all your needs" (Philippians 4:19).

Bill Crowder

We always have enough when God is our supply.

Love

Winds of Love

READ 1 JOHN 4:1–8

Whoever does not love does not know God, because God is love. —1 JOHN 4:8

Atop his barn, a farmer had a weather vane on which was written, "God is love." When friends asked why, the farmer said, "This is to remind me that no matter which way the wind blows, God is love."

When the warm *"south wind"* with its soothing and balmy breezes brings showers of blessing, God is love. "Every good and every perfect gift is from above" (James 1:17). When the cold *"north wind"* of trial and testing sweeps down upon you, God is love. "In all things God works for the good of those who love God" (Romans 8:28).

When the *"west wind"* blows hard upon you with its punishing intent, God is love. "The Lord disciplines the one he loves," (Hebrews 12:6). When the *"east wind"* threatens to sweep away all that you have, God is love. "God shall supply all your needs according to the riches of his glory" (Philippians 4:19).

Whenever we are discouraged and downhearted, let's recall that God still cares for us. What we are experiencing has either been sent or it has been allowed by Him for our good.

No matter which way the wind is blowing, God is love.

RICHARD DEHAAN

No affliction would trouble us if we knew God's reason for permitting it.

The Adventure

READ ESTHER 4:13–17

Who knows but that you have come to your royal position for such a time as this? —ESTHER 4:14

When I was about seven (long before the GPS era), I was in the car with my mom and two sisters when my mother pulled over to the side of the road to open up her road map to study it. "Are we lost, Mom?" I was worried.

"Oh, no," she replied cheerfully, quickly folding up the map. "We're on an adventure." My sisters and I exchanged doubtful glances as one of them whispered knowingly and with resignation, "We're lost."

Adventures can be fun—and scary. They usually involve a bit of the unknown. As we walk in fellowship with God, it's likely that our lives will have many unique adventures—opportunities to serve Him. If we're reluctant or scared and we turn down an opportunity, we miss out. Will God still get the job done? Of course. But someone else will receive the blessing.

In Esther 4, Mordecai encouraged young Queen Esther to help rescue the Jewish people. He cautioned: "If you remain completely silent . . . deliverance will arise for the Jews from another place, but you and your father's house will perish. Yet who knows whether you have come to the kingdom for such a time as this?" (v. 14 NKJV).

Esther was naturally frightened to take this assignment, for she faced possible death in confronting her husband the king. But God used her courage and her faith to deliver her people.

Trust God to show you the way. Adventure ahead!

CINDY HESS KASPER

Courage is fear that has said its prayers.

Hope

Ambition Under Control

READ 1 CHRONICLES 17:1–20

Then King David went in and sat before the LORD, and he said: "Who am I, LORD God, and what is my family, that you have brought me this far?" —1 CHRONICLES 17:16

When my husband was eighteen years old, he started a car-cleaning business. He rented a garage, hired helpers, and created advertising brochures. The business prospered. His intention was to sell it and use the proceeds to pay for college, so he was thrilled when a buyer expressed interest. After some negotiations, it seemed that the transaction would happen. But at the last minute, the deal collapsed. It wouldn't be until several months later that his plan to sell the business would succeed.

It's normal to be disappointed when God's timing and design for our lives do not match our expectations. When David wanted to build the LORD's temple, he had the right motives, the leadership ability, and the resources. Yet God said he could not undertake the project because he had killed too many people in battle (1 Chronicles 22:8).

David could have shaken his fist at the sky in anger. He could have pouted or plowed ahead with his own plans. But he humbly said, "Who am I, LORD God . . . that you have brought me this far?" (17:16). David went on to praise God and affirm his devotion to Him. He valued his relationship with God more than his ambition.

What is more important—achieving our hopes and dreams, or our love for God?

JENNIFER BENSON SCHULDT

True satisfaction is found in yielding ourselves to the will of God.

Because of Love

READ JAMES 2:14–26

Faith was working together with his works, and by works faith was made perfect. —JAMES 2:22 NKJV

This happened quite a few years ago now, but it still touches my heart. I came home from work one day to find a plate of peanut butter snack bars on the kitchen counter. Accompanying the delectables was a note from my twelve-year-old daughter Melissa to her grandparents. "Dear Grandma and Grandpa, I made these for you. Love, Melissa."

No one told her to do this. She didn't have to. She just did it.

But why? Was Melissa trying to gain their favor? Was she trying to make sure that they loved her? Was she trying to win Brownie points (well, snack-bar points) with her grandparents?

No, she cooked up this little confectionary delight just to show her grandparents she loved them. It was evidence of their close relationship. She did it because she is their granddaughter, not to somehow earn the right to be their granddaughter.

That's how it is with the good works we should do as followers of Jesus Christ. We don't do good works so we can win a place in heaven. Rather, our good deeds show evidence of our salvation and faith in Christ.

Jesus did all the work of providing salvation. But we still have to work. Why? Not to win His favor but to show our love. It's an outpouring of a grateful heart.

DAVE BRANON

Serving Christ under law is a duty;
serving under love is a delight.

Faith

Home

READ EPHESIANS 2:11–22

You are no longer foreigners and strangers, but fellow citizens with God's people. —EPHESIANS 2:19

A young African refugee who goes by the name of Steven is a man without a country. He thinks he may have been born in either Mozambique or Zimbabwe. But he never knew his father, and he lost his mother. She fled civil war, traveling country to country as a street vendor. Without ID and unable to prove his place of birth, Steven walked into a British police station, asking to be arrested. Jail seemed better to Steven than trying to exist on the streets without the rights and benefits of citizenship.

The plight of living without a country was on Paul's mind as he wrote his letter to the Ephesians. His non-Jewish readers knew what it was like to live as aliens and outsiders (2:12). Only since finding life and hope in Christ (1:13) had they discovered what it meant to belong to the kingdom of heaven (Matthew 5:3). In Jesus, they learned what it means to be known and cared for by the Father He came to reveal (Matthew 6:31–33).

Paul realized, however, that as the past fades from view, a short memory can cause us to forget that, while hope is the new norm, despair was the old reality.

May our God help us to live in security—to know each day that the belonging we have as members of His family comes by faith in Jesus Christ and to understand the rights and benefits of having our home in Him.

Mart DeHaan

Hope means the most to those
who have lived without it.

The Factory of Sadness

READ JOHN 16:28–33

[God] will wipe every tear from their eyes. —REVELATION 21:4

As a lifelong Cleveland Browns football fan, I grew up knowing my share of disappointment. Despite being one of only four teams to have never appeared in a Super Bowl championship game, the Browns have a loyal fan base that sticks with the team year in and year out. But because the fans usually end up disappointed, many of them now refer to the home stadium as the "Factory of Sadness."

The broken world we live in can be a "factory of sadness" too. There seems to be an endless supply of heartache and disappointment, whether from our own choices or from things beyond our control.

Yet the follower of Christ has hope—not only in the life to come but for this very day. Jesus said, "I have told you these things, so that in me you may have peace. In this world you will have trouble. But take heart! I have overcome the world" (John 16:33). Notice that without minimizing the struggles or sadness we may experience, Christ counters them with His promises of peace, hope, joy, and ultimate victory.

Great peace is available in Christ, and it's more than enough to help us navigate whatever life throws at us.

Bill Crowder

Our hope and peace are found in Jesus.

Love

What Fuels You?

READ 1 JOHN 4:11–21

Dear friends, since God so loved us, we also ought to love one another. —1 JOHN 4:11

Space shuttles are propelled out of the earth's atmosphere by a solid fuel mixture producing millions of pounds of thrust.

NASCAR features race cars that can travel more than two hundred miles per hour, powered by a highly volatile fuel mixture.

What fuels us as followers of Jesus Christ? What gives us the power to love as He loved? Only the indwelling Holy Spirit can motivate us to Christlike deeds of compassion, forgiveness, and self-sacrifice.

The apostle John wrote, "If we love one another, God lives in us and his love is made complete in us. This is how we know that we live in him and he in us: He has given us of his Spirit" (1 John 4:12–13).

A mother asked her young son to clean her shoes. He worked on them diligently until they were spotless and shiny. To show her appreciation, his mother gave him a dollar. When she went to put the shoes on, she found something wadded up in the toe of one of them. It was her dollar wrapped in a note that read: "Here's yur dallar, Mom. I done it for luv."

Fueled by the Holy Spirit, we too can serve others, motivated by Christ's love.

DAVID EGNER

We do not function well on anything but love.

Unconditional Love

READ 1 JOHN 4:7–10

This is love: not that we loved God, but that he loved us and sent his Son as an atoning sacrifice for our sins. —1 JOHN 4:10

Books on leadership often appear on bestseller lists. Most of them tell how to become a powerful and effective leader. But Henri Nouwen's book *In the Name of Jesus: Reflections on Christian Leadership* is written from a different perspective. The former university professor who spent many years serving in a community of developmentally disabled adults says: "The question is not: How many people take you seriously? How much are you going to accomplish? Can you show some results? But: Are you in love with Jesus? . . . In our world of loneliness and despair, there is an enormous need for men and women who know the heart of God, a heart that forgives, that cares, that reaches out and wants to heal."

John wrote, "This is how God showed his love among us: He sent his one and only Son into the world that we might live through him. This is love: not that we loved God, but that he loved us and sent his Son as an atoning sacrifice for our sins" (1 John 4:9–10).

"The Christian leader of the future," writes Nouwen, "is the one who truly knows the heart of God as it has become flesh . . . in Jesus." In Him, we discover and experience God's unconditional, unlimited love.

DAVID MCCASLAND

God's love in our heart gives us a heart for others.

Hope

God Is for Us!

READ EZEKIEL 36:8–15

What, then, shall we say in response to these things? If God is for us, who can be against us? —ROMANS 8:31

Think of how the Jews must have felt after mighty Babylon had swept in and had taken the southern kingdom of Judah captive. The land lay desolate. Jerusalem had been turned into a dusty heap of charred timbers and displaced stones. Nobles and princes had been carried away to a foreign land, and the few people left in the rubble were forced to live in poverty and misery. The nation was reaping the bitter fruits of wickedness and idolatry.

Things may have looked horrible, but this one thing was true: God had not abandoned His people. In a strange but pointed command, the Lord told His servant Ezekiel to prophesy to the mountains of Israel, "I am concerned for you and will look on you with favor" (36:9). To a despairing Jewish populace, those words must have kindled at least some hope. Although the people who heard it might never see the day themselves, they were reassured that Jehovah would someday restore their beloved nation.

As Christians, we too have a message from the Lord that can remind us that God is always for us—always there to redeem our losses. Paul stated it in Romans 8:31, "If God be for us, who can be against us?" When the dark consequences of our sin and failure engulf us, this truth can renew within our hearts a hope that is steadfast and sure. God is for us—that's a thought equal to life's most discouraging times!

DENNIS DEHAAN

No one is hopeless whose hope is in God.

OCTOBER
5

Atmosphere of Encouragement

READ ROMANS 15:1–7

Each of us should please our neighbors for their good, to build them up. —ROMANS 15:2

I'm encouraged every time I visit the fitness center near our house. In that busy place, I'm surrounded by others who are striving to improve their physical health and strength. Posted signs remind us not to judge each other, but words and actions that reveal support for others' conditioning efforts are always welcomed.

What a great picture of how things should look in the spiritual realm of life! Those of us who are striving to "get in shape" spiritually, to grow in our faith, can sometimes feel as if we don't belong because we're not as spiritually fit—as mature in our walk with Jesus—as someone else.

Paul gave us this short, direct suggestion: "Encourage one another and build each other up" (1 Thessalonians 5:11). And to the believers in Rome he wrote: "Each of us should please our neighbors for their good, to build them up" (Romans 15:2). Recognizing that our Father is so lovingly gracious with us, let's show God's grace to others with encouraging words and actions.

As we "accept one another" (v. 7), let's entrust our spiritual growth to God—to the work of His Spirit. And while we daily seek to follow Him, may we create an atmosphere of encouragement for our brothers and sisters in Jesus as they also seek to grow in their faith.

DAVE BRANON

A word of encouragement can make the difference between giving up and pressing on.

Love

Ambassador of Love

READ JOHN 3:9–21

"For God did not send his Son into the world to condemn the world, but to save the world through him." —JOHN 3:17

In my work as a chaplain, some people occasionally ask if I am willing to give them some additional spiritual help. Sometimes when I do this, I often find myself doing more learning than teaching. This was true when one painfully honest new Christian said to me with resignation, "I don't think it's a good idea for me to read the Bible. The more I read what God expects from me, the more I judge others who aren't doing what it says."

As he said this, I realized that I was at least partly responsible for instilling this judgmental spirit in him. At that time, one of the first things I did with those new to faith in Jesus was to tell them about things they should no longer be doing. Instead of showing them God's love and letting the Holy Spirit reshape them, I urged them to "behave like a believer."

Now I was gaining a new appreciation for John 3:16–17. Jesus's invitation to believe in Him in verse 16 is followed by these words. "For God did not send his Son into the world to condemn the world, but to save the world through him."

Jesus didn't come to condemn us. But by giving these new Christians a checklist of behaviors, I was teaching them to condemn themselves, which then led them to judge others. Instead of being agents of condemnation, we are to be ambassadors of God's love and mercy.

RANDY KILGORE

If Jesus didn't come to condemn the world, that's probably not our mission either!

Faith Now, Sight Later

READ 2 CORINTHIANS 5:1–10

Then Jesus told him, "Because you have seen me, you have believed; blessed are those who have not seen and yet have believed." —JOHN 20:29

Do you see dramatic evidence of God at work in your life, or is your life rather quiet and routine? Catherine Booth, who with her husband William organized the Salvation Army in 1865, stressed the need for being content to walk by faith. Even as she faced an illness that would take her life, she talked to a friend about the difference between faith and sight.

"One of the hardest lessons I've had to learn," she said, "is to discern between faith and realization. If I have had to conquer all through life by naked faith, bringing afterward perhaps very blessed realizations, I can only expect that it shall be the same now."

Catherine was prepared to pass through the valley of death's shadow sustained by "naked faith," without any reassuring sight of her Savior's face. She exemplified the confidence Paul spoke of in 2 Corinthians. "We are confident, I say, and would prefer to be away from the body and at home with the Lord" (5:8). Catherine concluded, "All our enemies have to be conquered by faith, not by realization." Then she asked, "Is it not so with the last enemy—death?"

Today, some are seeking high-voltage experiences to buttress their faith. But as Catherine learned, blessed are those who believe without having seen (John 20:29). Blessed are those for whom God's Word is sufficient.

VERNON GROUNDS

It is good to have things settled by faith before they are unsettled by feelings.

Hope

The Best Hope of All

READ ROMANS 8:31–39

Praise be to the God and Father of our Lord Jesus Christ! In his great mercy he has given us new birth into a living hope through the resurrection of Jesus Christ from the dead. —1 PETER 1:3

Medical doctors and psychologists agree that hope is vital to physical and mental health. This was borne out when a surgeon postponed an operation because his patient felt sure he was going to die on the operating table. The doctor knew the patient needed to go into the procedure with hope.

If hope has such great value when it relates to the things of this life, think of what it can do for a person if it encompasses both time and eternity. I saw this firsthand when I talked to an older believer who knew he was soon going to die. He had endured many medical problems. He couldn't talk clearly, but he managed to say, "Brother, each of those blows has been a boost. Each one has drawn me closer to Christ and made me more eager for heaven." Another Christian man, who is losing his battle against cancer, assured me that while he hopes medical science will find a cure, he is also looking forward expectantly to seeing his Savior when he enters Glory.

The world has no match for that kind of anticipation.

The Christian's hope is superior. It is based on the death of Jesus for our sins and His resurrection from the grave. We are assured of victory in this life and a glorious eternity in the next. That's why it's called a "living hope."

HERB VANDER LUGT

The ladder of hope has nothing to stand on here below; it is held up from above.

The Right Information

READ 1 THESSALONIANS 4:13–18

Brothers and sisters, we do not want you to be uninformed about those who sleep in death, so that you do not grieve like the rest of mankind, who have no hope. —1 THESSALONIANS 4:13

Our flight had been airborne about fifteen minutes when the pilot announced that the aircraft had a serious problem the crew was trying to analyze. A few minutes later, he announced that it was a vibration and that we would have to return to the airport. Then the flight attendants made a series of step-by-step announcements explaining what was going on and what would happen once we were on the ground. In an event that could have been terrifying, the fears of the passengers were relieved because we were given the right information.

In the first century, a group of believers in Thessalonica were afraid that their believing loved ones who had died were gone forever and would miss out on the second coming of Christ. For that reason, Paul wrote, "we do not want you to be uninformed about those who sleep in death, so that you do not grieve like the rest of mankind, who have no hope" (1 Thessalonians 4:13). Paul's words of comfort were intended to soften their fears by giving them the right information, which made all the difference in the world. While grieving their loss, they could still have hope of a coming reunion with those who were in Christ.

In seasons of loss, we too can find comfort and hope because the Bible has given us the right information.

BILL CROWDER

Death is not a period—it's only a comma.

Love

Serving Together

READ GALATIANS 5:13–16

You, my brothers and sisters, were called to be free. But do not use your freedom to indulge the flesh; rather, serve one another humbly in love. —GALATIANS 5:13

When Cristine Bouwkamp and Kyle Kramer got married in a spring wedding, they did something most of us wouldn't think of doing. Instead of hosting a "sit-down dinner," they held a simple reception at the church and invited their guests to help distribute food to people in need.

They bought a truckload of food and had it delivered to the church parking lot. Then they and their wedding guests served the people of the neighborhood. Cristine and Kyle said the first thing they wished to do as a married couple was to serve others. Because God had changed their lives so radically, they wanted to "bless God for blessing us with each other."

The Kramers chose a great start for their new marriage—blessing God by serving others. The apostle Paul encouraged the Christians of Galatia: "Through love serve one another" (Galatians 5:13 NKJV). Some of them believed that the ceremonial practices of the Old Testament were still binding on the church. So Paul reminded them that salvation is by grace through faith. It is by faith we live out our new life in Christ. He reminded them that the law was fulfilled in this: "Love your neighbor as yourself" (v. 14).

As followers of Jesus, we're here to serve Him out of love—to "bless God for blessing us."

ANNE CETAS

God blesses us so we can be a blessing to others.

Love Will Find a Way

READ 1 CORINTHIANS 13:4–13

Love never fails. But where there are prophecies, they will cease; where there are tongues, they will be stilled; where there is knowledge, it will pass away. —1 CORINTHIANS 13:8

Years ago I saw a cartoon that depicted a sour, disgruntled, elderly gentleman standing in rumpled pajamas and robe at his apartment door. He had just secured the door for the night with four locks, two deadbolts, and a chain latch. Later he noticed a small white envelope stuck beneath the door. On the envelope was a large sticker in the shape of a heart. It was a valentine. Love had found a way.

Only love can change a person's heart. The Russian author Dostoevsky, in his book *The Brothers Karamazov*, tells the story of a hardened cynic, Ivan, and his resistance to the love of God. On one occasion his brother Alyosha, a man of deep faith who was confounded by his brother's resistance, leans over and kisses Ivan. This simple act of love burned into Ivan's heart.

Perhaps you have a friend who is resisting the love of God. Show His love to that friend, just as God showed love to us when He brought salvation into the world through Jesus. Shower upon others the kind of love described in 1 Corinthians 13—a love that is patient, kind, humble, and unselfish.

Authentic love is a gift from God that we can keep on giving.

DAVID ROPER

God pours His love into our hearts to flow out to others.

Faith

Taking Shortcuts

READ LUKE 9:57–62

Then he said to them all: "Whoever wants to be my disciple must deny themselves and take up their cross daily and follow me." —LUKE 9:23

Sipping her tea, Nancy gazed out her friend's window and sighed. Spring rains and sunshine had coaxed a riotous expanse of color from a well-groomed flowerbed of lilies, phlox, irises, and evening primrose.

"I want that look," she said wistfully, "without all the work."

Some shortcuts are fine—even practical. Others short-circuit our spirit and deaden our lives. We want romance without the difficulties and messiness of committing to someone so different from ourselves. We want "greatness" without the risks and failures necessary in the adventure of real life. We desire to please God, but not when it inconveniences us.

Jesus made clear to His followers that there is no shortcut that avoids the hard choice of surrendering our lives to Him. He warned a prospective disciple, "No one who puts a hand to the plow and looks back is fit for service in the kingdom of God" (Luke 9:62). To follow Christ requires a radical altering of our loyalties.

When we turn in faith to Jesus, the work just begins. But it is oh-so-worth-it, for He also told us that no one who sacrifices "for me and the gospel will fail to receive a hundred times as much in this present age . . . and in the age to come eternal life" (Mark 10:29–30). The work of following Christ is difficult, but He's given us His Spirit to help us. And the reward is a full, joyful life now and forever.

TIM GUSTAFSON

Most things worth doing are difficult.

Love and Support

READ PHILIPPIANS 4:10–18

I thank my God every time I remember you. . . because of your partnership in the gospel from the first day until now. —PHILIPPIANS 1:3, 5

I received this note from a friend serving in an orphanage in a developing country: "Yesterday, as I was sitting at my office desk, I noticed a trail of ants on the floor. As I followed it, I was shocked to see that thousands of ants had blanketed the walls of our office building—inside and out. They swarmed everything. Fortunately, one of the workers . . . set to work. Less than an hour later, the ants were gone."

After telling this insect story, my friend wrote, "So, how was your day at work?" Sometimes we need reminders of the needs of those who've left behind the comforts and conveniences of home. God calls each of us to different paths of service, and some paths are bumpy. Working in an office overrun by ants isn't appealing, but my friend isn't there for the perks.

She and many other believers have had their hearts captured by Christ and think that abandoning "essential" comforts and conveniences is a small thing to do to honor Him who loves us. They need our support in the way Paul depended on his friends in Philippi—for fellowship (Philippians 1:5), for finances (4:16), and for care (4:18). When we encourage our friends who have left their familiar environments to serve God elsewhere, we show our love for the One who sent them.

Dave Branon

The glory of life is to love, not to be loved; to give, not to get; to serve, not to be served.

Hope

Victory Over Death!

READ JOHN 5:24–30

A time is coming when all who are in their graves will hear his voice and come out. —JOHN 5:28–29

An ancient painting I recently saw made a deep impression on me. Its title, *The Anastasis*, means "the resurrection," and the painting depicts in a stunning way the triumph of Christ's victory over death. The Lord Jesus, newly emerged from the tomb, is pulling Adam and Eve out of their coffins and into eternal life. What is so amazing about this artwork is the way it shows how spiritual and physical death, the result of the fall, are dramatically reversed by the risen Christ.

Prior to His death on the cross, the Lord Jesus predicted a future day when He will call believers into a new and glorified existence: "A time is coming when all who are in their graves will hear his voice and come out" (John 5:28–29).

Because of Christ's victory over death, the grave is not final. We naturally will feel sorrow and grief when those we love die and we are separated from them in this life. But the believer does not grieve as one who has no hope (1 Thessalonians 4:13). The witness of Jesus's resurrection is that all Christians will one day be taken from their graves to be clothed with glorified resurrection bodies (1 Corinthians 15:42–44). And so "we will be with the Lord forever" (1 Thessalonians 4:17).

DENNIS FISHER

Because Christ is alive, we too shall live.

Enemy Love

READ JONAH 3:10–4:11

"If you love those who love you, what credit is that to you? Even sinners love those who love them." —LUKE 6:32

When war broke out in 1950, fifteen-year-old Kim Chin-Kyung joined the South Korean army to defend his homeland. He soon found, however, that he wasn't ready for the horrors of combat. As young friends died around him, he begged God for his life and promised that, if allowed to live, he would learn to love his enemies.

Sixty-five years later, Dr. Kim reflected on that answered prayer. Through decades of caring for orphans and assisting in the education of North Korean and Chinese young people, he has won many friends among those he once regarded as enemies. Today he shuns political labels. Instead he calls himself a "loveist" as an expression of his faith in Jesus.

The prophet Jonah left a different kind of legacy. Even a dramatic rescue from the belly of a big fish didn't transform his heart. Although he eventually obeyed God, Jonah said he'd rather die than watch the Lord show mercy to his enemies (See Jonah 4:1–2, 8).

We can only guess as to whether Jonah ever learned to care for the people of Nineveh. Instead we are left to wonder about ourselves. Will we settle for his attitude toward those we fear and hate? Or will we ask God for the ability to love our enemies as He has shown mercy to us?

MART DEHAAN

Love conquers all.

Faith

Magic Eye

READ HEBREWS 11:1–10

Without faith it is impossible to please God, because anyone who comes to him must believe that he exists and that he rewards those who earnestly seek him. —HEBREWS 11:6

My nephew brought a book of Magic Eye images to a family gathering. Magic Eye images look like ordinary two-dimensional patterns, but when they're viewed a certain way, the flat surface appears three-dimensional.

We took turns trying to train our eyes to make the three-dimensional image pop out. One family member had trouble seeing the extra dimension. Several times I noticed he had the book open, looking at it from all different distances and directions. But even though he couldn't see the hidden image, he believed it was there because others had seen it.

His persistence made me think about the importance of having the same tenacity in matters of faith. The danger for those who doubt is that they stop looking for God because they believe He can't be found. Moses warned the Israelites that future generations would wander from God. He promised, however, that those who seek God with all their heart and soul would find Him (Deuteronomy 4:29). The book of Hebrews confirms that God rewards those who diligently seek Him (11:6).

If you struggle to believe, remember: Just because you don't see God right now doesn't mean He doesn't exist. He promises to be found by those who seek Him.

—JULIE ACKERMAN LINK

Because God is great, He will be sought;
because God is good, He will be found.

What Love Is

READ ROMANS 5:1–8

God demonstrates his own love for us in this: While we were still sinners, Christ died for us. —ROMANS 5:8

Years ago I asked a young man who was engaged to be married, "How do you know you love her?" It was a loaded question, intended to help him look at his heart's motives for the upcoming marriage. After several thoughtful moments, he responded, "I know I love her because I want to spend the rest of my life making her happy."

We discussed what that meant—and the price tag attached to the selflessness of constantly seeking the best for the other person, rather than putting ourselves first. Real love has a lot to do with sacrifice.

That idea is in line with the wisdom of the Bible. In the Scriptures there are several Greek words for *love*, but the highest form is *agape*—"love that is defined and driven by self-sacrifice." Nowhere is this more true than in the love our heavenly Father has shown us in Christ. We are deeply valued by Him. Paul stated, "God demonstrates his own love for us in this: While we were still sinners, Christ died for us" (Romans 5:8).

If sacrifice is the true measure of love, there could be no more precious gift than Jesus: "For God so loved the world that he gave his one and only Son" (John 3:16).

BILL CROWDER

The measure of love is what you are willing to give up for it.

The Price of Love

READ ISAIAH 53:9–12

He poured out his life unto death.
—ISAIAH 53:12

Our daughter burst into tears as we waved goodbye to my parents. After visiting us in England, they were starting their long journey back to their home in the US. "I don't want them to go," she said. As I comforted her, my husband remarked, "I'm afraid that's the price of love."

We might feel the pain of being separated from loved ones, but Jesus felt the ultimate separation when He paid the price of love on the cross. He, who was both human and God, fulfilled Isaiah's prophecy seven hundred years after Isaiah gave it when He "bore the sin of many" (Isaiah 53:12). In this chapter we see rich pointers to Jesus being the suffering Servant, such as when He was "pierced for our transgressions" (v. 5), which happened when He was nailed to the cross and when one of the soldiers pierced His side (John 19:34). Also we read that "by his wounds we are healed" (Isaiah 53:5).

Because of love, Jesus came to earth and was born a baby. Because of love, He received the abuse of the teachers of the law, the crowds, and the soldiers. Because of love, He suffered and died to be the perfect sacrifice, standing in our place before the Father. We live because of His love.

AMY BOUCHER PYE

Jesus was the perfect sacrifice who died to give us life.

Hope When the Journey Gets Tough

READ 2 CORINTHIANS 1:6–11

We should not trust in ourselves but in God who raises the dead. —2 CORINTHIANS 1:9 NKJV

Several years ago, Blair and Ronna Martin lost their energetic nine-year-old son Matti when he was dragged to his death by a family cow. I had a chance to meet this Kenai, Alaska, family and share in their grief. And I know how tough this tragedy has been for them.

I also know that they sought God's care and comfort for their pain. An observation made by Matti's mom is valuable for anyone walking through one of life's valleys. During one of her down times, Ronna was reading 2 Corinthians 1:9, which says, "We should not trust in ourselves but in God who raises the dead." She felt as if Jesus were telling her, "Ronna, I know the journey has been too much for you, and you are bone-weary. Do not be ashamed of your exhaustion. Instead, see it as an opportunity for Me to take charge of your life."

When the journey gets too tough to navigate, 2 Corinthians 1:9 is a reminder to us that we don't travel alone. We have the help of the One who showed us His power in the resurrection and who will demonstrate His power again when He raises believing loved ones like Matti to eternal life. "My strength and my hope have to be in Christ alone," Ronna said. That's a truth we all need as we travel the sometimes-difficult journey God has for us.

DAVE BRANON

The storms of life remind us to take shelter in the loving arms of our Savior.

Hope

The Best Things in Life

READ PROVERBS 23:1–18

Do not wear yourself out to get rich.
—PROVERBS 23:4

An old adage says, "The best things in life are free." There's a lot of truth in that. Some people, however, believe that the best things in life are expensive or perhaps elusive. Recently I saw a sign that made me smile and think. It said, "The best things in life are not things." What a great way to say it! The value of family, friends, and faith points us to the realization that what matters most in life is all wrapped up in people and the Lord.

Solomon was well qualified to speak about material things because he "was greater in riches and wisdom than all the other kings of the earth" (1 Kings 10:23). His advice? "Do not wear yourself out to get rich; do not trust in your own cleverness. Cast but a glance at riches, and they are gone, for they will surely sprout wings and fly off to the sky" (Proverbs 23:4–5). His recommended course of action was, "Apply your heart to instruction and your ears to words of knowledge. . . . There is surely a future hope for you, and your hope will not be cut off" (vv. 12, 18).

The best things in life are the eternal riches that come from God's goodness and grace in Jesus Christ. We do not hold them in our hands but in our hearts.

DAVID MCCASLAND

Our greatest riches are the riches we have in Christ.

Waiting . . .

READ LUKE 2:22–38

The Lord longs to be gracious to you; therefore he will rise up to show you compassion. For the Lord is a God of justice. Blessed are all who wait for him! —ISAIAH 30:18

Autumn is hunting season here in Michigan. For a few weeks, licensed hunters are allowed to go into the woods and hunt for various species of wildlife. Some hunters build elaborate tree stands high above the ground where they sit quietly for hours waiting for a deer to wander within range.

When I think of hunters who are so patient when it comes to waiting for deer, I think of how impatient we can be when we have to wait for God. We often equate "wait" with "waste." If we're waiting for something (or someone), we think we are doing nothing, which, in an accomplishment-crazed culture, seems like a waste of time.

But waiting serves many purposes. In particular, it proves our faith. Those whose faith is weak are often the first to give up waiting, while those with the strongest faith are willing to wait indefinitely.

When we read the Christmas story in Luke 2, we learn of two people who proved their faith by their willingness to wait. Simeon and Anna waited long, but their time wasn't wasted; it put them in a place where they could witness the coming of Messiah (vv. 22–38).

Not receiving an immediate answer to prayer is no reason to give up faith.

Julie Ackerman Link

Waiting for God is never a waste of time.

Love's Shaping Power

READ 1 JOHN 2:24–3:3

Dear friends, now we are children of God, and what we will be has not yet been made known. But we know that when Christ appears, we shall be like him, for we shall see him as he is. —1 JOHN 3:2

We as Christians may get discouraged at times by how unloving, impatient, and selfish we really are. From our hearts we cry out, "Will I ever be any different?"

In 1 John 2:24–3:3, John answers with an emphatic yes! We can change. Here's why: God has showered on us a marvelous love that allows all who trust Jesus as Savior to be called "children of God" (3:1). We also bear a unique family similarity that will burst forth one day into full-bloomed likeness (v. 2). In Christ we are already perfect; in our daily walk we are becoming more Christlike. And the hope that one day we shall be like Him motivates us to purify ourselves.

Dr. Ida Scudder, a missionary doctor in India for many years, was once asked by a Muslim woman, "Why is it you don't ever seem to lose your temper when others are abusive to you?" A Hindu friend who knew Dr. Scudder answered for her. "Don't you know why? It's because Dr. Ida's God is patient and loving, and she's like her God."

God is changing us, but we must confess our sins (1:9), keep His Word (2:5; 3:24), practice righteousness (2:29; 3:7), and love one another (4:7, 11). This will keep love's shaping power working in our lives.

DENNIS DEHAAN

Conversion of a sinner takes only a moment;
growth of a saint takes a lifetime.

The Best Life

READ JOHN 1:35–42

The first thing Andrew did was to find his brother Simon and tell him, "We have found the Messiah." —JOHN 1:41

A few months ago, I had to travel to Florida and back on business. On my flight home, I was pleasantly surprised to find that I had a seat with lots of legroom. It felt so good not to be scrunched into a small area. Plus, I had an empty seat beside me! The makings of a good nap.

Then I remembered those around me in their not-as-comfortable seats. I invited several others I knew to join me in a better spot but was surprised they all wanted to stay in their own seats for various reasons: They didn't want to be inconvenienced with a move or felt fine where they were.

As believers in Christ, we have a much more significant invitation to extend: We've received a new life of faith in Jesus, and we want others to experience it too. Some will want to do so, and others won't. In John 1:40 we read that Andrew had begun to follow Jesus. The first thing Andrew did was to find his brother Simon and invite him to meet Jesus, the Messiah, too (v. 41). Jesus offered them a wonderful new way of life of knowing Him and enjoying His promises: His forgiveness (Romans 3:24), continual presence (Hebrews 13:5), hope (Romans 15:13), peace (John 14:27), and a forever future in His presence (1 Thessalonians 4:17).

Won't you join in? Jesus gives the best life.

ANNE CETAS

If you want someone to know what Christ will do for him, let him see what Christ has done for you.

Faith

Is Faith an Escape?

READ HEBREWS 11:32–40

Join with me in suffering, like a good soldier of Christ Jesus. —2 TIMOTHY 2:3

In the late 1960s and 1970s, travel to the moon moved from fantasy to reality. Twelve human beings walked on its surface. But in 1952, when the Hayden Planetarium in New York advertised (in jest) that it would take reservations for that lunar trip of 240,000 miles, more than 24,000 people applied within a few days.

A psychologist who studied their letters concluded that most of them were eager to escape from their responsibilities and problems. One woman wrote, "It would be heaven to get away from this busy earth . . . and just go somewhere that's nice and peaceful, good, safe, and secure."

Many who don't believe in Christ think of Christians as emotionally weak people who are looking for an escape from real life now and pie-in-the-sky later. But biblical faith is not a pill that induces drug-like passivity. In Hebrews 11:32–38 we read about men and women who chose to endure torture rather than renounce their spiritual convictions. And today, bold missionaries throughout the world illustrate that following Christ can be very difficult.

While we may not experience great persecution for our faith, we do face our share hardships and trials. Our faith in Christ is not an escape; it gives us the strength to endure.

VERNON GROUNDS

Great faith is often built during great trials.

The Missing Factor

READ 1 CORINTHIANS 13

If I have the gift of prophecy and can fathom all mysteries and all knowledge, and if I have a faith that can move mountains, but do not have love, I am nothing. —1 CORINTHIANS 13:2

After accompanying his mother through a hospital stay, Joe Urschel, an editor for *USA Today*, said this about the medical treatment she received: "There is nothing to complain about there—only to marvel at. It's the room and board that's nightmarish. On one hand, the hospital gives you the kind of medical miracle that not many years ago was the stuff of science fiction, and on the other delivers the kind of care and comfort you wouldn't accept from the cheapest motel." Insensitive treatment by the hospital staff often left his mother in tears.

Mr. Urschel's experience, which is not typical of most good hospitals, reminds me of what the apostle Paul wrote to the Corinthians. He admired their skill and giftedness (1 Corinthians 1:4–7). Their church was one of miracles, changed lives, and success stories (1 Corinthians 6:9–11). They were enriched in knowledge and not lacking any gift (1 Corinthians 1:5–7).

But Paul rebuked the Corinthians for their lack of love (1 Corinthians 11:17–22). They were neglecting many common courtesies. In the middle of a miracle-minded church there was a missing factor. Without love, all of the knowledge, gifts, and organizational efforts were coming unraveled.

It's still true today. If love is missing, even miracles can leave the human spirit damaged.

MART DEHAAN

Without the ingredient of love, nothing is done well.

Hope

Hopeful Realists

READ MICAH 7:1–13

I will bear the L*ORD's wrath . . . He will bring me out into the light; I will see his righteousness.* —MICAH 7:9

A humorist wrote, "When I was feeling down, someone told me, 'Cheer up, things could get worse.' So I cheered up—and they did!"

Wishing someone a shallow "cheer up" seldom helps that person's distress. What people long for is reassuring news that life will soon change for the better. During my years as a pastor, though, I often had to tell very ill people that unless the Lord intervened they would soon die. That's hardly "cheer up" news.

In Micah's day, many people in Israel no doubt wanted to hear some good news. The ruthlessness and dishonesty of fellow-citizens, rulers, and even judges were frightening (Micah 7:2–3). The nation was so fractured that people could not even trust their closest friends or relatives (vv. 5–6). The decent citizens hoped the prophet would tell them that a revival was coming to bring positive changes in their land. Instead, he had to tell them that God's judgment was at hand: The Assyrians would soon invade.

The outlook was gloomy. But it was not hopeless. Micah saw beyond the judgment to a time when the nation would worship God and be blessed. He was mixing realism with hope. We too can be hopeful realists. With the eye of faith we can see through the hard times and see the eternal glory that God has in store for us.

HERB VANDER LUGT

Sorrow looks back, worry looks around,
but faith looks up.

OCTOBER
27

Run!

READ 2 TIMOTHY 2:14–26

Flee the evil desires of youth and pursue righteousness, faith, love and peace, along with those who call on the Lord out of a pure heart. —2 TIMOTHY 2:22

Everyone faces temptations, but not everyone handles them in the same way. Some people don't even try to resist. Others flirt with sin, thinking they can stop before they get in too deep. The Bible tells us, "do not think about how to gratify the desires of the flesh" (Romans 13:14), and in 2 Timothy 2:22 we are told to "flee the evil desires of youth."

Here are two ways of handling temptation. One leads to defeat, the other to victory. A boy named Bobby asked his mother if he could go play ball with his friends. She consented, but she knew that the boys had to pass their favorite "swimming hole" to get to the ballfield, so she told him not to go swimming. When Bobby left the house, however, he took his bathing suit with him–just in case! Well, you know what he did when he saw his friends in the pond. Bobby had invited temptation by taking his swimsuit with him.

How different the attitude displayed by the youngster who said, "When I go past a watermelon patch, I can't keep my mouth from watering, but I can run!" His action exemplifies what Paul was saying to young Timothy in today's Scripture reading. According to 1 Corinthians 10:13, God is faithful and will not allow us to be tempted beyond what we are able, but will with the temptation also provide a way out. When temptation comes, God will do His part. He will provide "a way out." But it's up to us to run!

RICHARD DEHAAN

Every temptation is an opportunity to flee to God.

Love

His Joy—His Love

READ ZEPHANIAH 3:14–20

The Lord *your God is with you, the Mighty Warrior who saves. He will take great delight in you; in his love he will no longer rebuke you, but will rejoice over you with singing.* —ZEPHANIAH 3:17

The documentary film *Young@Heart* gives a rollicking look at a senior chorus of twenty-four singers whose average age is eighty. Filled with humor and poignant moments, the film includes this remarkable singing group's deeply moving performance at a New England prison. When the concert concludes, the singers walk into the audience, greeting the surprised prisoners with handshakes and hugs.

The inmates' unexpected amazement at this personal touch reminds me of the book of Zephaniah in which the prophet brings a powerful message of God's presence and love to His people during a dark time: "The Lord your God in with you, the Mighty Warrior who saves. He will take great delight in you; in his love he will no longer rebuke you, but will rejoice over you with singing" (3:17).

According to Bible teacher Henrietta Mears, Zephaniah "begins with sorrow but ends with singing. The first of the book is full of sadness and gloom, but the last contains one of the sweetest songs of love in the Old Testament."

God's love for us is always astonishing, especially when it touches us at a low ebb of life. During our darkest times, the Lord comes to us with His joy, His song, and His love.

David McCasland

In God's garden of love, you are His forget-me-not.

The Power of Love

READ 1 JOHN 4:7–11

See what great love the Father has lavished on us, that we should be called children of God! And that is what we are! The reason the world does not know us is that it did not know him. —1 JOHN 3:1

On the chapel wall at Eagle Village, a residential treatment center for boys near Hersey, Michigan, the portraits of two twelve-year-old boys—blond-haired Rick and a black youngster named Rosy—have been displayed. The pictures recall a long-ago incident during a canoe trip on Lake Superior when some boys from Eagle Village pulled ashore to make camp.

Rosy spotted something floating in the water, so he pushed off in a canoe to retrieve it. Strong winds quickly blew him offshore. Alarmed, the staff started off in two canoes to rescue him. When Rick saw that his best friend Rosy was in danger, he went along. The high winds tossed all three canoes about, and they capsized. Miraculously, the staff members all made it to shore. But Rick and Rosy were both lost in the depths of Lake Superior. A plaque between the pictures tells the story.

Rick, who loved enough
to give his life for another.
Rosy, who was loved enough to
have another pay that price.

This story calls to mind "what manner of love the Father has bestowed on us." He loved us enough to give His Son to die in payment of the awful price of our sin. And we were loved enough so that He would willingly make that sacrifice. Truly, our salvation is the best demonstration of the power of love.

DAVID EGNER

The true measure of God's love is that
He loves without measure.

Hope

Open Door to Paradise

READ LUKE 23:39–43

Jesus answered him, "Truly I tell you, today you will be with me in paradise." —LUKE 23:43

In his insightful book *Seven Words*, W. R. Matthews calls the dying thief "the first captive of the cross." A slave to crime, that man found freedom in the final hours of his life. He admitted that God was right to punish his sin, and he asked to be remembered in Christ's kingdom. In simple faith he reached out to Jesus (Luke 23:40–42).

Right there from the cross, Jesus gave him in one decisive moment more than he asked for: forgiveness for his lawless deeds, companionship in his dying hour, and the assurance of a share in God's paradise—that very day!

What hope for all who feel they've been too bad too long to start over! What hope for the grieving parent who agonizes over a child who is living a rebellious life and faces an untimely death from the devastating effects of drugs or immorality! If there comes a moment of conviction of sin, which is the Holy Spirit's work (John 16:8), and a plea in faith to the Lord Jesus for mercy—no matter what the circumstances—He will have but one response: "You will be with me in paradise."

Repentance doesn't erase wasted years nor stay death's hand, but it always swings wide the door to heaven.

DENNIS DEHAAN

No one is too bad to be forgiven.

When Questions Remain

READ JOB 23:1–12

He knows the way that I take. JOB 23:10

On October 31, 2014, an experimental spacecraft broke apart during a test flight and crashed into the Mojave Desert in California. The copilot, Michael Alsbury, died while the pilot miraculously survived. Investigators soon determined what had happened, but not why. The title of a newspaper article about the crash began with the words "Questions remain."

We may experience sorrows for which no explanations are adequate. Some are catastrophic events with far-reaching effects while others are personal, private tragedies that alter our individual lives. We want to know why, but we seem to find more questions than answers. Even as we struggle with "Why?" God extends His unfailing love to us.

When Job lost his children and his wealth in a single day (Job 1:13–19), he sank into angry depression and resisted any attempted explanations by his friends. Yet he held out hope that someday there would be an answer from God. Even in the darkness Job could say, "[God] knows the way that I take; when he has tested me, I will come forth as gold" (23:10).

Oswald Chambers said, "There will come one day a personal and direct touch from God when . . . every suffering and pain, and wrong and injustice will have a complete and ample and overwhelming explanation."

Today, as we face life's unanswered questions, we can find hope in God's love and promises.

DAVID MCCASLAND

When we face unanswered questions,
we find help and hope in God's love.

Hope

Words for the Weary

READ ISAIAH 50:4–10

The Sovereign L*ORD* *has given me a well-instructed tongue, to know the word that sustains the weary.* —ISAIAH 50:4

A few days after his father died, thirty-year-old C. S. Lewis received a letter from a woman who had cared for his mother during her illness and death more than two decades earlier. The woman offered her sympathy for his loss and wondered if he remembered her. "My dear Nurse Davison," Lewis replied. "Remember you? I should think I do."

Lewis recalled how much her presence in their home had meant to him as well as to his brother and father during a difficult time. He thanked her for her words of sympathy and said, "It is *really* comforting to be taken back to those old days. The time during which you were with my mother seemed very long to a child and you became part of home."

When we struggle in the circumstances of life, an encouraging word from others can lift our spirits and direct our eyes to the Lord. The Old Testament prophet Isaiah wrote, "The Sovereign LORD has given me a well-instructed tongue, to know the word that sustains the weary" (50:4). And when we look to the Lord, He offers words of hope and light in the darkness.

DAVID MCCASLAND

Kind words can lift a heavy heart.

Trial by Fire

READ JAMES 1:1–12

Blessed is the one who perseveres under trial because, having stood the test, that person will receive the crown of life that the Lord has promised to those who love him. —JAMES 1:12

Last winter while visiting a natural history museum in Colorado, I learned some remarkable facts about the aspen tree. An entire grove of slender, white-trunked aspens can grow from a single seed and share the same root system. These root systems can exist for thousands of years whether or not they produce trees. They sleep underground, waiting for fire, flood, or avalanche to clear a space for them in the shady forest. After a natural disaster has cleared the land, aspen roots can sense the sun at last. The roots send up saplings, which become trees.

For aspens, new growth is made possible by the devastation of a natural disaster. James writes that our growth in faith is also made possible by difficulties. "Consider it pure joy," he writes, "whenever you face trials of many kinds, because you know that the testing of your faith produces perseverance. Let perseverance finish its work so that you may be mature and complete, not lacking anything" (James 1:2–4).

It's difficult to be joyful during trials, but we can take hope from the fact that God will use difficult circumstances to help us reach maturity. Like aspen trees, faith can grow in times of trial when difficulty clears space in our hearts for the light of God to touch us.

Amy Peterson

Trials and tests can draw us closer to Christ.

Love That Won't Quit

READ REVELATION 3:14–22

If anyone hears My voice and opens the door, I will come in and dine with him, and he with Me. —REVELATION 3:20

Day after day, the loving father came to the hospital, often with flowers in his hand. He would sit beside the bed of his comatose six-year-old daughter, talking to her about the wonderful world outside her window. Sometimes he would tell her a story. But in her unconscious state, the only sound she ever made was her labored breathing.

One day her nurse, touched by the father's unrewarded faithfulness, ventured to say, "It must be hard giving so much love when she's like this."

He quickly responded, "I'm going to keep on coming and bringing flowers and telling her stories even if she's oblivious to it. I love her whether or not she loves me back."

What a tender and poignant picture of God's love! Patiently, untiringly, He is in love with us. We may be unaware of His presence, as though we are spiritually comatose. But we don't have to be that way. What our loving Lord said to the church of Laodicea He says to each of us: "I stand at the door and knock. If anyone hears My voice and opens the door, I will come in and dine with him" (Revelation 3:20 NKJV).

Today, as always, God is reaching out to us. Let's respond now to the love that won't quit loving.

VERNON GROUNDS

God's love is persistent but never pushy.

Maintain Unity

READ EPHESIANS 4:1–6

Make every effort to keep the unity of the Spirit through the bond of peace. —EPHESIANS 4:3

A man stranded by himself on an island was finally discovered. His rescuers asked him about the three huts they saw there. He pointed and said, "This one is my home, and that one is my church." They asked about the third hut: "Oh," he said, "that was my *former* church." Though we may laugh at the silliness of this story, it does highlight a concern about unity among believers.

The church of Ephesus during the time of the apostle Paul was comprised of both rich and poor, Jews and Gentiles, men and women, masters and slaves. And where differences exist, so does friction. One concern Paul wrote about was the issue of unity. But observe what Paul said about this issue in Ephesians 4:3. He didn't tell them to be "eager to produce or to organize unity." He told them to endeavor "to keep the unity of the Spirit through the bond of peace." Unity already exists because believers share one body, one Spirit, one hope, one Lord, one faith, one baptism, and one God and Father of all (vv. 4–6).

How do we "keep the unity"? By expressing our different opinions and convictions with lowliness, gentleness, and patience (v. 2). The Spirit will give us the power to react in love toward those with whom we disagree.

Albert Lee

Unity among believers comes from our union with Christ.

Hope

When Morning Comes

READ HEBREWS 11:1–8

Now faith is confidence in what we hope for and assurance about what we do not see. —HEBREWS 11:1

It was very late when my husband and I stopped for the night at a country inn outside of Munich, Germany. We were delighted to see that our cozy room had a balcony, although an oppressive fog made it impossible to see into the darkness. But when the sun rose a few hours later, the haze began to fade. Then we could see what had been grimly shrouded the night before—a completely idyllic scene—peaceful and lush green meadows, sheep grazing with tiny tinkling bells about their necks, and big white clouds in the sky that looked exactly like more sheep—huge, fluffy sheep!

Sometimes life can get clouded over by a heavy fog of despair. Our situation may look so dark that we begin to lose hope. But just as the sun burns away a fog, our faith in God can burn away the haze of doubt. Hebrews 11 defines faith as "confidence in what we hope for and assurance about what we do not see" (v. 1). The passage goes on to remind us of the faith of Noah, who was "warned about things not yet seen," yet obeyed God (v. 7). And it reminds us of Abraham, who went where God directed even though he didn't know where that would be (v. 8).

Although we have not seen God and cannot always feel His presence, He is always present. He can give us hope in our darkest nights.

CINDY HESS KASPER

Faith is the radar that sees through the fog. —Corrie ten Boom

In Every Generation

READ PSALM 100

For the LORD is good and his love endures forever; his faithfulness continues through all generations. —PSALM 100:5

It may seem surprising when children don't follow their parents' example of faith in God. Equally unexpected is a person with a deep commitment to Christ who emerges from a family where faith was not present. In every generation, each person has a choice.

Samuel was a great man of God who appointed his two sons, Joel and Abijah, as leaders over Israel (1 Samuel 8:1–2). Unlike their father, however, they were corrupt and "turned aside after dishonest gain and accepted bribes and perverted justice" (v. 3). Yet, years later, we find Heman, Joel's son, appointed as a musician in the house of the Lord (1 Chronicles 6:31–33). Heman, Samuel's grandson—along with Asaph, his right-hand man and the author of many of the psalms—served the Lord by singing joyful songs (1 Chronicles 15:16–17).

Even though a person seems indifferent toward the faith so precious to his or her parents, God is still at work. Things can change in later years, and seeds of faith may spring to life in generations to come.

No matter what the family situation may be, we know that "the LORD is good and his love endures forever; his faithfulness continues through all generations" (Psalm 100:5).

DAVID MCCASLAND

God's faithfulness extends to all generations.

Love

Fear and Love

READ 2 SAMUEL 6:1–11

Let us be thankful, and so worship God acceptably with reverence and awe, for our "God is a consuming fire." —HEBREWS 12:28–29

For years I was troubled by God's harsh judgment on a man who made a seemingly honest mistake. We read in 2 Samuel 6:6–7 that Uzzah simply grabbed the ark of the covenant to keep it from falling off a cart. For that, the Lord struck him dead.

God had earlier given clear instructions about the sacred ark. Only the priests were to touch it (Numbers 1:51, 53; 4:15). Ignoring His commandments was not a minor matter.

Sobering scenes like this provide evidence of God's holiness. They vividly show the aspect of His character that concerns Him when He sees disobedience and sin.

Uzzah's death was a dramatic reminder that those who handled the ark incorrectly were guilty of flagrant irreverence. King David got the message. He made sure that God's instructions were carefully followed when he moved the ark to Jerusalem.

How aware are we of God's majesty and flawless character? Sometimes we enter His presence in worship and prayer with far less reverence than we would if we were meeting the President.

Our God of purity and holiness is gracious and merciful, but we must never forget that He is also "a consuming fire" (Hebrews 12:29). The more we fear His awesome power, the more we'll appreciate His perfect love.

HERB VANDER LUGT

No one knows the grace of God who does not know the fear of God.

Hope

The Hope of the Heart

READ ROMANS 4:13–15

He did not waver through unbelief regarding the promise of God, but was strengthened in his faith and gave glory to God. —ROMANS 4:20

Promises are the hope of our heart. A child's security depends on a parent's promise to keep him or her safe. A spouse can live with confidence because of a mate's promise of fidelity, loyalty, and love. Businesses depend on promises from employees, vendors, and clients. Countries remain safe when neighbors keep their promise to honor their borders.

Unfortunately, hearts and relationships are broken in all of those situations by unkept promises. There is one Promise Maker, though, who can be trusted completely and without fear. That one is God. He has given us hundreds of promises in His Word, and He keeps every one of them.

If anyone had reason to wonder if God could or would keep His promises, it was Abraham. But "against all hope, Abraham in hope believed" (Romans 4:18). We know that what God had promised him—that he and his wife would have a child when they were both past ninety years old—could not have happened without divine intervention.

Are you looking for hope? Then search the Scriptures diligently and claim the promises of God that apply to you. Promises truly are the hope of the heart, and God always keeps His word.

DAVE BRANON

The future always looks bright when viewed through the window of God's promises.

Christ-Centered Faith

READ COLOSSIANS 2:1–10

So then, just as you received Christ Jesus as Lord, continue to live your lives in him. —COLOSSIANS 2:6

Some Christians try to live from one dramatic mountaintop experience to another. Their relationship with the Lord is based on their feelings at the moment. They go from Bible conferences to seminars to Bible studies, trying to maintain an emotional high.

Author Creath Davis, referring to his early Christian life, wrote, "I felt that if something spectacular was not transpiring, my faith was weakening. As a result, I missed most of what was going on in the valleys, waiting to get back to the mountain."

What's an effective antidote for a feelings-centered faith? According to the apostle Paul in Colossians 2, being Christ-centered is the answer. Having received Christ Jesus by faith, we are instructed to continue to "live [our] lives in him" by faith (v. 6) through both the highs and lows of life. By walking in close fellowship with Him each day, we become "rooted and built up in him, strengthened in the faith" (v. 7). We grow steadily into maturity as we focus on Christ and what He has done for us—not on our feelings.

Mountaintop experiences can be beneficial, but nothing is more profitable than an ongoing, Christ-centered life of faith.

JOANIE YODER

True faith needs no feelings to rest upon.

Looking Up When You're Down

READ PSALM 42

Why, my soul, are you downcast? Why so disturbed within me? Put your hope in God, for I will yet praise him, my Savior and my God. —PSALM 42:11

We all have those moments in life when we're down. We all get the "blues." Nothing looks right to us. Everything seems to be going wrong. And no solution or relief is in sight. Speaking out of his own experience, the psalmist cried, "Why, my soul, are you downcast? Why so disturbed within me? Put your hope in God" (42:11). That's good advice for anyone who is facing discouragement.

In the book of Acts we are told about an experience in the life of the apostle Paul while he was on board ship headed for Rome. A violent storm raged for several days and threatened to plunge the boat and all its passengers to the bottom of the sea. One night, however, an angel of the Lord appeared and assured Paul that not a person on board would perish. Paul believed that message and told his fellow passengers about it: "Keep up your courage, men, for I have faith in God" (Acts 27:25). Like the psalmist in Psalm 42, Paul's hope was in the Lord.

Even when we are fearful, we have reason for cheer when look to our heavenly Father. After surviving the boat accident, Paul later wrote, "My God will meet all your needs according to the riches of his glory in Christ Jesus" (Philippians 4:19). Believe it. And the next time you're down, think of Paul's words and look up!

RICHARD DEHAAN

When you can't find a way out, look up!

Love

Greater Love Has No One

READ JOHN 15:9–17

Greater love has no one than this: to lay down one's life for one's friends. —JOHN 15:13

Melbourne, Australia, is home to the Shrine of Remembrance, a war memorial honoring those who died for their country. Built following World War I, it has since been expanded to honor those who served in subsequent conflicts.

It's a beautiful place, with reminders of courage and devotion, but the highlight of the shrine is a hall containing a carved stone that simply reads, "Greater Love Hath No Man." Every year on the eleventh day of the eleventh month at 11:00 a.m., a mirror reflects the sun's light onto the stone to spotlight the word *love*. It is a poignant tribute to those who gave their lives.

We honor the memory of those who paid the ultimate price for freedom. Yet the words on that stone carry a far greater meaning. Jesus spoke them the night before He died on the cross for the sins of a needy world (John 15:13). His death was not for freedom from political tyranny but freedom from the penalty of sin. His death was not just to give us a better life but to give us eternal life.

It is important to remember those who have given their lives for their country—but may we never forget to praise and honor the Christ who died for a dying world. Truly, there is no greater love than this.

BILL CROWDER

The cross of Jesus is the supreme evidence of the love of God.

By Faith

READ HEBREWS 11:1–16

All these people were still living by faith when they died. They did not receive the things promised; they only saw them and welcomed them from a distance. —HEBREWS 11:13

Every day Lisa and David Holden asked God for a baby. She said they prayed "sometimes with bitter disappointment, sometimes with a confidence that seemed infallible, and sometimes with frustration and a hurt so deep it ached." Lisa finally conceived, and a little guy named Peter was born.

Lisa and David had close friends who also wanted children. They too prayed fervently about their situation. Eventually they decided to adopt but were told they were too old. Both couples prayed in faith. One request was granted; the other was denied.

In Hebrews 11:11 we read, "By faith even Sarah, who was past childbearing age, was enabled to bear children." But in contrast, when the apostle Paul prayed that his unidentified "thorn in the flesh" be removed from him, the Lord responded, "My grace is sufficient for you" (2 Corinthians 12:9), and the "thorn" remained. Even Christ himself prayed to His heavenly Father that the cup of agony awaiting Him at Calvary might be taken from Him, but He added, "Yet not my will, but yours be done" (Luke 22:42).

O Lord, whether or not our deepest longings and most desperate prayers are granted, our faith is in you. Help us to desire your will above all else. Amen.

David Egner

When God's answer is negative,
His reason is affirmative.

Love

Pink Sheep

READ JOHN 10:7–18

"By this everyone will know that you are my disciples, if you love one another." —JOHN 13:35

While traveling on a road from Glasgow to Edinburgh, Scotland, I was enjoying the beautiful, pastoral countryside when a rather humorous sight captured my attention. There, on a small hilltop, was a rather large flock of pink sheep.

I know that sheep owners mark their animals with dots of spray paint to identify them—but these sheep really stood out. The owner had fully covered every animal with pink coloring. Everyone knew who those sheep belonged to.

Scripture calls followers of Christ "sheep," and they too have a unique identifying mark. What is the "pink coloring" in a Christ-follower's life? How can someone be identified as Jesus's own?

In the gospel of John, Jesus, the Good Shepherd, told us what that identifier is: Love. "Love one another. As I have loved you . . . . By this everyone will know that you are my disciples, if you love one another" (John 13:34–35).

In words and deeds, a believer should show love to all those around. "Dear friends," John writes, "since God so loved us, we also ought to love one another" (1 John 4:11). A Christian's love for others should be as obvious as pink wool on a flock of Scottish sheep.

DAVE BRANON

As followers of Christ, our love should make us stand out in a crowd.

Health-Giving Hope

READ 1 PETER 1:13–21

May the God of hope fill you with all joy and peace as you trust in him, so that you may overflow with hope by the power of the Holy Spirit. —ROMANS 15:13

It is well-known that our emotions can have a profound effect on our bodies. And the condition of our bodies can affect our emotions.

For example, an article in the journal published by the American Heart Association pointed to the negative physical consequences of hopelessness. It essentially said that those who had experienced extreme feelings of despair had a twenty-percent greater increase in arteriosclerosis (hardening of the arteries) over a four-year period. Other studies have also connected hopelessness with heart disease, heart attacks, and death.

The relationship between one's emotional well-being and physical condition, however, is not a modern discovery. In the Old Testament book of Proverbs, we read that "a cheerful heart is good medicine" (17:22) and that the wisdom found in God's words "are life to those who find them and health to one's whole body" (4:22).

A proper relationship to God and Scripture can benefit us spiritually, physically, and emotionally. The central concern of the gospel is to bring us into a right relationship with God through faith in Christ. Its blessed by-product is an abundant life filled with health-promoting hope—the assurance of total forgiveness of sins and eternal life with Christ.

VERNON GROUNDS

Hope in the heart puts a smile on the face.

NOVEMBER
15

Hope

Not in Vain

READ 1 CORINTHIANS 15:50–58

Therefore, my dear brothers and sisters, stand firm. Let nothing move you. Always give yourselves fully to the work of the Lord, because you know that your labor in the Lord is not in vain. —1 CORINTHIANS 15:58

A financial advisor I know describes the reality of investing money by saying, "Hope for the best and be prepared for the worst." With almost every decision we make in life there is uncertainty about the outcome. Yet there is one course we can follow where no matter what happens, we know that in the end it will not be a wasted effort.

The apostle Paul spent a year with the followers of Jesus in Corinth, a city known for its moral corruption. After he left, he sent a follow-up letter urging them not to be discouraged or feel that their witness for Christ was of no value. He assured them that a day is coming when the Lord will return and even death will be swallowed up in victory (1 Corinthians 15:52–55).

Remaining true to Jesus may be difficult, discouraging, and even dangerous, but it is never pointless or wasted. As we walk with the Lord and become a witness to His presence and power, our lives are not in vain! We can be sure of that.

DAVID MCCASLAND

Our life and witness for Jesus Christ are not in vain.

True Love

READ JOHN 15:9–17

"My command is this: Love each other as I have loved you." —JOHN 15:12

During the rehearsal for my brother's wedding ceremony, my husband snapped a picture of the bride and groom as they faced each other in front of the pastor. When we looked at the photograph later, we noticed that the camera's flash had illuminated a metal cross in the background, which appeared as a glowing image above the couple.

The photograph reminded me that marriage is a picture of Christ's love for the church as shown on the cross. When the Bible instructs husbands to love their wives (Ephesians 5:25), God compares that kind of faithful, selfless affection to Christ's love for His followers. Because Jesus sacrificed His life for the sake of love, we are all to love each other (1 John 4:10–11). He died in our place so our sin would not keep us separate from God for eternity. He lived out His words to the disciples: "Greater love has no one than this: to lay down one's life for one's friends" (John 15:13).

Many of us suffer from the pain of abandonment, rejection, and betrayal. Despite all of this, through Christ we can understand the sacrificial, compassionate, and enduring nature of true love. You are loved by God! Jesus said so at the cross.

JENNIFER BENSON SCHULDT

Nothing speaks more clearly of God's
love than the cross of Jesus.

Faith

Farsighted Faith

READ JOB 19:21–29

I know that my redeemer lives, and that in the end he will stand on the earth. And after my skin has been destroyed, yet in my flesh I will see God. —JOB 19:25–26

A skilled surgeon lost the idealism with which he began his practice. Again and again he corrected serious problems through surgery—only to see his patients die later from other ailments. He decided that all he was doing was postponing the inevitable.

In one sense, he is right.

Faith, however, looks beyond this life to eternity. I thought of this when visiting a thirty-two-year-old mother who had leukemia. She didn't like to think of the possibility of leaving behind a husband and young children. She prayed for a remission or a cure. Her loved ones and friends prayed with her. We didn't know what God would do. Yet she was full of faith. She told me she could be happy because she knew that nothing really bad could happen to her. She saw beyond death to the resurrection of the body, reunion with her loved ones, and a home in heaven. Hers was not a shortsighted idealism but a farsighted faith.

The thought of suffering and death can be frightening. Even Job complained bitterly about his trials and expressed negative sentiments about death. At other times, however, he saw that beyond the grave he would be vindicated and rewarded by God. And he never let go of that confidence.

Farsighted faith always focuses on God.

HERB VANDER LUGT

Faith sees God in the dark as well as in the light.

"I'm Really Scared"

READ PHILIPPIANS 4:4–9

Do not be anxious about anything, but in every situation, by prayer and petition, with thanksgiving, present your requests to God. —PHILIPPIANS 4:6

"I'm really scared." This was the poignant note a teenager posted to friends on Facebook as she told them of some upcoming medical tests. She was facing hospitalization and a series of procedures in a city three hours from home, and she was anxious as she waited for doctors to discover the source of some serious medical problems she was experiencing.

Who of us, in youth or later years, has not felt similar fears when facing unwanted life events that are truly frightening? And where can we turn for help? What comfort can we find from Scripture to give us courage in these kinds of situations?

The reality that God will go with us through our trial can help us to hope. Isaiah 41:13 tells us, "For I am the LORD your God who takes hold of your right hand and says to you, 'Do not fear; I will help you.' " In addition, God offers indescribable, heart-guarding peace when we present our difficulties to Him in prayer (Philippians 4:6–7).

Through God's unfailing presence and His peace that "transcends all understanding" (v. 7), we can find the hope and help we need to endure situations in which we are really scared.

DAVE BRANON

God is with us in all our struggles.

Love

God's Love on a Plate

READ HEBREWS 13:1–16

Do not forget to show hospitality to strangers, for by so doing some people have shown hospitality to angels without knowing it. —HEBREWS 13:2

During His life on earth, Jesus chose to identify with poor and destitute people. He lived as one who had no place to call home (Matthew 8:20), and His ministry was marked by compassion for the needy.

In her book *Hidden Art*, Edith Schaeffer tells of feeding the occasional vagrant who would stop at her back door and ask, "May I have a cup of coffee, ma'am, and maybe some bread?"

Edith would invite him to sit down, then she would go in to prepare a tray of food fit for a king: steaming soup and thick sandwiches, cut and arranged artfully on a plate with garnishes. The children would make a tiny bouquet, and if it was dusk they would add a candle.

In amazement the man would gasp, "For me?" "Yes," Edith would answer, "and coffee will be ready in a minute. This Gospel of John is for you too. Take it with you. It really is very important."

In my kitchen hangs this saying: "Food is God's love made edible." Certainly those vagrants at Edith's door experienced God's love through her and her family.

How about serving up God's love to someone? Through your generosity you will be serving Christ—and perhaps, you may be serving an angel in disguise (Hebrews 13:2).

JOANIE YODER

Food is God's love made edible.

Teens and Those Who Love Them

READ DANIEL 1:1–17

To these four young men God gave knowledge and understanding of all kinds of literature and learning. And Daniel could understand visions and dreams of all kinds. —DANIEL 1:17

Imagine yourself in Daniel's predicament. The king has told you, a Jewish teenager, what you're going to eat and drink. But there's a problem: God has said that the food on the king's menu is prohibited. Could you stand up to that kind of pressure?

Many people don't think teens have what it takes to do what's right in a case like this—or in similar situations where it would cost them something to take a moral stand. Parents often think that the teenage years are simply a time to endure. But instead of dwelling on the difficulties they will face, we ought to think of the opportunities we have to encourage them to do what is right.

I think Daniel, the teen who was challenged to stand up to the king in God's name, must have had people who taught him to make right choices. And it showed, for he boldly challenged the king's rules.

Many teens have the love for God and the wisdom from God that Daniel displayed. What they need is guidance and encouragement, not a prejudiced, negative attitude about the younger generation. Help the teens you know to develop the courage of Daniel.

DAVE BRANON

Children tend to rise to the level of their parents' expectations.

Faith

"Do Your Best"

READ ROMANS 12:1–8

We have different gifts, according to the grace given to each of us. —ROMANS 12:6

All Christians have unique, God-given abilities. Some believers, however, feel inferior because they don't have as much talent as someone else. None of us should think that way. God does not hold us accountable for what we do not have. He wants us to discover and develop the skills we do have.

In his book *Making the Most of Life*, J. R. Miller told about Leonardo da Vinci, the famous Renaissance artist. While da Vinci was still a pupil, his old and famous teacher asked him to finish a picture he had begun. Young da Vinci stood in such awe of his master's skill that at first he respectfully declined. But the old artist simply said, "Do your best." Leonardo took the brush and began. With each careful stroke, his hand grew more steady as his eye "awoke with slumbering genius." Soon he was completely caught up in his work. When the painting was finished, the master was carried into the studio to see it. There before him was a triumph of art. Embracing his student, he exclaimed, 'My son, I paint no more!' " Leonardo's talent surfaced when he did his best.

Of course, we cannot be a Leonardo da Vinci. But we don't have to be. In 1 Corinthians 4, the apostle Paul said that "it is required that those who have been given a trust must prove faithful" (v. 2). That means doing our best—and leaving the results with the One who gave us our talents. Who knows, we may surprise ourselves!

RICHARD DEHAAN

Don't rob yourself of being you by trying to do what others do.

What's Your Motive?

READ MATTHEW 6:1–16

"But if you do not forgive others their sins, your Father will not forgive your sins." —MATTHEW 6:15–16

A friend of mine carries his Bible everywhere. Some wonder whether he thinks of himself as a spiritual superman. Others think he must be. But my friend thinks otherwise. He says he carries his Bible not out of spiritual strength but because he knows how terribly weak he is.

He has had several "prodigal son" episodes when he fell into sin, but he is determined by God's grace to stay true to the Lord. He figures that as long as he carries the Bible in his hand, he'll be reminded of its warnings and promises, and he'll think twice before falling back into his old ways.

His reasoning brings to mind Jesus's words in Matthew 6. Although He was talking about charitable deeds, He set forth the principle that it is wrong to parade one's faith in public (v. 2). He also taught in Matthew 5:14–16 that it's important to let others see evidence of our faith.

The key to understanding this seeming contradiction is motive. If our desire is to *do* right—to give light—we're acting in the spirit of Christ. But if we desire to *seem* right—to get the spotlight—we have the wrong motive.

I'm thankful for the life of my friend. By carrying his Bible, he may be misunderstood, but I know his one motive is to do right. He alerts me to my own weakness and need for God's Word (Matthew 6:13).

May our actions today reflect a desire not to impress people but to please God.

MART DEHAAN

It's possible to do the right thing for the wrong reason.

Love

God's Little Blessings

READ PSALM 36:5–10

How priceless is your unfailing love, O God! People take refuge in the shadow of your wings. —PSALM 36:7

Our family was at Disney World several years ago when God handed us one of His little blessings. Disney World is a huge place—one hundred and seven acres huge, to be exact. You could walk around for days without seeing someone you know. My wife and I decided to do our own thing while our children sought out the really cool stuff. We parted at 9 a.m. and were planning a rendezvous around 6 p.m. This was in PC days: Pre-cell phone.

At about 2 p.m., Sue and I got a craving for tacos. We looked at our map and made our way to a Spanish-sounding place for Mexican food. We had just sat down with our food when we heard, "Hi, Mom. Hi, Dad." Our four amigos had, at the same time, a hankering for a hot burrito.

Ten minutes after they joined us, a violent summer storm ripped through the park with whipping winds, heavy rain, and loud thunder. My wife commented, "I'd be a wreck if the kids weren't with us during this!" It seemed that God had orchestrated our meeting.

Ever notice those blessings from Him? Ever spend time thanking Him for His concern and care? Consider how remarkable it is that the One who created the universe cares enough to intervene in your life. "How priceless is your unfailing love, O God!"

DAVE BRANON

Belonging to God brings boundless blessings.

Truth: Handle with Care

READ EPHESIANS 4:7–16

Instead, speaking the truth in love, we will grow to become in every respect the mature body of him who is the head, that is, Christ. —EPHESIANS 4:15

Pastor and author Calvin Miller (1936–2012) told of a woman in a church he pastored who became angry because he wouldn't let her son sing more solos in church. She jotted down in a notebook every instance in her contact with Miller in which he did things "that were not in the spirit of Christ." Several months later she showed him all he had done that was offensive to her. Miller remarked about that incident, "What amazed me was that her list was mostly true. She didn't say anything that was untrue, but what she said was unkind."

Speaking the truth without love can serve the cause of evil. Truth can be devastating. When clothed in love, however, it eliminates error, builds trust, and promotes the good of others. Miller states, "Malicious truth gloats like a conqueror. Loving truth mourns that it must confront and show a brother his error. Malicious truth struts at its power. Loving truth weeps to find that the correction it inspires may for a while cause great pain. Malicious truth cries, 'Checkmate, you are beaten!' Loving truth whispers, 'I correct you with the same pain you feel. But when the pain is over, we shall rejoice that honesty and love have been served.' "

God's Spirit of truth prompts us to speak the truth, but not without love. Only by yielding our tongues to Him can we handle truth with care.

DENNIS DEHAAN

A bit of love is the only bit that will put a bridle on the tongue.

Love

Love We Can Trust

READ LAMENTATIONS 3:13–26

Because of the LORD's great love we are not consumed, for his compassions never fail. —LAMENTATIONS 3:22

Perhaps the most painful statement a person can hear is, "I don't love you anymore." Those words end relationships, break hearts, and shatter dreams. Often, people who have been betrayed guard themselves against future pain by deciding not to trust anyone's love again. That settled conviction might even include the love of God.

The remarkable thing about God's love for us, though, is His promise that it will never end. The prophet Jeremiah experienced devastating circumstances that left him emotionally depleted (Lamentations 3:13–20). His own people rejected his repeated calls to respond to God's love and follow Him. At a low point, Jeremiah said, "My strength and my hope have perished from the LORD" (v. 18 NKJV).

Yet, in his darkest hour Jeremiah considered God's unfailing love and wrote, "Because of the LORD's great love we are not consumed, for his compassions never fail. They are new every morning; great is your faithfulness. I say to myself, 'The LORD is my portion; therefore I will wait for him' " (Lamentations 3:22–24). A person may vow to love us forever yet fail to keep that promise; however, God's love remains steadfast and sure. "The LORD your God goes with you; he will never leave you nor forsake you" (Deuteronomy 31:6). That's a love we can trust.

DAVID MCCASLAND

God's love never fails.

It's in the Word

READ PSALM 119:25–32

I run the path of your commands, for you have broadened my understanding. —PSALM 119:32

As optimistic as I try to be, I also know that life can be a dark and lonely place.

I've talked to teenagers who have a parent whose anger makes just going home after school a dreaded trip.

I've known people who can't escape the curtain of depression.

I've spent considerable time with others who, like my wife and me, are enduring life with the sudden death of a child.

I've seen what relentless poverty can do to people all over the world.

Despite knowing that these scenarios exist, I don't despair. I know that hope is available in Jesus, that guidance comes through the Spirit, and that knowledge and power are found in God's Word.

The words of Psalm 119 give us encouragement. When our soul is "laid low in the dust," we can be revived according to God's Word (v. 25). When our soul is full of sorrow, we can be strengthened by the same source (v. 28). When we are threatened by deceit, we can follow God's laws (vv. 29–30). We can be given new understanding through God's commands (v. 32).

Are life's demands overwhelming you? If so, you can find hope, guidance, and knowledge to help in our great God and in the promises of His Word.

DAVE BRANON

A well-read Bible makes a well-fed soul.

Love

How to Turn Hate into Love

READ MATTHEW 5:43–48

Hatred stirs up conflict, but love covers over all wrongs. —PROVERBS 10:12

The message of Jesus is simple yet astounding: Love your enemies. Do good to those who mistreat you. Repay evil with kindness. When a Christian lives by these principles, he will keep his heart free of hatred no matter how others feel toward him.

In January 1981, Colombian rebels kidnapped missionary Chet Bitterman, shot him, and left his body in a hijacked bus. Imagine how his parents and loved ones must have felt at the senseless death of this young man!

But in April 1982, as a demonstration of international good will, the churches and civic groups of Bitterman's native area, Lancaster County, Pennsylvania, gave an ambulance to the state of Meta in Colombia, where the young linguist was killed.

Bitterman's parents traveled to Colombia for the presentation of the ambulance. At the ceremony his mother explained, "We are able to do this because God has taken the hatred from our hearts."

This is the power of Christ in action! When we are wronged and ill will begins turning to hatred in our hearts, we need to ask God to change us and enable us to show kindness to the one who has wronged us. This is the way to turn hatred into love.

DAVID EGNER

Our hatred can turn into love when we do right to those who do us wrong.

"The Light of Life"

READ PSALM 14

The fool says in his heart, "There is no God." They are corrupt, their deeds are vile; there is no one who does good. —PSALM 14:1

What if we didn't have faith in God but accepted instead the God-denying theory of evolution? Suppose we had an atheistic view of life.

Cornell University biologist William Provine once declared in a public debate that a person who is a consistent Darwinian must conclude that there's no life after death, no ultimate foundation for ethics, no ultimate meaning for existence, no free will. That sounds like a rather empty life.

Instead of that bleak unbelief—no matter what is behind it—we can open our hearts and minds to have faith in God as He has revealed himself through His Son Jesus Christ. That gives us the freeing forgiveness of our sin through His death on the cross. Also, it not only assures us of a blessed eternity but also fills our here-and-now experience with measureless blessings of meaning and hope. We can know by the indwelling Holy Spirit that Jesus's words in John 8:12 are true: "I am the light of the world. Whoever follows me will never walk in darkness, but will have the light of life."

As we move along on our earthly pilgrimage, we don't need to stumble in the darkness of unbelief. Faith in Jesus Christ allows us to enjoy "the light of life."

VERNON GROUNDS

Unbelief is a fearful darkness that only the light of salvation can remove.

Faith

Obscured by Clouds

READ 2 CORINTHIANS 4:16–18

We fix our eyes not on what is seen, but on what is unseen. —2 CORINTHIANS 4:18

A rare supermoon appeared in November 2016—the moon in its orbit reached its closest point to the earth in over sixty years and so appeared bigger and brighter than at other times. But for me that day the skies were shrouded in gray. Although I saw photos of this wonder from friends in other places, as I gazed upward I had to trust that the supermoon was lurking behind the clouds.

The apostle Paul faced many hardships but believed that what is unseen will last forever. He said his "momentary troubles" achieve "an eternal glory" (2 Corinthians 4:17). Thus he could fix his eyes "not on what is seen, but on what is unseen," because what is unseen is eternal (v. 18). Paul yearned that the Corinthians' and our faith would grow, and although we suffer, that we too would trust in God. We might not be able to see Him, but we can believe He is renewing us day by day (v. 16).

I thought about how God is unseen but eternal when I gazed at the clouds that day, knowing that the supermoon was hidden but there. And I hoped the next time I was tempted to believe that God was far from me, I would fix my eyes on what is unseen.

AMY BOUCHER PYE

Faith sees things that are out of our sight.

The Land of "What Is"

READ PSALM 46:1–7

Brothers and sisters, we do not want you to be uninformed about those who sleep in death, so that you do not grieve like the rest of mankind, who have no hope. —1 THESSALONIANS 4:13

Even all these years after losing our seventeen-year-old daughter Melissa in a car accident in 2002, I sometimes find myself entering the world of "What If." It's easy, in grief, to reimagine the events of that tragic June evening and think of factors that—if rearranged—would have had Mell arriving safely home and living out her life as we had hoped and dreamed.

In reality, though, the land of "What If" is not a good place to be for any of us. It is a place of regret, second-guessing, and hopelessness. While the grief is real and the sadness endures, life is better and God is honored if we dwell in the world of "What Is."

In that world, we can find hope, encouragement, and comfort. We have the sure hope (1 Thessalonians 4:13)—the assurance—that because Melissa loved Jesus she is in a place that is "better by far" (Philippians 1:23). We have the helpful presence of the God of all comfort (2 Corinthians 1:3). We have God's "ever-present help in trouble" (Psalm 46:1). And we often have the encouragement of fellow believers.

We all wish to avoid life's tragedies. But when we do face hard times, our greatest help comes from trusting God, our sure hope in the land of "What Is."

DAVE BRANON

Our greatest hope comes from trusting God.

Love

Knowing Isn't Everything

READ 1 CORINTHIANS 8

Now about food sacrificed to idols: We know that "We all possess knowledge." But knowledge puffs up while love builds up. —1 CORINTHIANS 8:1

No one could accuse the Pharisees of Jesus's day of being ignorant of the Old Testament. They knew it so well that many of them went around telling others how they should be living. They became proud, arrogant, judgmental religionists (Matthew 23).

I must confess I can relate. After a couple of years of Bible college, I thought I knew everything. I remember making caustic remarks about some statements I heard in sermons. One time I was especially critical of a guest speaker who was filled with enthusiasm but not very well trained. My root problem was pride and a lack of love. I had knowledge but didn't know how to handle it. It took a rebuke from a fellow Christian to show me that my knowledge was doing more harm than good.

It is good to have Bible knowledge. We need to learn all we can about God's Word and how it applies to everyday life. But we can become proud of our knowledge. That's why Paul said, "Knowledge puffs up while love builds up" (1 Corinthians 8:1).

When we use what we know to promote ourselves rather than to build others up, we are motivated by pride, not by love.

Lord Jesus, help us to know and love.

DAVID EGNER

Knowledge minus love makes us proud;
knowledge plus love makes us Christlike.

For Sinners Only

READ ROMANS 3:19–31

This righteousness is given through faith in Jesus Christ to all who believe. There is no difference between Jew and Gentile, for all have sinned and fall short of the glory of God. —ROMANS 3:22–23

It's heartbreaking to realize that the majority of people in our world are spiritually lost and without Christ. Among them are the lovely and unlovely, the caring and uncaring, the eloquent and the crude. As we witness for Christ, we may wrongly assume that people with social graces are closer to God's kingdom.

However, pleasant people need Christ just as much as unpleasant ones, because no one has a spiritual advantage when it comes to salvation. Paul explained why in Romans 3: "There is no difference . . . for all have sinned and fall short of the glory of God . . . . For we maintain that a person is justified by faith apart from the works of the law" (vv. 22–23, 28).

Yes, salvation is God's free gift to sinners. And since all of us are sinners, the only "contribution" we make toward our salvation is the sin from which we need to be saved! Oswald Chambers said that the only way a person can be born again is to renounce all good. He wrote, "Any coward among us will give up wrong things, but will he give up right things?" We cannot rely on our own natural goodness.

We need to share with all kinds of people the salvation Christ offers, for as the apostle Paul said, "There is no difference."

JOANIE YODER

You can never speak to the wrong person about Christ.

DECEMBER
3

Hope

Good News

READ NAHUM 1:7–15

Look, there on the mountains, the feet of one who brings good news, who proclaims peace! —NAHUM 1:15

World news bombards us from the internet, television, radio, and mobile devices. The majority seems to describe what's wrong—crime, terrorism, war, and economic problems. Yet there are times when good news invades the darkest hours of sadness and despair—stories of unselfish acts, a medical breakthrough, or steps toward peace in war-scarred places.

The words of two men recorded in the Old Testament brought great hope to people weary of conflict. While describing God's coming judgment on a ruthless and powerful nation, Nahum said, "Look, there on the mountains, the feet of one who brings good news, who proclaims peace!" (Nahum 1:15). That news brought hope to all those oppressed by cruelty. A similar phrase occurs in the book of Isaiah: "How beautiful on the mountains are the feet of those who bring good news, who proclaim peace, who bring good tidings, who proclaim salvation" (Isaiah 52:7).

Nahum and Isaiah's prophetic words of hope found their ultimate fulfillment at the first Christmas when the angel told the shepherds, "Do not be afraid. I bring you good news that will cause great joy for all the people. Today in the town of David a Savior has been born to you; he is the Messiah, the Lord" (Luke 2:10–11).

The most important headline in our lives every day is the very best news ever spoken—Christ the Savior is born!

DAVID MCCASLAND

The birth of Jesus is the best news the world has ever received!

New Love in an Old Marriage

READ EPHESIANS 5:22–33

Wives, submit yourselves to your own husbands as you do to the Lord. . . . Husbands, love your wives, just as Christ loved the church and gave himself up for her. —EPHESIANS 5:22, 25

Success in marriage is not the result of some misty-eyed, magical feeling called "love." Yet to hear some people's reason for divorce, you'd think that's all it takes. "I don't love her anymore" sounds like an irrefutable argument. After all, when love dies, the marriage is dead—or is it? In Old Testament days, marriages were usually arranged by the parents, and often the couple fell in love after the vows were spoken. Yes, love is important, and a relationship without it is a heavy burden. But love is renewable.

A woman told psychologist George W. Crane that she hated her husband and wanted a divorce. "I want to hurt him all I can," she declared. "Well, in that case," said Dr. Crane, "I advise you to start showering him with compliments. When you have become indispensable to him, when he thinks you love him devotedly, then start the divorce action." The woman was intrigued by this novel approach. A few months later she returned and said all was going well. "Good," said Dr. Crane, "it's time to file for divorce." "Divorce?" she responded. "Never! I love my husband dearly."

As Christians, we are indwelt by the Holy Spirit, who gives the incentive and courage to find new ways of expressing love. New love in an old marriage is not just possible—it's essential!

DENNIS DEHAAN

God is the only third party in a marriage
who can make it happy.

Love

Jesus Loves You

READ JOHN 15:9–17

As the Father loved me, so have I have loved you. Now remain in my love. —JOHN 15:9

The substitute teacher was overwhelmed. She was helping to care for a small group of children at a school that specializes in students with severe disabilities. As she sat with a little boy who seemed extremely agitated, she leaned over to him and whispered in his ear, "Jesus loves you." Immediately the boy's agitation calmed, and he began to laugh and make happy sounds.

Have you ever thought about the significance of the words "Jesus loves you"? Can anything be more simple, yet more profound?

Consider what it means to have the Creator of all things know your name. Think of the comfort in knowing that the Great Physician has your best interests at heart. Ponder the security of knowing that the Good Shepherd is watching over you. Contemplate what it means that the Savior cared enough to die for you.

Ponder too what Paul said. He asked, "Who shall separate us from the love of Christ?" (Romans 8:35). The answer: Nothing in all creation "shall be able to separate us from the love of God which is in Christ Jesus our Lord" (v. 39).

What does it mean to have Someone like that love you? It means life and peace and hope and joy.

Jesus loves you. What else do you need?

DAVE BRANON

God loves everyone as if there were but one to love.

Coming Alongside

READ EXODUS 17:8–16

When Moses' hands grew tired, they took a stone and put it under him and he sat on it. Aaron and Hur held his hands up—one on one side, one on the other—so that his hands remained steady till sunset. —EXODUS 17:12

Her thirty classmates and their parents watched as Mi'Asya nervously walked to the podium to speak at her fifth-grade graduation ceremony. When the principal adjusted the microphone to Mi'Asya's height, she turned her back to the microphone and the audience. The crowd whispered words of encouragement: "Come on, honey, you can do it." But she didn't budge. Then a classmate walked to the front and stood by her side. With the principal on one side of Mi'Asya and her friend on the other, the three read her speech together. What a beautiful example of support!

Moses needed help and support in the middle of a battle with the Amalekites (Exodus 17:10–16). "As long as Moses held up his hands [with the staff of God in his hands], the Israelites were winning, but whenever he lowered his hands, the Amalekites were winning" (v. 11). When Aaron and Hur saw what was happening, they stood beside Moses, "one on one side, one on the other," and supported his arms when he grew tired. With their support, victory came by sunset.

We all need the support of one another. As brothers and sisters in the family of God, we have so many opportunities to encourage one another on our shared journey of faith. And God is right here in our midst giving us His grace to do that.

ANNE CETAS

Hope can be ignited by a spark of encouragement.

Love

Sandal Love

READ 1 JOHN 3:16–24

Dear children, let us not love with words or speech but with actions and in truth. —1 JOHN 3:18

A young woman backpacking in Colorado encountered another woman hobbling down a mountain trail. On one foot she wore an improvised shoe made of green twigs wrapped with a strip of cloth.

"Lost one boot crossing a stream," she explained. "Hope I can get down the mountain before dark."

The first hiker reached into her own pack and took out a sport sandal. "Wear this," she said. "You can mail it to me when you get home."

The woman gratefully accepted the sandal and set off down the trail. A few days later the sandal arrived in the mail with a note saying: "I passed several people who noticed my predicament, but you're the only one who offered any help. It made all the difference. Thanks for sharing your sandal with me."

The Bible says love can be seen and touched—it's tangible. It may be as big as the Good Samaritan's care for an injured man (Luke 10:30–37) or as small as a cup of cold water given in Jesus's name (Matthew 10:42).

Real love takes action. The Bible says, "Let us not love with words or speech but with actions and in truth" (1 John 3:18).

On the trail of life today, when we meet a hobbler, let's offer a sandal in love.

DAVID MCCASLAND

You may give without loving, but you can't love without giving.

Hope Restored

READ PSALM 145:14–21

The LORD *upholds all who fall and lifts up all who are bowed down.* —PSALM 145:14

What happens when the hope we have because of our faith grows dim? When our circumstances or our memories or our thoughts lead us into feelings of depression or even despair, what do we do?

Can I tell you about a dark episode in my life? It crept up on me gradually—before I could even notice. As I look back now, I wonder how it ever could have happened. I could see nothing to be hopeful about. Inside, I had given up. I couldn't express it in words. I could only reach out to God for help.

As you might suspect, God came to my rescue. And his help came in several forms. For instance, friends who had no idea what I was going through sent me encouraging notes. Also, the two or three people I risked telling about my struggle were very supportive and my family stood with me. I received gentle, firm help from a counselor.

Sunlight began to peek through the dark clouds. It grew brighter as I continued to work and pray and think. I found great hope in Psalm 145:14, and slowly the Lord lifted me up.

When we are so discouraged that we think there is no hope, God is there. We can call out to the Lord for help, even if we can't put it into words. He will keep His promise. In His time, and in His way, He will lift us up.

DAVID EGNER

No one is hopeless whose hope is in God.

Faith

God's Gift—Not for Sale

READ TITUS 3:1–7

He saved us, not because of righteous things we had done, but because of his mercy. He saved us through the washing of rebirth and renewal by the Holy Spirit. —TITUS 3:5

A shoe store owner in a large city decided to conduct an experiment. He placed two identical pairs of shoes side by side in his shop window and put the following sign above them: "There is absolutely no difference in this merchandise. One pair sells for $16.95 and the other for $32.95. We just want to see which price you prefer." Three out of every four people suspected trickery and insisted on paying the larger amount.

A transaction involving the loss of a mere $16 is trivial indeed when compared to the eternal issues of our personal relationship to Christ and the destiny of our souls.

Salvation through Jesus Christ is based on grace, and it is described by the apostle Paul as "the gift of God" (Romans 6:23). Many people often reject it, however, saying, "It's just too easy. There must be more to do than just believe." They turn to the false substitute of salvation by works.

If you are thinking about salvation and about knowing that you will spend eternity in heaven, don't be fooled. Scripture says, "To him who does not work but believes on Him who justifies the ungodly, his faith is accounted for righteousness" (Romans 4:5 NKJV).

Take the free gift! You'll be eternally grateful.

PAUL VAN GORDER

We are saved by God's grace, not by our goodness—
by Christ's dying, not by our doing.

The Love of God

READ PSALM 8

What is man that You are mindful of him, and the son of man that You visit him? —PSALM 8:4 NKJV

A highly acclaimed astronomer was giving an address on recent discoveries about the vast workings of our universe. The information was amazing!

When the astronomer fielded questions, someone asked, "Professor, after all you have told us about the complexity of our universe, do you think a God great enough to make such a world could be concerned about us mortals?" After careful thought, the professor answered, "It depends on how great your God is!"

Planet earth is a mere speck of dust traveling through space. And we, its passengers, might well be viewed as less noticeable than the tiny, almost invisible insects that we unwittingly trample underfoot. But God is not like man. His power is so great that He sees us, knows us, and cares for us. He seeks us, and He meets our need. Yes, this all-powerful God loves us.

The Christian faith affirms that the God who created and sustains the universe is great enough to know you, the creature He has made. He is great enough to care about you personally.

When I think how small and helpless we are in God's expansive and awesome creation, I'm thankful that His love is as great as His power.

RICHARD DEHAAN

God loves His children not because of who they are but because of who He is.

Hope

Our Living Hope

READ JOHN 6:39–54

Praise be to the God and Father of our Lord Jesus Christ! In his great mercy he has given us new birth into a living hope through the resurrection of Jesus Christ from the dead. —1 PETER 1:3

The morning after my mother died, I was reading the Bible and talking to the Lord about my sadness. The *Our Daily Bread* Bible-In-One-Year reading for that day was John 6.

When I came to verse 39, the Lord whispered comfort to my sad heart: "This is the will of him who sent me, that I shall lose none of those he has given me, but raise them up at the last day." Mom's spirit was with the Lord already, but I knew that one day she would be given a new body.

As I continued reading, I noticed three other times in John 6 that Jesus said He will raise His people from the dead at the last day. He was repeating this truth to those who were listening long ago as well as to my heart that day.

Our hope of resurrection will be realized when Jesus returns. "In a flash, in the twinkling of an eye, at the last trumpet. For the trumpet will sound, the dead will be raised imperishable, and we will be changed" (1 Corinthians 15:52). After the resurrection, believers in Jesus will receive their new bodies and rewards for their faithful service (1 Corinthians 3:12–15; 2 Corinthians 5:9–11).

The resurrection is the living hope of the Christian. Do you have that hope?

ANNE CETAS

The risen Christ will come from heaven
to take His own to heaven.

Room 5020

READ GENESIS 50:15–20

"You intended to harm me, but God intended it for good to accomplish what is now being done, the saving of many lives." —GENESIS 50:20

Jay Bufton turned his hospital room into a lighthouse.

The fifty-two-year-old husband, father, high school teacher, and coach was dying of cancer, but his room—Room 5020—became a beacon of hope for friends, family, and hospital workers. Because of his joyful attitude and strong faith, nurses wanted to be assigned to Jay. Some even came to see him during off-hours.

Even as his once-athletic body was wasting away, he greeted anyone and everyone with a smile and encouragement. One friend said, "Every time I visited Jay he was upbeat, positive, and filled with hope. He was, even while looking cancer and death in the face, living out his faith."

At Jay's funeral, one speaker noted that Room 5020 had a special meaning. He pointed to Genesis 50:20, in which Joseph says that although his brothers sold him into slavery, God turned the tables and accomplished something good: "the saving of many lives." Cancer invaded Jay's life, but by recognizing God's hand at work Jay could say that "God intended it for good." That's why Jay could use even the ravages of cancer as an open door to tell others about Jesus.

What a legacy of unwavering trust in our Savior even as death was knocking at the door! What a testimony of confidence in our good and trustworthy God!

DAVE BRANON

By God's grace, we can have our best witness in the worst of times.

Love

A Love that Won't Let Go

READ HOSEA 11

How can I give you up, Ephraim? . . . My heart is changed within me; all my compassion is aroused. —HOSEA 11:8

An elderly man lay in a hospital, with his wife of fifty-five years sitting at his bedside. "Is that you, Ethel, at my side again?" he whispered.

"Yes, dear," she answered.

He softly said to her, "Remember years ago when I was in the Veteran's Hospital? You were with me then. You were with me when we lost everything in a fire. And Ethel, when we were poor—you stuck with me then too." The man sighed and said, "I tell you, Ethel, you are bad luck!"

It's only a humorous story, but it reminds us how we can twist the facts and fail to recognize the love and loyalty of someone who cares about us.

In Hosea 11, we read that God's people had spurned the love that gave them birth as a nation and cared for them through many crises. Instead of loving Him in return, they burned incense to carved images (v. 2), refused to repent (v. 5), and were bent on backsliding (v. 7). But even in His anger, when discipline became necessary, God did not stop loving them. He said, "My heart is changed within me; all my compassion is aroused" (v. 8).

If you have strayed far from God, you may wonder how He can keep loving you. Remember the love that sent Jesus to die for your sins so you could be forgiven. God's love will not let you go.

DENNIS DEHAAN

A child of God is always welcomed home.

The Gift of the Magi

READ MATTHEW 2:1–12

"Where is the one who has been born king of the Jews? We saw his star when it rose and have come to worship him." —MATTHEW 2:2

A young married couple had more love than money. As Christmas neared, both struggled to find a gift that would show how much they cared for the other. Finally, on Christmas Eve, Della sold her long, knee-length hair to buy Jim a platinum chain for the watch he had inherited from his father and grandfather. Jim, however, had just sold the watch to buy a set of expensive combs for Della's hair.

Author O. Henry called the couple's story "The Gift of the Magi." His creation suggests that even though their gifts became useless and may have caused them to look foolish on Christmas morning, their love made them among the wisest of those who give gifts.

The wise men of the first Christmas story also could have looked foolish to some as they arrived in Bethlehem with gifts of gold, frankincense, and myrrh (Matthew 2:11). They weren't Jewish. They were outsiders, Gentiles, who didn't realize how much they would disturb the peace of Jerusalem by asking about a newly born king of the Jews (v. 2).

As with Jim and Della's experience, the magi's plans didn't turn out the way they expected. But they gave what money cannot buy. They came with gifts, but then bowed to worship One who would ultimately make the greatest of all loving sacrifices for them—and for us.

MART DEHAAN

God's gift of grace is priceless.

DECEMBER
15

Faith

No Risk

READ EPHESIANS 2:1–10

For it is by grace you have been saved, through faith—and this is not from yourselves, it is the gift of God. —EPHESIANS 2:8

A colleague recently shared an experience I don't intend to try personally—bungee jumping. I found his description of the event both fascinating and terrifying. To think of jumping headfirst from a bridge hundreds of feet in the air suspended only by a giant rubber band is not my idea of a good time. But his leap was not without support. He described not one, but two heavy-duty harnesses that secured him to his lifeline—and to safety. The careful design and proven testing of those harnesses gave him great confidence as he leaped off the bridge.

As I listened, it occurred to me that for the follower of Christ, living in a sinful world is not a blind "leap of faith." We too have a pair of protections that can secure us in even the darkest times of life. In Ephesians 2:8–9, Paul wrote these words, "For it is by grace you have been saved, through faith—and this is not from yourselves, it is the gift of God—not by works, so that no one can boast."

It's in these twin harnesses—God's grace and our faith in the finished work of Jesus—that our relationship with God safely rests. In the strength of these provisions, salvation is not a risky leap into the void. It's an exercise of confidence in God's Word and His unfailing love and protection.

BILL CROWDER

We can expect God's peace when we accept God's grace.

Finding New Hope

READ 1 KINGS 19:1–18

Why, my soul, are you downcast? Why so disturbed within me? Put your hope in God, for I will yet praise him, my Savior and my God. —PSALM 42:5

A woman who was widowed for the second time felt the loss deeply. She saw little reason to go on living.

One day she got into the car with her young grandson. After securing him properly, she started the car without fastening her own seatbelt. When the five-year-old politely pointed this out to her, she told him she didn't care about her safety because she wanted to go to Jesus and Grandpa. The boy replied, "But Grandma, then you would leave me!"

God used this youngster to bring to her the realization that He still had service for her to perform, and that her situation was not as hopeless as it seemed to be.

During almost fifty years of ministry, I've seen many despairing people come to the place where they felt there was no way out. Like Elijah, they wanted to die (1 Kings 19:4). God sustained them, however, and showed them that He still had work for them to do. They discovered that the situation was not as dark as they had thought and that God had a reason for them to go on living.

We don't need to give in to despair! Let's remind ourselves of God's goodness and love, and go to Him in prayer. He can meet our needs. He'll lead us in paths of love and light and joy where we will find new hope.

HERB VANDER LUGT

No one is hopeless whose hope is in God.

Love

You Are Never Alone

READ JOHN 14:15–21

"I will not leave you as orphans; I will come to you." —JOHN 14:18

Jesus is just as real today as He was when He walked on this earth. Even though He doesn't move among us physically, by the Holy Spirit He is here, there, everywhere—a continuous, living presence—outside of us and inside of us.

That may be a terrifying thought for some. Perhaps you don't like yourself, or you're contemplating all the bad things you've done. Insecurity and sin can create a sense of fear, awkwardness, and clumsiness in Jesus's presence. But think of what you know about Him.

Despite what you are or what you may have done, He loves you (Romans 5:8; 1 John 4:7–11). He will never leave you nor forsake you (John 14:18; Hebrews 13:5). Others may not think much of you or invite you to spend time with them, but Jesus does (Matthew 11:28). Others may not like the way you look, but He looks at your heart (1 Samuel 16:7; Luke 24:38). Others may think you're a bother because you're old and in the way, but He will love you to the end (Romans 8:35–39).

Jesus loves you in spite of all the conditions that cause others to turn away. He wants to change you to be like Him, but He loves you as you are and will never abandon you. You are family; you will never, ever be alone.

DAVID ROPER

If you know Jesus, you'll never walk alone.

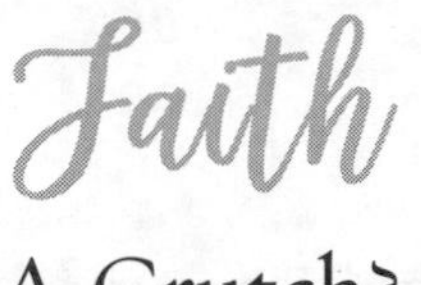

A Crutch?

READ 2 CORINTHIANS 4:8–15

We are hard pressed on every side, but not crushed; perplexed, but not in despair. —2 CORINTHIANS 4:8

Have you ever heard skeptics say that the Christian faith is nothing more than a crutch—that the only reason people claim to trust Jesus is that they are weaklings who have to make up "religion" to get by?

Apparently those skeptics haven't heard about the doctor in one Far Eastern country who spent two-and-a-half years in jail being "reeducated" because he professed faith in Christ. Then, after his release, he was arrested again—this time for his efforts at his church.

And perhaps those skeptics haven't heard about Paul. After trusting Christ, he was arrested, flogged, mocked, and shipwrecked (2 Corinthians 11:16–29).

These believers were not looking for a crutch. No, they had something deep and essential in their hearts. They had a personal relationship with God—a relationship born of faith in the work of Jesus on the cross. As a result, they became children of the King—eager to sacrifice everything for the privilege of proclaiming Him. They were not limping along looking for something to hold them up.

A crutch? Hardly. Faith in Christ is not about safety and caution. It's about believing Jesus and trusting Him no matter what. It's about taking up a daily cross (Luke 9:23) and living for the Savior.

DAVE BRANON

Because Jesus bore the cross for us,
we willingly take it up for Him.

DECEMBER
19

Hope

Everlasting Hope

READ PSALM 146

Blessed are those whose help is the God of Jacob,
whose hope is in the Lord their God. —PSALM 146:5

When the Christmas season rolled around just two months after my mother died, holiday shopping and decorating sat at the bottom of my priority list. I resisted my husband's attempts to comfort me as I grieved the loss of our family's faith-filled matriarch. I sulked as our son, Xavier, stretched and stapled strands of Christmas lights onto the inside walls of our home. Without a word, he plugged in the cord before he and his dad left for work.

As the colorful bulbs blinked, God gently drew me out of my darkness. No matter how painful the circumstances, my hope remained secure in the light of God's truth, which always reveals His unchanging character.

Psalm 146 affirms what God reminded me on that difficult morning: My endless "hope is in the Lord," my helper, my mighty and merciful God (v. 5). As Creator of all, He "remains faithful forever" (v. 6). He "upholds the cause of the oppressed," protecting us and providing for us (v. 7). "The Lord lifts up those who are bowed down" (v. 8). He "watches over" us, "sustains" us, and will always be King (vv. 9–10).

Sometimes, when Christmas rolls around, our days will overflow with joyful moments. Sometimes, we'll face loss, experience hurt, or feel alone. But at all times, God promises to be our light in the darkness, offering us tangible help and everlasting hope.

Xochitl Dixon

God secures our hope in His unchanging character.

Degrees of Faith

READ LUKE 7:1–10

Then he touched their eyes and said, "According to your faith let it be done to you." —MATTHEW 9:29

Not all Christians exercise the same degree of faith. Some people seem to think their problem is too big for God to solve. Others are sure that God is all-powerful, but they're not confident that He will do what is best for them. Still others affirm, "I know what God can do, and I'll trust Him to do what He has promised." These various attitudes range from a weak and tentative faith to a firm confidence that takes God at His word and believes He is good.

As we study the ministry of Jesus, we see varying degrees of faith in those who came to Him. He cast out a mute spirit from a son whose father wavered between faith and doubt (Mark 9:17–24). He healed a leper who knew He could but was not sure He would (Mark 1:40–45). And He healed the servant of a centurion who was so sure of the outcome that he asked Jesus merely to speak the word from afar (Luke 7:1–10).

These examples don't teach that God always answers according to the strength of our faith. Rather, in His wisdom He responds to any degree of faith. His ultimate goal is to lead us to trust Him completely. Because of who Jesus is, He can turn the weakest faith into strong faith.

DENNIS DEHAAN

Our faith in God grows greater as we recognize the greatness of our God.

Faith

Nothing for Something

READ ROMANS 4:1–8

To the one who does not work but trusts God who justifies the ungodly, their faith is credited as righteousness. —ROMANS 4:5

If you're looking for a great deal, you'll want to be careful when you examine the ad for a national donut store chain:

"Free! Three muffins when you buy three at the regular half-dozen price."

If that rather confusing statement means you end up buying six muffins for the price of six, it's not exactly a bargain!

So many of the seemingly great buys in our world are like deceptive advertisements. You receive nothing for something, when you thought it would be the other way around.

Think about it in spiritual terms. Various religions require a long list of activities in exchange for what amounts to hopelessness.

One religion, for example, expects its adherents to eat only leftovers, never injure a living thing, and denounce all preferences of sounds, colors, smells, and people. In return for all this meaningless (and impossible) self-denial, the individual hopes to be reincarnated to a better life.

In reality, spiritual rewards are God's to give, and He does so on the basis of His grace. Only God's plan of salvation offers something that is truly free (Romans 4:5). Jesus paid the price for our redemption; all He asks is that we put our faith in Him. Any other plan is nothing for something.

DAVE BRANON

If we could earn our salvation, Christ would not have died to provide it.

He Never Stops

READ HOSEA 10:9–15

Sow righteousness for yourselves, reap the fruit of unfailing love, . . . for it is time to seek the LORD. —HOSEA 10:12

The Old Testament book of Hosea is the story of God's faithful love for His unfaithful people. In what seems strange to us, the Lord commanded Hosea to marry a woman who would break her marriage vows and bring grief to him (Hosea 1:2–3). After she deserted Hosea for other men, the Lord told him to take her back—to "love her as the LORD loves the Israelites, though they turn to other gods" (3:1).

Later, Hosea was called upon to tell the Israelites that because of their rebellion against the Lord, they would be carried away into captivity by a foreign power. "The roar of battle will rise against your people, so that all your fortresses will be devastated" (10:14).

Yet in the midst of the Israelites' sin and punishment, the grace of God toward His people was never exhausted. In a grace-filled exhortation, He said: "Sow righteousness for yourselves, reap the fruit of unfailing love, and break up your unplowed ground; for it is time to seek the LORD, until he comes and showers his righteousness on you" (10:12).

Even when we have "planted wickedness" and "reaped evil" (10:13), God never stops loving us. Whatever our situation today, we can turn to the Lord and find forgiveness to make a new start. His love never fails!

DAVID MCCASLAND

No force is greater than the power of God's love.

Love

Love Changes Us

READ ACTS 9:1–22

At once he began to preach in the synagogues that Jesus is the Son of God. —ACTS 9:20

Before I met Jesus, I'd been wounded so deeply that I avoided close relationships in fear of being hurt more. My mom remained my closest friend until I married Alan. Seven years later and on the verge of divorce, I toted our kindergartner, Xavier, into a church service. I sat near the exit door, afraid to trust but desperate for help.

Thankfully, believers reached out, prayed for our family, and taught me how to nurture a relationship with God through prayer and Bible reading. Over time, the love of Christ and His followers changed me.

Two years after that first church service, Alan, Xavier, and I asked to be baptized. Later, during one of our weekly conversations, my mom said, "You're different. Tell me more about Jesus." A few months passed and she too accepted Christ as her Savior.

Jesus transforms lives . . . lives like Saul's, one of the most feared persecutors of the church until his encounter with Christ (Acts 9:1–5). Others helped Saul learn more about Jesus (vv. 17–19). His drastic transformation added to the credibility of his Spirit-empowered teaching (vv. 20–22).

Our first personal encounter with Jesus may not be as dramatic as Saul's. Our life transformation may not be as quick or drastic. Still, as people notice how Christ's love is changing us over time, we'll have opportunities to tell others what He did for us.

Xochitl Dixon

A life changed by Christ's love is worth talking about.

No Hope but God

READ ROMANS 5:1–5

If we hope for what we do not yet have, we wait for it patiently. —ROMANS 8:25

In his book *Through the Valley of the Kwai*, Scottish officer Ernest Gordon wrote of his years as a prisoner of war (POW) during World War II. This six-foot, two-inch man suffered from malaria, diphtheria, typhoid, beriberi, dysentery, and jungle ulcers; and the hard labor and scarcity of food quickly plunged his weight to less than one hundred pounds.

The squalor of the prison hospital prompted a desperate Ernest to request to be moved to a cleaner place—the morgue. Lying in the dirt of the death house, he waited to die. But every day, a fellow prisoner came to wash his wounds and to encourage him to eat part of his own rations. As the quiet and unassuming Dusty Miller nursed Ernest back to health, he talked with the agnostic Scotsman of his own strong faith in God and showed him that—even in the midst of suffering—there is hope.

The hope we read about in Scripture is not a vague, wishy-washy optimism. Instead, biblical hope is a strong and confident expectation that what God has promised in His Word He will accomplish. Tribulation is often the catalyst that produces perseverance, character, and finally, hope (Romans 5:3–4).

More than seventy-five years ago, in a brutal POW camp, Ernest Gordon learned this truth himself and said, "Faith thrives when there is no hope but God" (see Romans 8:24–25).

CINDY HESS KASPER

Christ, the Rock, is our sure hope.

DECEMBER
25

Hope

An Amazing Love

READ MALACHI 1:1–10; 4:5–6

"I have loved you," says the L*ORD*. —MALACHI 1:2

The final major historic acts of the Old Testament are described in Ezra and Nehemiah as God allowed the people of Israel to return from exile and resettle in Jerusalem. The City of David was repopulated with Hebrew families, a new temple was built, and the wall was repaired.

And that brings us to Malachi. This prophet, who was most likely a contemporary of Nehemiah, brings the written portion of the Old Testament to a close. Notice the first thing he said to the people of Israel: "'I have loved you,' says the LORD." And look at their response: "How have you loved us?" (1:2).

Amazing, isn't it? Their history had proven God's faithfulness, yet after hundreds of years in which God continually provided for His chosen people, they wondered how He had shown His love. As the book continues, Malachi reminds the people of their unfaithfulness (see vv. 6–8). They had a long historical pattern of God's provision for them, followed by their disobedience, followed by God's discipline.

It would be time, soon, for a new way. The prophet hints at it in Malachi 4:5–6. The Messiah would be coming. There was hope ahead for a Savior who would show us His love and pay the penalty once and for all for our sin.

That Messiah indeed has come! Malachi's hope is now a reality in Jesus.

DAVE BRANON

Those who put their trust in Jesus will have eternal life.

Nothing Left but God

READ 2 CHRONICLES 20:3–17

Do not be afraid or discouraged because of this vast army. For the battle is not yours, but God's. —2 CHRONICLES 20:15

A wise Bible teacher once said, "Sooner or later God will bring self-sufficient people to the place where they have no resource but Him—no strength, no answers, nothing but Him. Without God's help, they're sunk."

He then told of a despairing man who confessed to his pastor, "My life is really in bad shape." "How bad?" the pastor inquired. Burying his head in his hands, he moaned, "I'll tell you how bad—all I've got left is God." The pastor's face lit up. "I'm happy to assure you that a person with nothing left but God has more than enough for great victory!"

In 2 Chronicles 20:3–17, we read that the people of Judah were also in bad shape. They admitted their lack of power and wisdom to conquer their foes. All they had left was God! But King Jehoshaphat and the people saw this as reason for hope, not despair. "Our eyes are on you," they declared to God (2 Chronicles 20:12). And their hope was not disappointed as He fulfilled His promise: "The battle is not yours, but God's" (v. 15).

Sometimes we feel that our self-sufficiency is gone. As we turn our eyes on the Lord and put our hope in Him, we have God's reassuring promise that we need nothing more.

JOANIE YODER

When all you have is God, you have all you need.

Hope

God's Restraint

READ PSALM 76:1–12

Surely your wrath against mankind brings you praise, and the survivors of your wrath are restrained. —PSALM 76:10

Augustine said that God "judged it better to bring good out of evil, than not to permit any evil to exist." Thus God takes the worst evil that men and women can do to us and turns it into good. Even the wrath of ungodly men brings praise to Him (Psalm 76:10).

God has not promised that your life will be easy—indeed it may not be. But He has promised to sustain you in your struggle and uphold you with His mighty arm. If you trust Him, He will empower you to make your way bravely through extraordinary difficulty with faith, hope, and love. The trials God permits in your life will lead to His praise and glory, if only you will abide in Him.

Furthermore, there will be a restraint and a respite. The Hebrew text is somewhat obscure in Psalm 76:10. Literally it reads, "Surely the wrath of man will praise You; the remnant of wrath [God] will bind." God will use men's wrath to bring glory and praise to himself, but when that purpose is fulfilled He will then restrain it.

God will not allow us to be pressed beyond endurance. That is His sure promise. When the lesson has been learned, when the revelation of God's glory is complete and our soul has been tried and proven—then God will raise His hand and save us. He will say, "No more."

DAVID ROPER

In every desert of trial, God has an oasis of comfort.

Like a Little Child

READ MATTHEW 18:1–5; 19:13–14

And he said: "Truly I tell you, unless you change and become like little children, you will never enter the kingdom of heaven." —MATTHEW 18:3

One evening many years ago, after saying a goodnight prayer with our two-year-old daughter, my wife was surprised by a question. "Mommy, where is Jesus?"

Luann replied, "Jesus is in heaven and He's everywhere, right here with us. And He can be in your heart if you ask Him to come in."

"I want Jesus to be in my heart."

"One of these days you can ask Him."

"I want to ask Him to be in my heart now."

So our little girl said, "Jesus, please come into my heart and be with me." And that started her faith journey with Him.

When Jesus's disciples asked Him who was the greatest in the kingdom of heaven, He called a little child to come and join them (Matthew 18:1–2). "Unless you change and become like little children," Jesus said, "you will never enter the kingdom of heaven. . . . And whoever welcomes one such child in my name welcomes me" (vv. 3–5).

Through the eyes of Jesus we can see a trusting child as our example of faith. And we are told to welcome all who open their hearts to Him. "Let the little children come to me," Jesus said, "and do not hinder them, for the kingdom of heaven belongs to such as these" (19:14).

DAVID MCCASLAND

Our faith in Jesus is to be like that of a trusting child.

Faith

What Cancer Can't Do

READ 1 CORINTHIANS 15:35–49

But thanks be to God! He gives us the victory through our Lord Jesus Christ. —1 CORINTHIANS 15:57

One of the most dreaded sentences a patient can hear is, "You have cancer." These words bring a chill to the heart. Progress is being made in treating this disease, but recovery can be long and painful, and many don't survive.

An enthusiastic believer in Christ, Dan Richardson, lost his battle with cancer. But his life demonstrated that even though the physical body may be destroyed by disease, the spirit can remain triumphant. This poem was distributed at his memorial service:

Cancer is so limited . . .
It cannot cripple love,
It cannot shatter hope,
It cannot corrode faith,
It cannot eat away peace,
It cannot destroy confidence,
It cannot kill friendship,
It cannot shut out memories,
It cannot silence courage,
It cannot invade the soul,
It cannot reduce eternal life,
It cannot quench the Spirit,
It cannot lessen the power
of the resurrection.

If an incurable disease has invaded your life, refuse to let it touch your spirit. Your body can be severely afflicted, and you may have a great struggle. But if you keep trusting God's love, your spirit will remain strong.

DAVID EGNER

Our greatest enemy is not disease, but despair.

Why Keep the Faith?

READ 2 TIMOTHY 3

But as for you, continue in what you have learned and have become convinced of, because you know those from whom you learned it. —2 TIMOTHY 3:14

Many Christians are on the front lines of some very important battles. Some are speaking out on social issues and moral decline. Others are helping to relieve suffering and battling the effects of poverty. Still others are trying to make a difference in government or entertainment.

Sometimes these battles are won, but often they are lost. It can be a discouraging effort. When we lose a skirmish on the front lines of today's battles, how does that affect us? We may feel discouraged, but we need not feel hopeless. We know Christ will win ultimately, and we can be encouraged because there are some things that can't be taken away from us:

- Jesus Christ's continual presence with us (Hebrews 13:5).
- The Lord's promise of eternal life (Titus 1:2).
- The Holy Spirit's indwelling (1 Corinthians 6:19).
- Access to our heavenly Father through prayer (Ephesians 2:18).
- Spiritual gifts to serve the body of Christ (1 Corinthians 12).

It hurts to lose a battle in the daily fight for what is right. But as Paul made clear in 2 Timothy 3, it should come as no surprise. We are called only to be faithful. And when we contemplate what Christ has given to us, we'll never have to wonder why we should keep the faith.

DAVE BRANON

Having the Holy Spirit on the inside prepares you for any battle on the outside.

DECEMBER
31

Faith

God Is Faithful

READ LAMENTATIONS 3:1–24

Because of the L*ORD's great love we are not consumed, for his compassions never fail. They are new every morning; great is your faithfulness. I say to myself, "The* L*ORD is my portion; therefore I will wait for him."* —LAMENTATIONS 3:22–24

At the end of every year, I set aside some time to review the previous twelve months and record God's faithfulness to me and my family. I may leaf through a calendar, my appointment book, or prayer diary to jog my memory. Then, on a piece of paper labeled "God's Faithfulness" I'll write everything that comes to mind as evidence of God's love and care. It's a wonderful way to look back at the year and look forward to a fresh beginning.

My list will certainly include instances of God's grace and provision. But it will also chronicle God's presence during times of difficulty and disappointment. And it must include my failures and sins, which He has been "faithful and just" to forgive (1 John 1:9).

The prophet Jeremiah found that God's trustworthiness appeared as a light during the darkness of desperate circumstances. In his lament over the destruction of Jerusalem, Jeremiah wrote, "Because of the LORD's great love we are not consumed, for his compassions never fail. They are new every morning; great is Your faithfulness" (Lamentations 3:22–23).

Today, why not take time to record God's faithfulness to you and thank Him for it.

DAVID MCCASLAND

Adding up your blessings will multiply your joy.

Our Daily Bread Writers

JAMES BANKS. Pastor of Peace Church in Durham, North Carolina, James has written several books for Discovery House, including *Praying the Prayers of the Bible* and *Prayers for Prodigals*.

JOHN BLASE. An editor for Multnomah Publishers, John has written several books, including *Touching Wonder: Recapturing the Awe of Christmas* and *All Is Grace: A Ragamuffin Memoir* with Brennan Manning. John's articles first appeared in *Our Daily Bread* in early 2019. He and his wife have three children.

HENRY BOSCH (1914–1995). Henry was the first managing editor of *Our Daily Bread* and one of its first writers. Throughout his life, he battled illness but turned his weaknesses into spiritual encouragement for others through his devotional writing.

MONICA BRANDS. Monica has a master of theological studies from Calvin Seminary in Grand Rapids. She has worked with children with special needs. Monica grew up in Minnesota in a family with eight children. She began writing for *Our Daily Bread* in 2017.

DAVE BRANON. An editor with Discovery House, Dave has been involved with *Our Daily Bread* since the 1980s. He earned his master of arts degree in English from Western Michigan University. Dave has written nearly twenty books, including *Beyond the Valley* and *Living the Psalms Life*, both Discovery House publications.

ANNE CETAS. After becoming a Christian in her late teens, Anne was introduced to *Our Daily Bread* right away and began reading it. Now she reads it for a living as senior content editor of *Our Daily Bread*. Anne began writing articles for *ODB* in 2004.

POH FANG CHIA. Like Anne Cetas, Poh Fang trusted Jesus Christ as Savior as a teenager. She is an editor and a part of the Chinese editorial review committee serving in the Our Daily Bread Ministries Singapore office.

WINN COLLIER. Pastor of All Souls Church in Charlottesville, Virginia, Winn has established a writing career with books such as *Restless Faith: Hanging On to a God Just Out of Reach* and *Holy Curiosity: Encountering Jesus' Provocative Questions*. His first *Our Daily Bread* articles appeared in early 2019. He and his wife, Miska, have two sons.

BILL CROWDER. A former pastor who is now vice president of ministry content for Our Daily Bread Ministries, Bill travels extensively as a Bible conference teacher, sharing God's truths with fellow believers in Malaysia and Singapore and other places where ODB Ministries has international offices. His Discovery House books include *Windows on Easter* and *Let's Talk*.

LAWRENCE DARMANI. A noted novelist and publisher in Ghana, Lawrence is editor of *Step* magazine and CEO of Step Publishers. He and his family live in Accra, Ghana. His book *Grief Child* earned him the Commonwealth Writers' Prize as best first book by a writer in Africa.

DENNIS DEHAAN (1932–2014). When Henry Bosch retired, Dennis became the second managing editor of *Our Daily Bread*. A former pastor, he loved preaching and teaching the Word of God.

KURT DEHAAN (1953–2003). Kurt was a vital part of the ministry founded by his grandfather Dr. M. R. DeHaan. Kurt faithfully led *Our Daily Bread* as the managing editor for many years, and often wrote for other ministry publications until his sudden death in 2003 of a heart attack while jogging. He and his wife Mary (who died in 2014) had four children: Katie, Anna, Claire, and Nathan.

MART DEHAAN. The former president of Our Daily Bread Ministries, Mart followed in the footsteps of his grandfather M. R. and his dad Richard in that capacity. Mart, who has long been associated with *Day of Discovery* as host of the program from Israel, is now senior content advisor for Our Daily Bread Ministries and co-host of *Discover the Word*.

RICHARD DEHAAN (1923–2002). Son of the founder of Our Daily Bread Ministries, Dr. M. R. DeHaan, Richard was responsible for the ministry's entrance into television. Under his leadership, *Day of Discovery* television made its debut in 1968.

XOCHITL DIXON. Xochitl (soh-cheel) equips and encourages readers to embrace God's grace and grow deeper in their personal relationships with Christ and others. Serving as an author, speaker, and blogger at xedixon.com, she enjoys singing, reading, motherhood, and being married to her best friend, Dr. W. Alan Dixon Sr.

DAVID EGNER. A retired Our Daily Bread Ministries editor and longtime *Our Daily Bread* writer, David was also a college professor during his working career. In fact, he was a writing instructor for both Anne Cetas and Julie Ackerman Link at Cornerstone University.

DENNIS FISHER. For many years, Dennis was senior research editor at Our Daily Bread Ministries, using his theological training to guarantee biblical accuracy. He is also an expert in C. S. Lewis studies. He and his wife, Janet, a former university professor, have retired to Northern California.

VERNON GROUNDS (1914–2010). A longtime college president (Denver Seminary) and board member for Our Daily Bread Ministries, Vernon's life story was told in the Discovery House book *Transformed by Love*. Dr. Grounds died at the age of 96.

TIM GUSTAFSON. Tim writes for *Our Daily Bread* and serves as an editor for Discovery Series. As the son of missionaries to Ghana, Tim has an unusual perspective on life in the West. He and his wife, Leisa, are the parents of one daughter and seven sons.

C. P. HIA. Hia Chek Phang and his wife, Lin Choo, reside in the island nation of Singapore in Southeast Asia. C. P. came to faith in Jesus Christ at the age of thirteen. During his early years as a believer, he was privileged to learn from excellent Bible teachers who instilled in him a love for God's Word. He is special assistant to the president of Our Daily Bread Ministries, and he helps with translating resources for the ministry. He and his wife have a son, daughter-in-law, grandson, and granddaughter.

KIRSTEN HOLMBERG. Kirsten has been a part of the *Our Daily Bread* writing team since March 2017. She lives in the northwest part of the United States, and in addition to her writing, she has a ministry of speaking to various church, business, and community groups. She is the author of *Advent with the Word: Approaching Christmas through the Inspired Language of God*.

ADAM HOLZ. Adam's first *Our Daily Bread* articles appeared in January 2018. His main job is as senior associate editor of Focus on the Family's media review website, *Plugged In*. He has written a Bible study called *Beating Busyness*. He and his wife, Jennifer, have three children.

ARTHUR JACKSON. Having grown up in Kansas City, Arthur returned home after spending nearly three decades in pastoral ministry in Chicago. He began writing for *Our Daily Bread* in 2017. He serves as director of two ministries—one that cares for pastors and one that seeks to plant churches worldwide. He and his wife, Shirley, have five grandsons.

CINDY HESS KASPER. An editor for the Our Daily Bread Ministries publication *Our Daily Journey* until her retirement in 2018, Cindy began writing for *Our Daily Bread* in 2006. She and her husband, Tom, have three children and seven grandchildren.

RANDY KILGORE. Randy spent most of his twenty-plus years in business as a senior human resource manager before returning to seminary. Since finishing his master of divinity in 2000, he has served as a writer and workplace chaplain. He is the author of *Made to Matter: Devotions for Working Christians*. Randy and his wife, Cheryl, and their two children live in Massachusetts.

LESLIE KOH. Born and raised in Singapore, Leslie spent more than fifteen years as a journalist in the busy newsroom of local newspaper *The Straits Times* before moving to Our Daily Bread Ministries. He has found moving from bad news to good news most rewarding, and he still believes that nothing reaches out to people better than a good, compelling story. He likes traveling, running, editing, and writing.

ALBERT LEE. Albert was director of international ministries for Our Daily Bread Ministries for many years. Albert's passion, vision, and energy expanded the work of the ministry around the world. Albert grew up in Singapore and took a variety of courses from Singapore Bible College, as well as serving with Singapore Youth for Christ from 1971–1999. Albert appreciates art and collects paintings. He and his wife, Catherine, live in Singapore and have two children.

JULIE ACKERMAN LINK (1950–2015). A book editor by profession, Julie began writing for *Our Daily Bread* in 2000. Her books *Above All, Love* and *100 Prayers Inspired by the Psalms* are available through Discovery House. Julie lost her long battle with cancer in April 2015.

DAVID MCCASLAND. Living in Colorado, David enjoys the beauty of God's grandeur as displayed in the Rocky Mountains. An accomplished biographer, David has written the award-winning *Oswald Chambers: Abandoned to God* and *Eric Liddell: Pure Gold.*

KEILA OCHOA. In addition to her work with *Our Daily Bread*, Keila assists with Media Associates International, a group that trains writers around the world to write about faith. She and her husband have two children.

AMY PETERSON. Amy has a BA in English Literature from Texas A&M and an MA in Intercultural Studies from Wheaton College. Amy taught English as a Second Language for two years in Southeast Asia before returning stateside to teach at Taylor University. She is now pursuing an M.Div. at Duke Divinity School. She is the author of the book *Dangerous Territory: My Misguided Quest to Save the World.*

AMY BOUCHER PYE. Amy is a writer, editor, and speaker. The author of *Finding Myself in Britain: Our Search for Faith, Home, and True Identity*, she runs the Woman Alive book club in the UK and enjoys life with her family in their English vicarage.

HADDON ROBINSON (1931–2017). Haddon, a renowned expert on preaching, served many years as a seminary professor. He wrote numerous books and hundreds of magazine articles. For a number of years he was a panelist on Our Daily Bread Ministries' radio program *Discover the Word.*

DAVID ROPER. David lives in Idaho, where he takes advantage of the natural beauty of his state. He has been writing for *Our Daily Bread* since 2000, and he has published several books with Discovery House, including *Psalm 23* and *Teach Us to Number Our Days.*

LISA SAMRA. Lisa calls Grand Rapids home after growing up and attending both college (University of Texas) and seminary (Dallas Theological Seminary) in the Lone Star State. A journalism major in college, she continues her love of writing through *Our Daily Bread*. She and her husband, Jim, who pastors the church founded by Dr. M. R. DeHaan, have four children.

JENNIFER BENSON SCHULDT. Jennifer, a Chicagoan, writes from the perspective of a mom of a growing family. She has written for *Our Daily Bread* since 2010.

JULIE SCHWAB. Julie plans to use her recently earned master of arts degree from Liberty University to continue her love of writing about God's Word and life in Christ. Julie's first *Our Daily Bread* articles appeared in the publication in 2017 when she was an intern from Cornerstone University.

JOE STOWELL. As president of Cornerstone University, Joe has stayed connected to today's young adults in a leadership role. A popular speaker and a former pastor, Joe has written a number of books over the years, including *Strength for the Journey* and *Jesus Nation*.

HERB VANDER LUGT (1920–2006). For many years, Herb was senior research editor at Our Daily Bread Ministries, responsible for checking the biblical accuracy of the booklets published by ODB Ministries. A World War II veteran, Herb spent several years as a pastor before his ODB tenure began.

PAUL VAN GORDER (1921–2009). A writer for *Our Daily Bread* in the 1980s and 1990s, Paul was a noted pastor and Bible teacher—both in the Atlanta area where he lived and through the *Day of Discovery* TV program.

MARVIN WILLIAMS. Marvin's first foray into Our Daily Bread Ministries came as a writer for *Our Daily Journey*. In 2007, he penned his first *Our Daily Bread* article. Marvin is senior teaching pastor at a church in Lansing, Michigan.

JOANIE YODER (1934–2004). For ten years, until her death, Joanie wrote for *Our Daily Bread*. In addition, she published the book *God Alone* with Discovery House.

Scripture Index

Help us get the word out!

Our Daily Bread Publishing exists to feed the soul with the Word of God.

If you appreciated this book, please let others know.

- Pick up another copy to give as a gift.
- Share a link to the book or mention it on social media.
- Write a review on your blog, on a bookseller's website, or at our own site (ourdailybreadpublishing.org).
- Recommend this book for your church, book club, or small group.

Connect with us:

@ourdailybread

@ourdailybread

@ourdailybread

Our Daily Bread Publishing
PO Box 3566
Grand Rapids, Michigan 49501 USA

books@odb.org